Network Management

Problems, Standards and Strategies

Data Communications and Networks Series

Consulting Editor: Dr C. Smythe, Surrey University

Network Management

Problems, Standards and Strategies

Franz-Joachim Kauffels

Translated by Stephen S. Wilson

ADDISON-WESLEY
PUBLISHING
COMPANY

Wokingham, England · Reading, Massachusetts · Menlo Park, California · New York
Don Mills, Ontario · Amsterdam · Bonn · Sydney · Singapore
Tokyo · Madrid · San Juan · Milan · Paris · Mexico City · Seoul · Taipei

Translated from the German edition *Netzwerk-Management: Probleme, Standards, Strategien* published by Datacom-Verlag.

Cover designed by Chris Eley and
printed by The Riverside Printing Co. (Reading) Ltd.
Printed in Great Britain by The Bath Press, Avon

First printed 1992.

British Library Cataloguing in Publication Data
A catalogue record for this book is available from the British Library.

Library of Congress Cataloging-in-Publication Data
A catalog record for this book is available from the Library of Congress.

Preface

Network management. Scarcely any other theme in data communications has risen so forcefully in so short a time to become the centre of so much discussion and interest. There are two reasons for this: firstly, the almost exponentially increasing number of networked computers and secondly, the increasing heterogeneity.

The ideal world of centrally oriented data processing with an omniscient, omnipotent host in the middle has been subject to as great a change as the euphoria for individualism of the early days of the PC.

It is not an exaggeration to say that the growing together of the various DP worlds towards the scenario of decentralized data processing is also a social process.

Individual DP, in which personal computers are not networked, knows nothing of control mechanisms. However, even the centrally oriented management aids of large centralized networks are not adequate for all today's problems.

The data processing of the 1990s is based on the concept of workgroup computing, where a workgroup is a social and/or economic unit with at most 50–100 members who work with locally-networked PCs and share a server which provides them with basic application-oriented services. The workgroup LAN and its services are very much determined by the needs of the workgroup. All workgroup LANs are connected over a company-wide backbone network which provides the workgroup server with additional services, including those of the classical data centre. The backbone forms an internetwork, which is usually a completely new structure to the company.

This book attempts to build a bridge between old and new network-management concepts, taking particular account of the distributedness and integration within the framework of OSI and manufacturer strategies. It should alert the reader to the latest problems and solutions.

The book is not intended as a competitor to existing excellent presentations of classical network management approaches and solutions. Instead, it should be viewed primarily as a teaching aid to an understanding of new network management paths.

Today, the topics of network management, data protection and operating systems are in most cases considered separately. In the author's opinion, this is the wrong approach. It is actually the task of network management to guarantee the integrity of the overall information processing. However, in distributed networks, the functional units belonging to the network are primarily resources which should be managed by the operating system. It is the lack of capability of current operating systems, conceived 15–25 years ago, which makes network management in the broader sense necessary for the management of network resources. Accordingly, new concepts of network management should be related to new concepts in the development of operating systems.

One important aspect is integration. The book describes a number of important manufacturer concepts for integrated network management and attempts to assess how far these schemes are really equipped to face the problems of the years ahead. In addition, an explicit classification of multivendor management environments is undertaken.

Apart from introductions to the book and to the problem, three topic areas are covered: classical network management, the management of open heterogeneous systems according to OSI and SNMP, and manufacturers' strategies for the management of future distributed system environments.

The first edition of this book was primarily a response to the massive requirement for information in this area. The considerable success of the first edition meant that the presentation could be extended in the second edition to include, in particular, more details of the specific tasks of network management and descriptions of the latest manufacturer concepts. The second German edition is at the same time the basis for this first international edition.

Even a new edition of a book demands constructive criticism from its readers and the author and the publisher would welcome any such feedback.

For simplicity, the pronoun 'he' is used to relate to both male and female throughout the book.

The author would like to thank DATACOM Verlag and in particular Frau Lindig and Herrn. Pröfener, together with Addison-Wesley Publishers, and in particular Tim Pitts, for their problem-free cooperation. The author would also like to thank Dr Stephen S Wilson for his careful, empathetic and stylistically-faithful translation.

Euskirchen bei Bonn. Summer 1991   Dr Franz-Joachim Kauffels

Contents

Trademark notice

Chapter 1

Communication – quo vadis?

- Development of data processing – network nightmares

- Communication – quo vadis?

- The structure of the book

This chapter begins with a summary of the current basic problems of modern data processing, which largely stem from an unduly biased consideration of information processing in terms of raw functionality.

Only after major harm had been done, was the problem of improving the organization of data processing seriously considered, when distributed data processing crystallized as a synergy of purely-centralized and purely-decentralized data processing as an infrastructural basis.

Section 1.2 is concerned with the question: 'Communication – quo vadis?' in the areas of networks, protocol hierarchies and operating systems. This section is intended for all readers with a certain basic knowledge of data communication who wish learn about the latest trends by way of attunement and preparation for the main theme of network management.

In particular, we discuss the far-reaching role of the operating system and the cooperation of processes in it; this is an aspect which is often criminally neglected in the communications literature (including that by the author). However, since network management is very closely connected with the system management for a given operating system and since the topic is covered methodically in the next chapter (including in terms of the operating systems), reference to the appropriate section is recommended.

The chapter ends with a section on the structure of the book.

1.1 Development of data processing – network nightmares

This book is relatively technically oriented. However, today's problems associated with the management of industry-wide information processing systems and their underlying networks cannot be solved by technology alone.

Instead, a balanced synergy of technical, organizational and human components should lead to a gradual solution of the urgent requirements. In the later chapters of the book, we describe the views of data-processing (DP) and network manufacturers and international standardization bodies, since, so-to-speak, these groups form an intellectual melting pot in which management systems for network and system management are shaped. Thus, we guide those interested through the maze of concepts, standards and products and give them an idea of the underlying concepts and the interrelationship with classical views of technical network management.

In this introduction, the author would like to make a pithy reference to some of today's most important non-technical problem areas, which may be explained by organizational weaknesses and natural human behaviour, together with the lack of adaptation of the technology to this behaviour. The author does not wish to become embroiled in socio-psychological discussions, which are beyond his competence. Instead, he has brought together and evaluated (admittedly subjectively) a number of observations of 'real life'. However, this subjective evaluation is supported by statistics and third-party observations.

The remarks and the evaluations are sometimes painful for those concerned and not always flattering. But that is scarcely the point. Unlike in other areas of networking, the quality of a solution is crucially dependent on how closely the organization and the personnel are associated. During his lectures, the author's remarks often come under fire from three groups of people. One group consists of those who are too disappointed to buy high-tech products for their problem, which would then enable them to proceed effortlessly. The second group consists of those who believe that the inability to learn (we discuss this later), the irresponsibility and the lack of flexibility of users and those in responsibility are problems that are easily overcome with good words and who reject the use of software techniques to limit the data systems facilities to those absolutely necessary in the immediate area of work as inhuman. The third group consists of those fortunate people who actually have no problems or do not wish to have any and are angry to be startled pointlessly from their contentedness.

All readers who can count themselves in these groups should jump to Section 1.2, with the consolation that, even without Section 1.1, the book would not have been cheaper.

The current, relatively heated discussion of network management, the manufacturing concepts which began far too late, the enthusiastic generation of future scenarios, the frantic attention to data protection, data security and reliable information processing are all evidence that, to put it simply, many users and even the developers in the manufacturing companies have in the past been too strongly set on the raw functionality of their overall information processing. They have paid too little attention to infrastructural problems and above all to problems associated with growth.

In all honesty, many swimmers on the pure PC wave must acknowledge not having looked beyond the individual performance. It is very soothing, in the sense of soporific, to know that one is backed by a computer centre which will undertake the important work in case of emergency.

Office automation prophets have wanted to cover the office world with a blanket coverage of multifunction workstations. Because of the variety of possible uses of personal computers and personal systems, they have even managed this. While this may be gratifying from the purely functional point of view, the various side effects of purely decentralized data processing are equally unpleasant. The dangers to the integrity of the data and the processing, which may be introduced completely unwittingly, range from simple inability to handle devices, supported by DOS's complete lack of the most elementary security measures (C: format!), to the introduction of viruses by game programs as a result of the magical allure of playing during work time.

These dangers are also added to by attacks on data, devices or infrastructural aids such as operating systems and communication protocols, for which a certain degree of knowledge is required.

Finally, there are deliberate attacks by professionals, which though similar, are only executed when the target is worthwhile.

Not all these dangers can be excluded today while at the same time preserving economic information processing. As a solution, one basic approach is to bring together the worlds of purely-central and purely-decentralized data processing. Here, PCs and personal systems are linked together via simple local area networks. These LANs are embedded in the host environment, instead of, for example, terminal subsystems.

Does this alone actually solve the problem? Let us remain at the low end, the PC LAN.

Today's PC networks provide a large number of functions at a particularly cost-effective price. They are, in the meantime, relatively easy to bring into operation; however, the pleasure of a hastily installed network is often only short-lived. Is this the fault of the LAN or of the software? Often it is not the fault of either. When large datasets disappear, software is stolen or a virus is introduced, or when someone has knowledge of nearly all the secret business correspondence, we rarely have to look to technology for the cause.

Suppose a network with many PCs is placed in a closed hall and that no one is allowed to work on it; then no violations of the integrity of the information processing occur.

Naturally, there are also technical risks associated with PC LANs, which have been adequately described in (Kauffels, 1985), (Ruland, 1988), (Ruland, 1989) and (Ruland, 1990). However, there are currently grave organizational deficiencies.

All PC LAN software packages provide a number of simple-to-implement standard utilities for execution of network management, data protection and data security, either for the immediate environment of the PC LAN or oriented towards the servers. On further investigation, these are rarely used. This is primarily due not to the maliciousness of users but rather to shallow or undertrained administrators, who often do not know who is allowed to do what on the network and which utilities are available for particular tasks.

People who don't know what they want usually get something which is not what they had intuitively imagined. Instead of access rights being distributed in a proper matrix-like fashion, all users are made 'supervisors' and thus may access everything. It was even a basic philosophy of Plato that women and potatoes should be public property. Within the last 2000 years doubts have been raised about this notion. As far as data and resources are concerned, it seems that Plato, reinforced by Murphy, again rules the day. There is still a platonic attitude to data protection; there is much enthusiasm about how wonderful it would be, but there is no action!

For some years, data processing has been in a state of radical structural change. Services, and thus also the implicit power of the computer centre, are being increasingly decentralized with the increasing spread of the personal computer; naturally, completely new application areas are also being opened up. However, in many cases, this decentralization does not apply to the knowledge about proper integrated information processing including data protection and data security. Here, there are often considerable holes. No one would leave the company's money in twenty pound notes in the drawers of an employee's desk. We often do this today with information. It also has a value, which may be distinctly pecuniary or of a legal, ethical or other nature.

At the beginning of the PC craze, many people, including experts, were fully convinced that decentralization could go so far that mainframes or computer centres might be completely dispensed with. This turned out to be a fallacy. On the one hand, there are many applications where a mainframe is still required for the processing, while on the other hand the use of PCs involves completely new problems (for example, relating to data protection, the securing of the processing integrity, the securing of data consistency, etc.), which, with the present state of knowledge, depending on their magnitude, can only be overcome using mainframes (Figure 1.1).

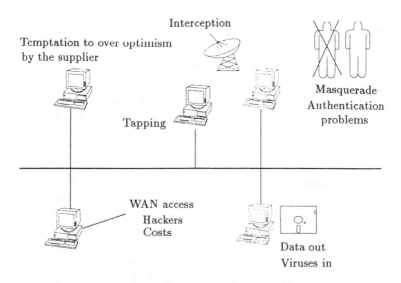

Figure 1.1   Risks for PC LANs (selected).

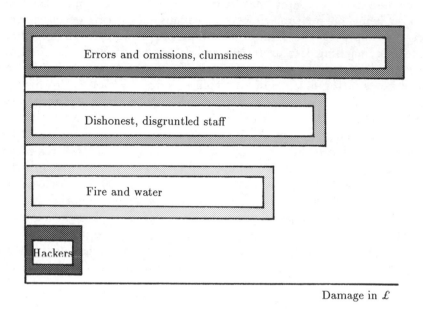

Damage in £

Figure 1.2 Evaluation of risks for an office environment.

We have even had to learn that as the capabilities of PCs increase the additional problems do not on the whole decrease but even increase likewise. This is not because of the devices themselves but because of the people who ultimately have to use them.

Current evaluations of the risks for time-sharing systems which regard unskilled users as one of the main sources of trouble are very optimistic (Figure 1.2). Recent assessments of the National Computer Crime Center (Figure 1.3) show that the threat from unskilled users continues to increase and that more than 60% of losses of data and programs and the consequent direct and indirect (in the form of hindrances to manufacturing) damage may be attributed to this. Figure 1.3 compares the NCCC assessment with an old IBM assessment for time-sharing systems. Here, for the purposes of comparison, the damage has been normalized to show a relatively similar distribution of its causes. The overall damage today is considerably higher because of the greater number of devices. The figure is also normalized for office environments. The damage and risks in manufacturing, construction or security-relevant areas are different.

It is interesting that the component of the damage attributable to hackers or viruses remains relatively constant. It is quite clear that when data is lost or other damage occurs, the blame seldom lies with technology.

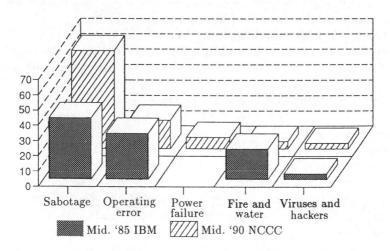

Figure 1.3   Installation base – unrestrained growth. IBM's analysis (1985) of multiuser systems is shown in the foreground, with the NCCC's assessment (1990) for the PC environment in the background.

In fact, small and medium-sized catastrophes are more often the result of various forms of human error, from planning to applications.

There are three serious problem areas which the author has encountered time and again during his work as a strategic consultant.

Problem 1: increasingly unskilled users

If we compare the structure of data processing and the spread of terminals over, for example, the last eight and the next two years, we see that the number of devices installed in the user area has doubled practically every two years in a continuing trend. Averaged over the relevant areas, the number of employees has increased comparatively little. While in the beginning, there was a tendency to hand data processing over to trained personnel, with the fall in prices and the PC craze the trend now is to distribute devices relatively chaotically. Often, however, staff are not trained in the necessary numbers because proper training, with the consequent absence of staff from the workplace, is much more expensive than the hardware and software. Of course, there are exceptions to this rule; some offices and even some industrial and commercial concerns do train and educate their staff properly, but you need a magnifying glass to find these. Particular attention should be paid to appropriate, responsible and reasonable training, as

Dr. Drols commented in his noteworthy speech at the 1990 Token Ring conference (Drols, 90). Amongst other things, he suggested that training today suffered from being entrusted to unprofessional pedagogues. Translated from the Greek, pedagogy means 'bringing up children'. The fact is that training must take on a different orientation, since it involves the education of adults. For example, an adult absorbs considerably less information than a child and even then the information must be properly presented.

Unfortunately, however, a consume or die mentality currently prevails. This is heightened by the fact that application programs on PCs are becoming increasingly powerful in almost breathtaking numbers, with a consequent increase in the demands on the users. In the area of business graphics, there are already calls for simplicity instead of ever-increasing graphical beauty and diversity.

Is this just pure stubbornness or inflexibility on the part of those responsible, to whom the sole blame for the poor structure of their data processing, the lack of training and the resulting deficiencies may be apportioned? Is it only a generation problem, which can be solved by pensioning off the older staff and replacing them by gifted young data-communication personnel, following the example of several American companies? Are the masses simply lazy as some entrepreneurs popularly make out?

In this problem area, the blame cannot be apportioned to any single cause, instead it is largely due to a mixture of the effects of Problem 2.

Problem 2: ignorance of problem 1

Problem 1 could be very neatly solved over a suitable period, were it not permanently ignored. The manufacturers of data processing equipment will find it difficult to argue with the decision takers: 'Your staff is increasingly unskilled and proper training is too expensive. Buy our machines and their fantastic user surfaces and all will be well'. Today's arguments are integration, acceptance and increasing productivity. This also includes an expensive training program and a background host that saves the day. In many cases, the decision takers are unknowingly misled. There is a trend to buy solutions to problems that do not really exist, thus creating new problems which at first go unnoticed. The most harmless software packages may contain fantastic functions, which no one needs and which can lead to very grave errors or to disproportionate and senseless expense in fishing out the necessary basic functions from amongst the extended functions.

This leads to the following false conclusions:

2a   Better devices necessarily lead to better information processing and higher productivity.

2b   Our staff are so good that firstly they are more highly motivated by the new machine and secondly, because of the improved user interfaces they scarcely need training.

2c   Our staff acquire the necessary knowledge on the fly.

2d   The software package we are buying contains functions which we do not yet require, together with the functions that we actually do require. We shall need these functions tomorrow and they are included in the price.

The staff realize this and in many cases are prone to overestimate themselves; one has the increasing impression that this is a part of survival, since the prospects are small for those without DP knowledge and it is better to say that one knows something about it even when one does not. Later, when one's job is secure, this lack of knowledge is less important and anyway, did one have it before or not? In any case, how important are a few data and game programs to the company?

Staff too draw the wrong conclusions:

2e   There is not much one can do wrong in data processing when everything is so modern.

2f   I am too old for data processing, nothing will change in the 25 years before I retire.

2g   The data is as valuable as the floppy disk on which it is stored. If I lose it I buy a new disk.

2h   (Larry syndrome[1]) The couple of minutes I spend running a game program do no harm to the company.

The fact that a game program may introduce invisible viruses is seemingly irrelevant. The view that data may actually be valuable in the company-wide context is rare.

The individualization of data processing over recent years has meant that terms such as methodicalness, comprehensibility and integrity have disappeared from the minds of those in responsibility and their staff until, that is, the first data catastrophes and virus show-downs become public.

Unfortunately, things have developed in the wrong direction. When a consultant tells a manager that there is a new virus which uses an algorithm which the manager cannot understand and that can be combatted with an anti-virus program which uses an equally incomprehensible algorithm, the manager is very pleased. He praises the consultant, buys the anti-virus program and has peace of mind because he has done something for data protection. The manager does not realize that whilst the consultant was talking an army of clerks has perpetrated a vast number of small errors which destroy more data than the virus itself. If the consultant mentions

---

[1]Larry is a typical, highly sophisticated, time-consuming computer game.

this, he is at best met with incredible astonishment and the comment that this might happen anywhere else but not here. Thus, the deficiency clearly lies in the form of the organization and of the corresponding decision-taking hierarchy which are simply not suited to the application of new technologies.

This cannot be changed here and now. However, the author believes that most of the readers of this book are exactly the people who each and every time have to clear up the mistakes of others: namely they are network and system administrators. Neither the decision takers, nor even the staff, have to repair the damage resulting from their wrong decisions or lack of skill. If there is any doubt, the DP personnel are always to blame. Since most devices will in the future be networked in some way, much of the problem comes down to the network management level.

Problem 3: inadequacy of network management

As we shall see in the book, current aids to network management are modest. They relate primarily to the management of the physical network and the devices within that network. However, the physical network is the least problem if it is carefully planned, constructed and monitored. Management of the users and restriction of their capabilities to what is absolutely necessary is a major problem. A user should always have the resources which he needs to accomplish his tasks; these should be available to him in an appropriate quality, so that he can carry out his work properly. There should be no games and/or other resources which would only lead to him fooling around electronically instead of doing his job.

The author notes that this functional view of the staff and the associated basic Taylorism often goes uncontradicted. The counter argument suggests that one should motivate and stimulate staff by providing them with facilities on their computers with which they may play and learn; this will increase their ease with data processing and improve the use of company-wide resources. The author believes this to be dangerous. It is like giving automatic cars to 12- to 14-year olds to give them a taste for being in traffic. In the most fortunate cases, it is the car repairers who would benefit. There are four dimensions to the problem: lack of integration, ignorance of standard aids, the view that network management is unproductive and the view that the more modern the system the simpler it is to manage.

3a   There is no integration. There are now many tools for controlling homogeneous subnetworks. As we shall see in this chapter, the data processing environment is becoming increasingly heterogeneous. There is a lack of overall management tools. Such tools form the subject of this book.

3b   Existing standard aids are not used. It is shocking to find that, for example, in a large PC network in Novell's NetWare, all users have the rights of a supervisor. This is not the fault of the manufacturer of the network software. As we shall see in Chapter 2, in addition to products similar to those of other manufacturers, this manufacturer also produces efficient utilities for allocating multilevel rights, for user management and for controlling the security policy defined in this way. In order to be able to use these sensibly one (the system administrator) must first consider who should be able to do what in which fields and why, and how and with what rights the resources should be allocated to the users. To do this, one draws up a matrix in which the resources and the users are represented by rows and columns and the matrix entries correspond to rights. This should be broken down into the individual user profiles and presented to the network software. It seems that this procedure is far too demanding. Here we would finally have a buck which is passed to the network administrators, since there is a real product which the manufacturers have supplied with sensible facilities and the users are keen to use it. However, this is too simple, for there are too few administrators, and they have too little time.

3c   There is a view that network management is unproductive. It is currently difficult for anyone proposing network management to those in charge to calculate the corresponding economy and increase in efficiency. This will already be known from existing networks. The decision takers will insist on seeing that networking also requires equipment, devices, software and personnel which cost money and which apparently have no return even though this is always politely expressed. It is only possible to get things moving if one can show that, soon (as US studies of electronic data processing have shown), if the data processing is not operational for a long time, the only decisions that will be left to the decision makers will concern the management of bankruptcy. The author estimates that according to the tasks of the workstations, every 50–200 networked PC workstations require a moderately well-trained, low-level system administrator to configure the network, introduce new users, answer users' questions, keep the printers stocked with paper, monitor the network physically and logically, carry out small repairs and keep the system permanently operational. Thus, this administrator has nothing to do with an existing computer centre. It is clear that managers are not happy when they see that the networking of 100 desktop PCs, which were previously quietly run without networking, requires a further member of staff.

    This also leads to the general tendency to automate network management as far as possible, and when possible to centralize it. This holds the promise of savings on staff and on cost. However, it should be clear that the increasing complexity of management tools leads to a requirement for increasingly well-qualified personnel and thus increases the cost of individual staff.

3d   There is a view that the more modern the network, the simpler it is to manage. We have become accustomed to the fact that as consumer and capital goods are technically improved their maintenance decreases in relevance. The valve-changing radioman belongs as much to the past as the car mechanic who optimally tunes the carburettor by feel and ear. Nowadays we may drive our cars up to 50 000 km before they need servicing.

The same should apply to modern networks. However, the exact opposite is the case: the more complex and modern the network, the more difficult it is to manage. We shall see why this is in Section 1.2 and Chapter 2. Often, the simplest basic control elements found in old networks such as SNA terminal networks or TRANSDATA networks are now missing. On the other hand, even more demands are being placed on networks (although comparatively fewer than on cars or radios).

These basic problems with their offshoots essentially characterize the organizational and personnel difficulties associated with the aspects of networked data processing of interest here.

The author does not claim that he can give perfect exemplary solutions. He will be satisfied if this sensitizes some users or speaks to them from the heart. This book can only introduce those aids which may in the future provide technical solutions to today's problems.

In the concept of distributed data processing as a synergy of central and decentralized data processing, another component, on which we now concentrate, comes into play, namely that of a communication network which is heterogeneous in wide areas. Here, the technical aspects are less interesting than the logical ones, since in the end, the data processing, whether central or decentralized, is based on a set of more or less cooperating processes. As far as the use of networks with ever improving reactions is concerned, whether these processes are implemented on a single computer or on several computers is increasingly irrelevant.

The diversity of communication networks corresponds to their possible uses. But what happens if the communication network becomes so large and diverse that an individual or a small group can no longer take in the network and its components at a glance? What happens when errors occur which involve a combination of logical and technical elements? How does one master the historically increased heterogeneity? How can the data network be (or be made) secure in the broadest sense? How can one assess which components are likely to fail next? How can performance bottlenecks be prevented? How can the network be extended? What limiting conditions should be taken into account in the next extension but one, so as not to endanger the next extension? Is there a sensible way of calculating costs?

These are the network nightmares! They apply not only to network managers and system administrators, but also, sooner or later, to all those

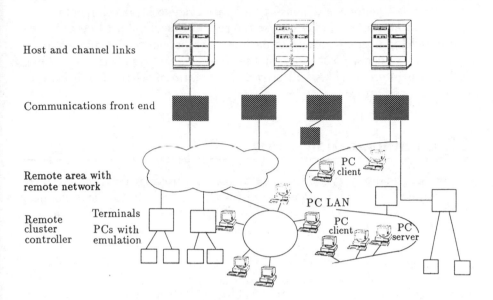

Host and channel links

Communications front end

Remote area with
remote network

Remote   Terminals
cluster   PCs with
controller   emulation

PC
client

PC LAN

PC
client

PC
server

Figure 1.4   Distributed data processing.

responsible for information processing. Sometimes they even apply to you, if you are honest about it.

Network management is an example of a subarea of information processing to which little attention was paid until very recently. Only the occurrence of major problems, only the rampant heterogeneous growth of communication networks, only the threat to national security interests from hackers have contributed to forcing the manufacturers of computers, PCs and networks to think about possible solutions going beyond a simple monitoring of the technical network and to develop solution strategies, albeit very late.

These strategies and the associated area form the subject of this book. However, the author can state in advance that the actual integration of all management components is not currently achievable.

The author could have written a highly technical and specialized book, which would not have achieved the aim of informing as many interested parties as possible about more recent developments in a compact manner. An awareness of the technical relationships of networks and communications protocols is assumed as a prerequisite. However, most chapters begin with a discussion of the area associated with the relevant management strategies.

Regrettably, the current discussion almost always loses sight of the overall context of the approach. Everyone is concerned with their local environment and is happy when this is in some way operational. This restriction is the greatest enemy of integrated network management.

The author would like to use the rest of this chapter to describe the major development trends and to outline a projection for the coming years.

Every reader must individualize this collective projection according to his own interests. This will provide a scenario of what he will have to manage in the future.

1.2 Communication – quo vadis?

There are many very different standpoints from which the area of responsibility of network management may be viewed. In the next chapter, we shall take a largely functionally-oriented approach. Before that, it is useful to cast an eye over current trends in data processing and communication.

The general route of march is towards distributed data processing. In the past, neither purely-centrally-oriented DP nor purely-individual DP alone has proved able to solve the problem of information processing with economical use of the resources.

The topics of current interest include the development of networks, communication protocols and operating systems together with infrastructural and application-oriented aspects.

1.2.1 The network tangle

In the past, the development of networks has presented us with almost incomprehensible variety. It is largely thanks to international standardization that the conceptual proliferation has been held within tolerable bounds (Figure 1.5).

In general, in local area networks, distinction must be made between voice- and non-voice-oriented communication. The once highly valued applicability of local area networks to telephony, and the suitability of private branch exchanges (PBXs) for narrow PC linkage, have turned out to be uneconomic. The concepts of LANs and PBXs both currently have a fixed place in companies and a fixed task area. The decision of what to implement on what is based on functional, practical and economic grounds. Data traffic over a PBX is always worthwhile if a narrow-band channel is (or can be) permanently used or if it can be used to attach devices to a LAN which are so unfortunately located that it would be uneconomic to extend the LAN to them. The use of a PBX as a system for transmission between PCs or other computers should always be rejected (or may be

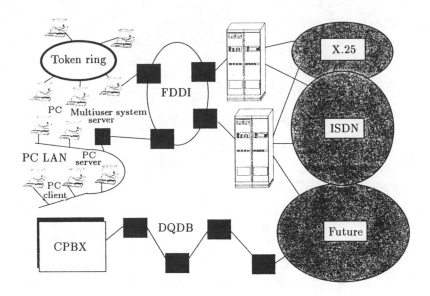

Figure 1.5   The network tangle.

impossible) if bursty traffic with high data rates is required. Today it is still possible to puzzle over, for example, whether or not the standard protocols between PCs (for example, NetBios) can also run over a PBX. The first attempt to harmonize file systems (as is best done using the Network File System (NFS) or Novell's NetWare 386) shows the absurdity of this undertaking. Nevertheless, there will be a large amount of communications software in the coming years (for example, for the office environment) which will not require this and will operate, for example, with the ISDN data rate.

There is an easy knockout criterion for PBXs, namely the remote loading of diskless workstations. It has long been recognized that these diskette drives present a basic problem as far as data protection is concerned. It is easy to use these drives to smuggle information out of a company or an office simply by transporting the diskette or to introduce viruses in the opposite direction. Nearly all manufacturers of LAN-capable PCs also produce so-called diskless workstations, which have no diskette drive and in many cases no hard disk. These LAN workstations have to be fully-remotely loaded. If one could use the full ISDN channel rate of 64 kbit/s without interruption, it would take 80 seconds to load a PC with 640 kbytes of memory, which is still tolerable. However, the loading server can only load one or two PCs simultaneously so that remote loading of n PCs would take a total of $1.5n$ minutes, which cannot be tolerated. The LAN solution with its broadcasting features is clearly preferable here.

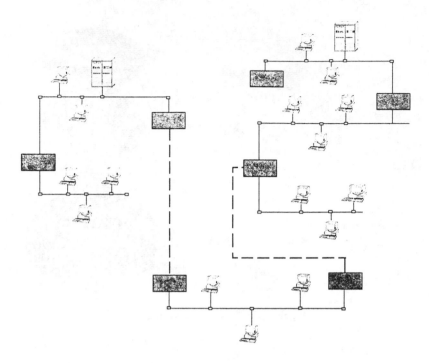

Figure 1.6   Ethernet networks.

In local area networks in the narrower sense, the IEEE standard 802, which above all produced the market favourites, Token Ring and Ethernet (Figures 1.6, 1.7) is definitive. Both groups of systems have an open product-basis which provides the user with a great deal of freedom to adjust his LANs to his circumstances.

For most applications, which of the standard systems is used is now a relative indifference, especially because the interoperability of Token Ring and Ethernet systems can be guaranteed by recent products such as the IBM 8209 LAN bridge provided the other software prerequisites agree. Individual segments or rings should not become too large, for performance reasons, fast bridges or routers may be used to interconnect several subnetworks.

This leads to the development in the local area of a new, previously unimportant, logical network, namely the internetwork. The internetwork is formed from the set of bridges and routers and the communication systems linking these. The internetwork must also be managed and should not be viewed as a loose collection of devices.

The connections in the internetwork may be of various types. In the future, the ISDN S2M multiplex interface will be available to smaller

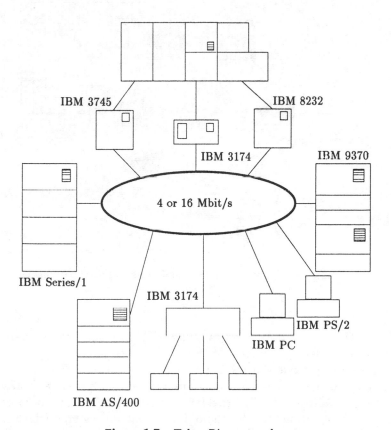

Figure 1.7   Token Ring networks.

applications; this may be implemented or provided by the latest generation of PBXs.

Another alternative for more sophisticated applications is the use of a high-speed network as a backbone. Here the *Fibre Distributed Data Interface* (FDDI) (see Figure 1.8) is blossoming into a standard solution for private internetworks. FDDI may also be used as a LAN for larger computers, even in the framework of channel extension.

As long as one remains in the private area, the planning stages are relatively straightforward. Only the creation of a private internetwork which uses public ground requires long, painful proceedings with the PTT. It is likely that only research establishments, universities and other similar organizations can hope for a reasonable, cost-effective and more-or-less acceptable outcome of this process in the near future. For the average user

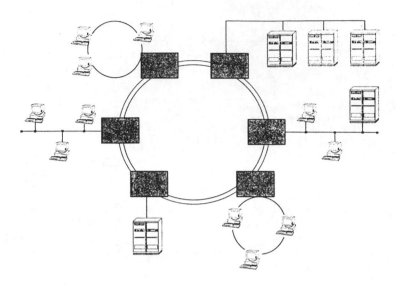

Figure 1.8 FDDI connectivity for mainframes and their peripherals.

an FDDI *Metropolitan Area Network* (MAN) still has prohibitively high compensation costs.

This also provides for a smooth technical transition from small desktop systems to mainframes in the computer centre. Is that all? Must we now manage LANs and the internetwork environment? That would be fine, except that firstly this includes the old terminal subsystems which have a strong hold due to slow innovation cycles and secondly, we are, as before, at a purely-technical level. Thus, this is far from the end of the story.

Since this book is principally concerned with computer communication, we shall only touch on PBXs. The next generation of PBXs are no longer the cellar-filling monstrosities of before. PBX technology is increasingly developing towards distributiveness, which means that even a large PBX now forms an internetworking environment where the individual components of the PBX installation may be interpreted as local integrated systems with routers. In the past, the manufacturers of PBX systems have always assumed that the users would basically prefer to telephone without problems than use complicated device controls; thus, they have designed stable, centrally-oriented management systems around their equipment, which permit a handful of people to manage and operate tens of thousands of connections with permanent reliability. These management systems are specially tailored to the equipment and are not the subject of this book. Occasionally, there are points of contact between the management of PBXs and network management, above all in the operation of terminal subsystems.

We return to this problem area again in the section on AT&T's UNMA strategy (Section 7.2).

The future equivalent of FDDI for distributed PBXs is the *Distributed Queue Double Bus* (DQDB). DQDB is primarily a synchronous communications control protocol for the management of bidirectional queues when accessing two serial buses running in opposite directions. It may (but need not) be implemented in fibre optic technology. DQDB is essentially technology independent. Pilot versions run at 140 Mbit/s, but this is certain to rise. DQDB is primarily optimal for synchronous data traffic with regular demands on a limited narrow bandwidth. FDDI on the other hand operates optimally for bursty traffic with occasional demands for higher data rates.

The prospects for integration in the area of infrastructural networks, in which FDDI and DQDB belong, have been temporarily thrown away (for the next 5–10 years). The FDDI II standard proposal, which would have considered both forms of traffic appropriately, was rejected for the most unfathomable reasons, but mainly as a result of the economics which, regrettably, characterize standardization today. The fruits of the most valuable scientific work are not normally raised to the standard, which, roughly speaking, goes to those who over the longest time have fed the most standardizers and sent them to vote. For there is a vote at the end, and many working drafts by committed working groups are voted into the wastepaper basket.

This is also, for example, the main reason why, contrary to many hopes in that direction, a far-reaching standard for in-house cabling has not been defined. The technical reasons often paraded for this are so-to-speak 'twaddle'. The business interests in tying the client down for as long as possible by constricting the manufacturer-specific cable system are so strong here that there is an invincible aversion between the individual interest groups. Only acts of desperation, such as those by the user group on cabling founded by the company ComConsult of Aachen can help.

As far as networks are concerned, we only reach quieter waters when we leave the local area. Here, the main service providers are the PTTs, and their strategy is technically clear: ISDN. Since ISDN is, in particular, enriched by value-added services, it is of no further interest here. For the next five years, ISDN will provide a stable, coverall, universal and economical transport vehicle for data transmission, regardless of all discussions on the form of the higher layers and the services associated with them. It is also clear that the old connections provided for the previous DATEL services, as permanent or virtual, fixed and switched connections, will be around for a long transition period. This also accords with the wishes of the user, who naturally wants to implement his information and communications strategy gradually rather than suddenly. This view is also quite reassuring for the network manager who may continue with a management based on virtual connections with which he is familiar from the remote area (for example, from the control of remote terminal clusters). The internal mail technologies such as ATM (Asynchronous Transfer Mode) are only of marginal interest.

The future will show how far new service providers will penetrate the market for remote connections, given the new legal rulings and how far the telecommunications companies will extend their provision. It is clear that these developments must be closely oriented towards developments in the international and in particular the European area, for cross-frontier data traffic will become increasingly important with the removal of boundaries.

Here, the route of march is clearly signposted: ISO/OSI. Only protocols and standards released in accordance with the guidelines of the open communications reference model by the international standardization bodies may be the basis for long-term stable international communications policies in the remote area. Implementations from the various manufacturers must be harmonized in corresponding test centres.

1.2.2 The protocol maze

We now come to the second theme, the protocol chaos. We shall have to get used to the fact that, even in the medium and longer term very different communication protocol stacks will coexist, in the same way as the network of the future will not consist of a large Token Ring, but of a variety of subnetworks thrown together by the internetworking environment (Figure 1.9).

Let us start from the current situation. Although the talk is all about ISO/OSI, the number of protocols actually realized, and thus the overall usage, is very small. Data processing in computer centres and associated networks in the coming years will clearly take place against the background of manufacturer-linked network architectures such as SNA from IBM, DECnet from DEC or TRANSDATA from Siemens. SNA and TRANSDATA were designed for the control of large terminal networks and thus have highly-developed management mechanisms in that sense. However, they were overrun by the PC craze, and the radical structural change to incorporate adequate treatment of the new components such as PCs and LANs has clearly caused a lot of trouble in all areas. This is also true for DEC, whose DNA concept was directed from the start towards cooperation between DEC operating systems rather than towards the control of units.

The development of the LAN operating systems, which are now so common for PC LANs, was largely encouraged by the large vacuum left by the manufacturers in this area. Workers in companies such as Novell or 3Com would even today be diving for sport into salt lakes rather than determining the world market for PC LANs and operating systems had not a very deep sleep cost IBM one of its own commodities.

It is now impossible to picture life in the future without NetWare and 3+Open, the LAN Manager, VINES, Topse and PC LAN programs.

ISO/OSI	Standards	DoD family		SAA family	Novell	
Application	X.400 FTAM	SMTP		DCA/DIA	Btrieve MHS Compiler	
Presentation	ASN.1	FTP TELNET		SNADS	Netware kernel	
Session	ISO 8326/27	DNS/NSP		APPC interface		
Transport	ISO 8072/73	TCP	UDP	LU 6.2	IPX SPX	NetBios
Network	X.25 WAN	ICMP	EGP			
		IP ARP RARP		PU 2.1		
Data link	X.25 WAN ISO 8802 LAN	ARPANET ETHERNET TOKEN RING		Token Ring Local Area Network Ethernet	Any of around 80 different LANs	
Physical	X.25 WAN ISO 8802 LAN	ARCNET X.25 PDN others		or SDLC		

Figure 1.9   The protocol maze.

They help us to implement more convenient and increasingly-ergonomic application programs in PC subLANs. From the point of view of the network management, this is not a bad thing provided these systems develop further and in so doing provide suitable assistance for communication with other environments such as SNA or OSI and for network management. Here at least, the market favourites are on the right path. This software provides a great deal of impetus to network management today. For example, the LAN Ranger which runs on the AppleTalk is a graphically-oriented package of control software, in which a ranger on his horse rides through the representation of the LAN, searches for problem points, finds them and suggests solutions.

Dedicated computer scientists may turn their noses up at this. However, one should realize that, with the drastic growth of the degree of networking, more and more people are becoming administrators without the relevant basic training; thus, such superficialities are at present, in many cases, the only viable way of achieving network management. A LAN ranger who draws his pistol to defend a bridge which one wishes to knock out is always better than a bridge knocked out by mistake which causes errors.

In addition to the classical protocols in the relatively homogeneous

Table 1.1   ISO/OSI protocol hierarchy.

ISO/OSI

Application	Application-supporting services Network management	X.400 FTAM
Presentation	Conversion of data into standard formats Interpretation of these common formats	ASN.1
Session	Interprocess connection Process synchronization	ISO 8326/27
Transport	Logical end-to-end connections abstracted from the technical communications system	ISO 8072/73
Network	Network routing Data flow control	X.25 WAN
Data link	Logical connections with data packets Elementary error-detection mechanisms	X.25 WAN ISO 8802 LAN
Physical	Communication aids to physical transmission	X.25 WAN ISO 8802 LAN

areas, in recent years the TCP/IP protocol suite which had already been laid to rest has made a glorious comeback. Today, this provides one of the few bases for communication in a heterogeneous environment. The TCP/IP protocols of layers 3 and 4 support simple application-oriented basic services such as file transfer, electronic mail and virtual terminals. They are also promoted by UNIX development and are available in all important operating systems. The joke is that, in principle, anything that one might want to do with protocols, standards and implementations using the OSI model can be done in simpler form with TCP/IP. Anyone now looking for a small, neat, economic solution is more likely to make a strike with TCP/IP than in the ISO/OSI area. This may change in the next five years, but that was the hope five years ago. A *Simple Network Management Protocol* (SNMP) has also been developed for TCP/IP and a description of this occupies a corresponding space in this book (Chapter 6).

Despite its awkward and slow development, the protocol stack of the OSI model (Table 1.1) is the most important for future orientation. The development of the application-supporting basic services in the last two to three years has shown that acceptance by the potential users is an important motivating force.

March 1990 may be celebrated as the date for the final breakthrough of OSI. Why this date? It was then that IBM proposed the last bastion against OSI, the OSI Communications Subsystem (OSI/CS), a powerful basis for implementing OSI protocols on IBM mainframes (Table 1.2).

Table 1.2 SNA and OSI.

OSI	FTAM	X.400	EDI	
NetView	OSI/CS	ISO 9596 Mgmt. ISO 9594 Dir ISO 8650 ACSE	CICS /VS	TSO /ISPF
		ISO 8823 kernel ISO 8825 ASN.1		
		ISO 8327 all		
		ISO 8073 0,2,4		
		ISO 8473 CNLS ISO 8878 CONP		
ACF/VTAM				

Internally, IBM is still adhering to SNA, which is certainly appropriate in most areas, but it has opened its very strongly represented world of mainframe platforms to OSI, for logically advanced communication between heterogeneous systems. This *perestroika* has also pleased the TCP/IP community.

In the meantime, the management of OSI environments causes difficulties. Even if the functionality of the communications components is there, the management is unclear. One reason for this is surely because in the past the OSI authorities have criminally ignored the management to the extent that there will be no stable standard before 1992 and no stable implementations before 1994/95. The IBM solution at this point is rigorous: OSI/CS will be handled and managed under NetView like any other communications resource. Other manufacturers instead include OSI network management as a possible module in their overall strategy. However, the main reason why there will be difficulties with OSI management for some time yet is actually the heterogeneous environment. Suppose that two computers, each with their own communications subsystem (for example, an IBM mainframe with MVS and SNA and a Siemens computer with BS 2000 and TRANSDATA), communicate by means of OSI protocols. Both computers control their own network resources with their own management systems. The few aspects which may arise from the use of common basic OSI services may be loosely controlled by the computers involved. Where should the OSI management be located? Clearly, the OSI management would to some extent deprive the host-based management of power. If there is a functioning management system on one side and a relatively uncertain picture, the OSI NM on the other, then it is clear where the control lies.

In the future, the question of OSI network management will increasingly arise when there is increased heterogeneity or where the ratio of OSI services and protocols to specific services is altered in favour of the OSI services.

Another reason for the use of OSI network management is the heterogeneity of the management tools which demands integration.

1.2.3 The operating system – funfair

Going a step further, the roles played by the operating systems in communication scenarios are certainly of interest. Quite simply, the problem of communication is blown up in many ways inappropriately: from the point of view of the operating system, a communications subsystem is primarily only a further facility for data input and output.

As far as the creation of distributed application environments is concerned, this view is however no longer appropriate. The communications subsystem becomes the basis for process communication.

Often in discussions of networks and communication, the term 'process communication' is qualified by the key words 'program-to-program'. It is almost always clear that scarcely anyone knows exactly what this means. Here, the very quality of the implementation of such communication determines the performance and the reliability of a whole network concept. Accordingly, we would like to draw attention to this point here. However, since this book is not about operating systems as such, the author recommends (Deitel and Harvey, 1984) or (Maekawa, Oldehoeft and Oldehoeft, 1987) for more details.

Current applications in computer systems which are not networked to other computer systems for the purposes of cooperation, run hidden from the users using a set of so-called processes.

The concept of a process first reaches planners and users intuitively through terms such as 'multitasking'. Multitasking is generally seen as the capability of an operating system to execute several tasks in a quasi-parallel fashion on a single computer. This is the opposite of the sequential processing of several programs one after the other on a single computer. The computer itself usually has only one so-called processor. The operating system accordingly contains a component which ensures that the processing of tasks may be interleaved in time and overlapped. From the outside, each task appears to have exclusive use of the processor.

This virtualization is a normal procedure in the technology of computers, operating systems and networks. Every subscriber in a time-sharing system appears to have the whole computer to himself. In virtual file systems, the various storage media are so cleverly linked together that one has the impression of an almost infinite memory which can operate at the rate of the main memory; in data transmission, signal currents are multiplexed.

Virtuality is also nothing new; it was already used in very different areas a long time ago. This even goes so far that on very large machines pretence is made of the existence of very different (virtual) machines offering full facilities (for example, multitasking). Thus, the capacity of a machine is decomposed into manageable parts.

However, there is a large area of data processing which the concept of virtuality has only penetrated to a small extent: personal computers. The original concept of the PC envisaged a user with only one task on a (small) machine. Thus, one process and the DOS operating system were sufficient; however, it was only possible to run one application at a time.

This was long thought to be sufficient. However, the ever increasing requirements on PC applications and the simultaneously increasing requirements for user friendliness have led to bottle-necks: programs for user support or for external communication must be able to run virtually simultaneously with application programs. Moreover, when one generates a document, the ability to work almost simultaneously with the word processing and the graphics program without having to chop and change between programs is practical. Equally, it is very impractical to have only a very small fixed limit for the main memory. Anyone who wants to run programs which may require more space, is left with no choice but to write the programs in such a way that they write to and read from the hard disk – that is in principle a task for the operating system.

The development of OS/2 has, regardless of the final acceptance of this operating system, shown that the days of 'single user – single application – single process – single machine' operating systems are over, at least conceptually.

Instead, there is increasing talk of use of the UNIX operating system, which was originally developed for small mainframes, on PCs. UNIX incorporates the most important concepts of virtuality.

We now return to processes and to multitasking. Why is it not immaterial whether a set of tasks (application programs, requests) is interleaved in a quasi-parallel fashion or executed in a strict consecutive sequence. The capacity of the processor is the same. The use of multitasking is associated with a major characteristic of task implementations, namely the fact that the execution of a program consists of phases. There are at least two classes of such phases, namely phases in which the program actively uses the processor and phases in which the program waits for something to happen (for example, the completion of an input/output operation or the occurrence of an event such as the satisfaction of a condition).

In a sequential execution, the wait phases decrease the effectiveness of the processor, since it is not doing anything useful. In the wait phases another program could make better use of the processor. Basically however, the execution of independent programs at this level must not be allowed to become dependent on the state of each program. This would lead to unfairness. The control of the use in empty phases must therefore be implemented by a component which is not itself one of the external requests passed to the system for execution.

An operating system is a collection of components which, in the broadest sense, control the use of a computer or make the computer usable in the first place. The component which controls multitasking belongs to this collection.

However, in general, one does not just set a program running and wait for the start of the next empty or wait phase. Instead, the available processor time is divided into static or dynamic time slices, which are generally shorter than the processing time for a very small task.

The requests, represented by program blocks, must enter the queue for the processor. If they are ready in time for a time slice, that's good, if not, they have to wait until they get another time slice. The overall management is usually refined by various program classes and priorities. We shall not go into that further.

Implicit dependencies, such as a general slowing down when a lot of programs place a heavy load on the processor, can never be totally ruled out.

Thus, the execution of large programs is always interrupted. This leads to another aspect: when the execution of a program is interrupted and it is desired to continue it later, it is very impractical to page the whole program (or parts of it) in or out or to represent partial results disproportionately.

During its execution, a program may be permanently described by its so-called overall state. The overall state before the beginning of the program execution is also called the static environment and is described by the individual states (the content) of the memory locations used by this program. These memory cells contain the program data and the program itself. However, the overall state also includes, for example, the memory cell (used by the operating system) which points to the address of the next instruction of the program to be executed (local instruction counter, instruction address register).

Whenever a program instruction is executed, the overall state changes, or at least, the local instruction counter changes. However, in relation to the size of the overall state, this change is very small. Now a program is executed in blocks, it is not always necessary to consider the full overall state, since in principle, at the end of a time slice, one only needs to consider that part of the overall state which has actually been affected.

Taken together, these considerations lead to the requirement for a halfway between program and processor to which all these concepts may be anchored: the *process*.

The process is a virtualization of a number of actions in the computer system. Such actions are generally associated with changes of state. Firstly, the linking of a program block to a process made available by the operating system leads to an action in the computer system which (we assume) corresponds to the execution of a desired sequence of operations.

In addition, there are a number of operating system processes which do a great deal for the user and the system without being immediately noticed (for example, memory management, system management, control of units, etc.). However, one would soon notice if these programs were not working.

Communication between application programs and users means, above all, communication between processes. This aspect is almost completely neglected in the literature. A communication connection between processes is usually called a session. In the ISO/OSI terminology, this is layer five, far beyond the communications subsystems. In the IBM world, the APPC concept provides a facility for process communication. Misleadingly, APPC is an abbreviation for 'Advanced Program-to-Program Communication'. It sometimes seems as though processes are suppressed like unpleasant shadows of the past.

Thus, all discussions on fast transport subsystems such as Token Ring are hollow words if the interprocess communication is badly implemented, since this largely determines what comes through 'end-to-end'.

In addition to data exchange, another major task of interprocess communication is the synchronization of concurrent processes via shared memory or pipes.

Programming languages, such as the DoD's Ada already exist, in which a problem solution may be directly expressed in terms of parallel tasks, which in the ideal case may be executed concurrently. The increased spread of such concepts will inevitably result in the requirement that a compiler for a distributed applications environment should have appropriate utilities to permit the implementation of these programming language concepts (including the synchronization mechanisms which they contain). Such utilities include powerful interprocess communication.

It is evident that, even in the future, in terms of numbers, most operating systems will have been conceived more than ten years ago (for example, MVS, VM, VMS, BS 2000, AIX, UNIX System V, BSD UNIX, OS/2 and DOS), (Figure 1.10).

The literature contains references to an operating system called Pilot which was developed by Xerox as a single-user multitasking operating system for the legendary Alto and Dorado computers between 1970 and 1975, in the same overall context as Ethernet. The latter has shot into the charts, although scarcely anyone has heard of Pilot. Thus, Microsoft and IBM can now sell OS/2 as new to almost everyone. The author does not really want to become embroiled in a conceptual comparison of OS/2 and Pilot. It could turn out that OS/2 is actually 'OS/half', where the other half with the well-developed communication is missing.

Thus, in the near future, we shall have to live with operating systems which support distributiveness at best inappropriately, and which when they do support it at all make comparatively little use of it. The only exceptions to this are the workstation concepts with operating systems such as Sun OS. However, surprisingly, even IBM has licensed a concept for a true distributed operating system. The system in question is the LOCUS offshoot TCF in the AIX framework.

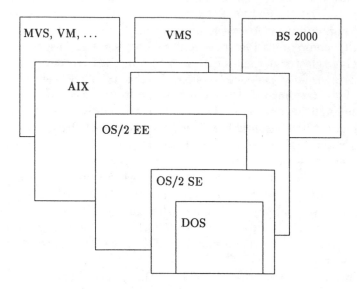

Figure 1.10 Operating systems – funfair.

Were we in a physically rigid, coherent mainframe, the management of the global resources and part of the management of the logical links would unquestionably be assigned to the spectrum of tasks of the computer's operating system.

The fact is that so many problems today arise because different operating systems on different computers are forced to interoperate using software utilities. These software utilities are, for example, called 'implementations of the main layers of a communications architecture'. They are used to create domains in which neither of the operating systems of the two machines is able to take decisions. These are the new main problem areas of network management, which go beyond the classical monitoring of network installations.

This mode of operation will continue as long as there exist heterogeneous environments of different machines and operating systems.

However, there is a completely different approach, which involves controlling a decentralized system via a uniform operating system on all components: the *distributed system.*

The distributed system should not be presented as though one takes an operating system and implements a copy of it on every computer in the distributed environment; instead, every computer has its own operating system kernel which supports the remainder of the overall system. From a logical point of view, a distributed system has a single operating system.

Distributed systems and solutions to all common related problems have been known in research for some time. Moreover, operative prototypes, experimental systems and for some restricted groups of computers (so-called workstations) even production products have also existed for some time. As with other concepts in the past, this will only be of interest when IBM provides an implementation.

This is now the case: TCF in the AIX framework is the first commercially-available distributed system from IBM. It certainly has deficiencies and, moreover, is not fully general. The UNIX standardization committee, the *Open Software Foundation* (OSF) is currently attempting to define a *Distributed Computing Environment* (DCE). At the moment, it seems that OSF will prefer the proposal of Digital and Hewlett Packard for the DECorum toolset to the already-established procedures of Sun, namely Remote Procedure Call (RPC) and Network File System (NFS). The DECorum DCE splits into two parts, namely, the fundamental distributed services, which are development tools for application programs in the distributed environment (such as remote procedure calls, naming and directory services, security software, tools for PC integration and support for execution environments for parallel programs) and data sharing services which consist of distributed file services and printer support. The selection of DECorum does not appear particularly fortunate since the Sun Open Network Computing/NFS range already has an installed base of almost 100 000 systems. However, IBM, DEC and HP want to develop DECorum products. It will of course be some time before these reach the user.

Because of TCF and DCE, it is now possible to talk about distributed systems without being deplored by most listeners or readers for one's lack of realism. However, distributed systems are no longer restricted to the level of small or medium systems. A first step towards distributed systems in the world of IBM mainframes is provided by the ESCON connections and the Sysplex (SystemComplex) which actually connects several MVS mainframes together into a logical unit. DEC also has a similar technology called the VAX cluster.

Distributed systems are the basis for future data processing. With an innovation and replacement cycle of between five and fifteen years for the most important system environments, it is highly likely that they will replace all other heterogeneous composite schemes. This thesis is daring, but well-grounded. The current uncertainty about distributed systems is comparable with the uncertainty associated with first attempts in the area of electronic document archiving. Users did not then trust electronic archiving and preferred to produce a hard copy. Today, users are not yet happy with the thought that their processes and data are spread somewhere around the system and can no longer be run or found on their workstations or on a server or a multiuser system.

Many network management problems arise in the context of a decentralized environment which is controlled by a distributed system; not any more.

However, it should be clear that here and now, the alternative possibility of developing applications based on a distributed system and simply throwing away everything to date is only open in very few cases. Conventional operating systems with 'one computer kingdom wide' will be the main workhorses for application-oriented data processing for at least ten years. Applications on distributed systems will only develop gradually.

Between true single-computer operating systems and distributed systems there will be metasoftware which will link single-computer operating systems together, more or less elegantly into pseudo distributed systems. Well-known examples of this include packages such as NetWare from Novell or the LAN Manager from Microsoft in the PC LAN environment.

When taking decisions in the information processing framework, there are two basic points of view which one may adopt:

- *The application-oriented decision.* One looks for an application program which optimally covers the needs of the application problem in hand. Then one selects an operating system and hardware on which to run the application program. This includes, if necessary, a network and metasoftware.

- *The decision oriented to the system infrastructure.* One looks for an operating system which determines the future nature of the information-technology infrastructure. All machines acquired and all networks must support this system appropriately.

Usually, one is not free to choose one's point of view. This applies not only to the system technology, but also to everything else from the cabling problem upwards.

Nevertheless, the two points of view may be conceptually analyzed. A stubborn adherence to one or the other is highly likely to result in at most the second-best solution.

In shaping the future working environment for information technology, the system-infrastructure oriented approach should not be replaced by the cobbling together of incomplete and emergency solutions.

1.2.4 Infrastructural aspects

The fact is that, because of the operating system properties described above, relatively little use is made of communication systems today. Basically, everything, whether electronic mail, remote job entry or dialogue, reduces to file transfer (Figure 1.11).

Recently, the author read that, as one would expect, a screen has 80 characters per line, while a punched card also has 80 characters per line. This inertia is clearly inherent in all areas.

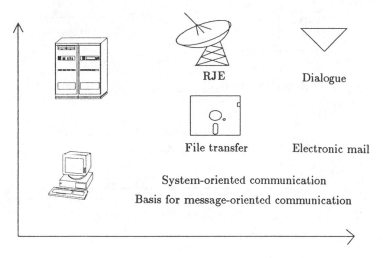

Figure 1.11   Current data processing requirements.

However, Erhard tells us that 'the network part of a metaphorically-defined continuum represents a different concept and adaptation of reality', whence 'every workstation is a physical representative of practical globality on the desk top' (Erhard, 1990).

Thus, indirectly, Erhard shows us the only way ahead: in order to secure an apparent plan for the future development of data processing in the area for which we are responsible, we must take the philosopher's words on this in all seriousness. In this way, we should use the reality of what we want to do as a fundamental basis for decision in the further development of the utilities available to us today. Little by little, based on our objectives, we must use the message-oriented basis for communication for system-oriented communication in such a way that the infrastructural aids to implementing the global user surface are adequately supported (in the sense of distributed transaction processing, distributed databases and integrated network management), regardless of whether we are dealing with a distributed system or a collection of incoherent components with corresponding structural communications software (Figure 1.12).

Only then will all users get what they actually need, an easy-to-master, ergonomically-optimal collection of tools for their daily work.

Here, network management has the important task of simplifying work with the overall system as far as possible.

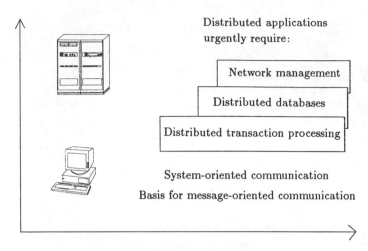

Figure 1.12   Future DP requirements.

1.3 The structure of the book

The content of this book is essentially based on a series of articles on network management which the author wrote between 1989 and 1991 for the journal DATACOM. The series has been completely rewritten, rearranged and brought up-to-date. Many additional details which were not in the original series have been introduced. The form of the series only allowed for very loose didactics and not for deeper motivation.

The next chapter provides a systematic introduction to the problem of network management using a logical-function model for computer systems.

Chapters 3 and 4 are devoted to the classical manufacturer-linked concepts for network management exemplified in the frameworks of SNA, DECnet, SINEC and TRANSDATA. This will provide the reader with an ample grasp of what these concepts involve.

Chapters 5 and 6 are devoted to the concepts for heterogeneous environments, OSI network management and TCP/IP SNMP.

Chapter 7 describes the manufacturers' strategic plans and how they intend to use OSI management for their own ends. The various different approaches are compared.

The author wishes to reach as many interested parties as possible with this book, regardless of their prior knowledge. Thus, all the main chapters contain a description of the relevant management environment and the current trends relating to this environment.

Chapter 2

Network management – systematic introduction to the problem

- The classical areas of responsibility of network management

- Network management: delimitation and formation of concepts

- Digression: distributed systems

- Summary of network and system management requirements

- Summary

After the non-technical presentation of the basic problems of data processing and the development of communication systems and operating systems in Chapter 1, this chapter provides an introduction to the problem of network management. Starting from classical environments consisting of host systems and local or remote terminals, the network management requirements are gradually extended.

The yardstick is not an organizational philosophy or a greatly outworn strategy but simply the picture of the distributed operating system. Under this, networks are just normal resources.

The author has a particular reason for this approach: the problem of distributed systems has been scientifically well-known for a decade and researched as far as possible. Most current problems only arise because a network today is a confused mixture of heterogeneous components with different operating systems and different software communication utilities. The ultimate objective is to provide the users at their workplaces with the aids they need, in such a way that they will not be permanently confused by the processing in very different environments.

When one thinks through the basic concepts of integration, a single system image stands at the end. The system, which consists of the various distributed components, computers and networks appears to all users as a homogeneous unified system (in terms of the totality of its services which are similarly available everywhere).

In about ten to fifteen years, we should be in possession of generally-distributed operating systems with such single system images. Then the major part of today's urgent problem will disappear.

However, we must make do until then. Integrated network management today consists of providing (if necessary by hand) the heterogeneous scattered networked systems with the capabilities which they currently do not have.

Starting from this baseline, the steps which must be taken on the road to the objective become clear.

Only a few subareas of computer science and computer technology have undergone such massive development over recent years as the technologies of computer and system interconnection.

The interaction of computer science, telecommunications and messaging technology has been a catalyst for new forms of communication between digital information processing devices, including, for example, high-speed data transfer over local area networks and remote connection via satellite channels.

The network requirements are growing in at least two dimensions:

- The number of stations per network is permanently increasing.
- The logical complexity (functional level) of the functions to be performed by the network is increasing.

Moreover, there are additional problems associated with the connection of largely-heterogeneous networks.

While the communications-engineering side of networks is on the whole clear, in the area of operation-supporting functions there are uncertainties similar to those associated with the general formulation of the application-oriented aspects of computer networks.

The logical complexity of network systems varies and ranges from terminal networks, through server-concept-oriented networks and open systems to distributed systems. In many cases there is a confused mixture of differently organized subnetworks. Accordingly, the requirements as far as the management of such network systems are concerned are of a varied nature. However, they are founded on common ground.

After this brief introduction, we first describe the classical task areas of network management. This comprises everything that is intuitively included in the management of, for example, a large terminal network. Then we come to the operating-system-oriented narrowing down of the concepts when we follow a more technically-oriented approach, initially omitting human factors so as to explain the problem from the technical side. The problem of logical control of terminal networks, local area networks (including the most important examples), open systems and the particular requirements of distributed systems is handled separately. Extensive use is made of cabling problems to clarify the overall context.

Section 2.3 is a digression into distributed systems, in which the reasons for using distributed computers are illustrated using the most important operating system constructions. Any reader who finds this too far removed from real problems should skip this section and read on from Section 2.4, where we attempt to summarize the network management problem area in terms of three dimensions: the network, the users and the technology security. This provides an overall introduction which is independent of the logical network type.

2.1 The classical areas of responsibility of network management

Firstly, we must describe the tasks of network management more exactly. For this, we stay initially with the classical areas of responsibility.

If we consider the management of a networked system globally, there is a division into external and internal functions. The external functions are those which cannot be executed in full by the system itself and which must be executed by people such as administrators or repairmen, with the system itself playing at best a supporting role. The internal functions are executed by the system itself and guarantee its efficiency in terms of its functionality, reactions and reliability.

In this connection, Terplan (Terplan, 1987) also notes that there are three factors which are critical to the successful management of communication networks: methods, tools and human resources.

All three must be valued appropriately. The methods of network management depend very heavily on the network and its structure. However, they should not depend directly on the size of the network, since then the network manager encounters problems when the network grows.

For those who want to deny everything possible about networks, one thing they do with certainty is grow! Here, in Germany, networks are still comparatively small. Thus, we can take advantage of the fact that others before us (for example, in the United States) have already had to manage even larger networks. Nevertheless, one should not labour under false illusions: with the rapid advance of the personal computer a tenfold increase in the number of networked computers must be reckoned with in the next five to seven years. This tenfold increase means that we can no longer 'manage by hand' as many today still believe.

Network management tools are also becoming more powerful. Where previously a network manager had to be content with a few terminals and consoles, he now has powerful systems available to him. However, he must obtain these and install them. In many companies, offices and other installations, it is still the general view that network management is valuable, useful and beneficial although it should cost nothing since it does not increase productivity. One might assert that in these companies or installations the network will not need to grow and the productivity will not need to increase, because, with such a lack of foresight they will soon not need to produce more if they plan so blindly in other areas. However, there is another problem: data protection, data security and network management are very closely related, as is now clear to many people. We shall discuss these aspects in more detail later.

Finally, in the author's opinion, the human factor is most problematic. One imagines the typical manager as being young, dynamic and liable to a coronary. The latter certainly applies to the network manager, since he is the first to see the limits on the number of stations, subnetworks and switching equipment which he can sensibly monitor. If he performs badly millions of pounds may be irrecoverably lost, for example in tasks with rapid transactions.

The classical SNA manager sits in a control centre with numerous screens. He clutches himself, graphically, the data systems of part of his organization crash. For, in the future, up to 70% of the organization's office staff (this percentage will be equipped with data systems over the next years) will be waiting for the data processing to become operational again. Presumably, in the future, workstations will not be as vulnerable as in the days of the unintelligent console, since they will be able to carry on working autonomously for a while. However, a long standstill is deadly.

Current network management products support the administrators, (as we shall now call the actual people involved in the overall network management process) but are only of limited use. Above all, when they are set complicated tasks these program systems tend to generate too much information which they forward largely unfiltered to the administrators. This requires even more highly qualified administrators – a trend which should not continue uninterrupted since otherwise the market for qualified administrators will be even narrower than today. Manufacturers and researchers see a way out in self-learning reacting systems as in the artificial intelligence (AI) area.

We shall discuss these aspects later and we now turn to more functional elements in order to get closer to the methods.

There are five groups of network management functions for the currently existing communication networks with a more classical tree structure (see for example, (Sloman, 1984)):

- *Operational management.* This describes the group of functions which are used in the operational area to prepare and manage the network resources.

- *Maintenance.* This includes all functions which may be used for error prevention, error detection and error recovery in the network.

- *Configuration management.* This involves utilities and functions for planning, extension and modification of the configuration and maintenance of the configuration information.

- *Performance management.* This involves utilities and tools to measure and improve the network performance.

- *User administration.* This group contains means of ensuring that the usage of the network is properly managed (including access management, control of usage, accounting utilities and also information services).

As far as the general structure of computer network systems is concerned, the ISO reference model ((DIN, 1982), (Effelsberg and Fleischmann, 1986), (Beyschlag, 1988)) and the resulting standards provide a reference point for the status of the technology and part of the development work.

Since, however, according to this, only protocols which are needed to control the exchange of information between systems, are candidates for a standardization, only those management activities which imply an actual exchange of information between systems will be seen as belonging to the architectural framework. Other management activities which are local to a system will not be considered in this context.

Since such a division cannot always be uniquely drawn up (for example, the execution of a user authorization may be viewed as local to a system or network wide, according to the type of the network and the application), this standpoint is in many cases inappropriate to a closed consideration of the overall problem. In due course, we shall learn what the members of the ISO committees think about network management.

2.2 Network management: delimitation and formation of concepts

Corresponding to the heterogeneous forms and environments of networks there are many different ideas about the concept of network management. For comparison, it is advisable to delimit these.

The conception and perception of network management in this book are introduced via the tasks of an operating system of an individual closed machine *per se* and the additional functional demands when components (such as controllers for remote peripheral devices) are swapped-out, as is normal for networked systems with remote terminals, subnetworks and PCs. This view is then extended to include open systems, local area networks (including heterogeneous systems) and finally distributed systems. The objective as far as distributed systems are concerned may be viewed as forward-looking, everything else is so-to-speak 'on the way'.

2.2.1 Classification of networks from the logical function viewpoint

The usual classification of networks according to the technical structure and the classes of remoteness is only useful in the network-management context when we are actually dealing with message-oriented resources. Above a functional layer such as layer 3 of the ISO reference model there is another logical-function view which takes into account the tasks of the network and the capabilities of the components.

For the classification of networks from the logical-function viewpoint we form four classes. This subdivision into classes is a mixture of statistics (which will be the most common system classes today and in the future?) and necessary didactics (how can one clear a path through the various facets of the network management?) and represents a confused mix of functional and device-specific characteristics. Nevertheless, it appears to the author to provide an appropriate cross-section.

2.2.1.1 Class 1: terminal networks

The network consists of a central computer, remote data processing computers and terminal controllers together with the end devices and the message-oriented components which connect these components (lines, LANs, data switches); the control is central; the nodes have limited capabilities. Example: SNA network with one domain (Figure 2.1).

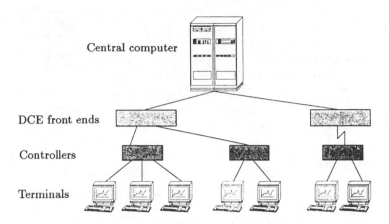

Figure 2.1   Class 1 network: terminal network.

2.2.1.2 Class 2: server networks

Here, two groups of nodes (workstations and servers) are connected by a message transport system. Servers provide services which may be used by the workstations. All nodes have their own independent control, from a workstation viewpoint the cooperation with the server is controlled by the latter; there is no network control, however, a server may take on control tasks. Example: PC networks with NetWare (Figure 2.2).

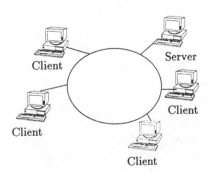

Figure 2.2   Class 2 network: server network.

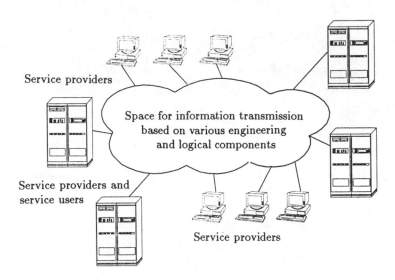

Service providers

Service providers and service users

Space for information transmission based on various engineering and logical components

Service providers

Figure 2.3   Class 3 network: open systems.

2.2.1.3 Class 3: open systems

Computers may belong to these systems if they adhere to a set of hardware and software agreements, provided they are connected to the computers already in the system by a communication link. They may then use a range of services provided in the system and may also provide services. Users are normally connected to these computers indirectly via class 1 or class 2 networks. Control of the individual nodes is carried out by the latter, control of the network installations is in most cases carried out by a network operator. A user of a service is in the main subordinate to the control of the service provider. Example: DFN (Figure 2.3) or other research networks.

2.2.1.4 Class 4: distributed systems

A distributed system consists of a set of computers (nodes) and a system of connections which permits the exchange of messages between the points. The main characteristics of a distributed system are (Figure 2.4):

- Variety of components.
- Several processors.
- A system-wide operating system.
- Transparency.
- Distributed control based on the principle of cooperative autonomy.

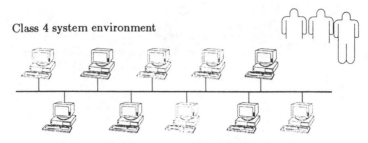

Class 4 system environment

Network and computers fused into a unit
Distributed system transparent to the user

Figure 2.4   Class 4 network: distributed systems.

In a real networked environment an increasing number of heterogeneous mixtures of the above classes will occur over a period of time. For example, a system may begin as a class 1 network such as an SNA network with a single domain. Eventually, with the introduction of Token Rings and PS/2 as end systems instead of terminal clusters, a new class of systems will essentially be formed, namely that of class 1 networks with class 2 subsystems in the end area. The control of the previously-pure class 1 network must adapt itself to this. Later on, someone thinks of an X.25 connection to permit access to a service such as X.400. Suddenly there is a new class of systems comprising class 1 networks with class 2 subsystems in the end system area in very large class 3 integrated networks. Finally, the core computer of the class 1 network might be replaced by a distributed system.

If one now concentrates on the management, there are commonalities between the classes and features specific to each class, and it may be assumed that in a mixture of two or more network types, the class-specific characteristics add together.

2.2.2 Operating systems of closed information-processing installations

The transition from individual isolated computer systems to host systems in class 1 networks involves consequences on the form of the operating system of the dominant machine in these networks. These consequences are described below.

An operating system of an individual computer system (Figure 2.5) converts a number of hardware and software resources into a coherent set

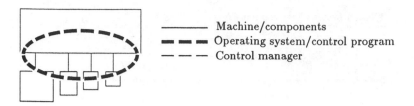

Figure 2.5   Isolated computer.

of objects and supports the execution of operations on these objects by:

- Unique object identification
- Object access mechanisms and protection against unauthorized access
- Partitioning of shared objects and synchronization
- Error control
- Bottle-neck detection and avoidance mechanisms
- Inter-object communication
- Allocation of objects
- Generation, withdrawal, linking, suspension and termination of process objects.

A large number of corresponding mechanisms are implemented for this.

The operating system has an overall view of the components. Based on an operating-system kernel oriented towards the machine, a hierarchical design may be used to create a system consisting of parts with precisely delimited capabilities and facilities, which is appropriate to a particular task area.

The operating system is then constructed in a modular fashion according to well-known software-engineering techniques. The functionality of each individual module of an operating system layer is made available via appropriate interfaces.

Here, various components are responsible for the management of the control and the optimal use of resources together with the recovery from errors which may be detected but not removed by subordinate functional units.

A component hierarchy of such an operating system contains machine-oriented and high-level layers.

The management facilities of an operating system are found in almost all layers of the component hierarchy. The position within the hierarchy determines the potential, capabilities and duties of a facility. We distinguish between two broad cases:

(1) Operating-system components in low layers have relatively short or direct paths into the machine, but their global functionality is heavily restricted by their position. In a strict design, they cannot see beyond their own layer and are thus unable to take general decisions. Thus, they are not able to execute general management functions. On the other hand, they are possible sources of information about the states of resources, to which they are closer than the components of the higher layers. Thus, they are designed to filter information in an appropriate fashion and to forward it as necessary to the components of the higher layers.

(2) Operating-system components in higher layers have access to the information produced as described above and thus obtain a complete overall picture. In addition, it is also useful to have a relatively direct access from the operator or user to the system management at a suitably protected interface.

In a small number of cases a large machine may simply consist of a single homogeneous kernel, which is only connected by an internal bus to controls (inside the machine) for peripheral devices. Since the introduction of terminal concepts such as SNA, remote, hierarchically-ordered intelligent devices (controllers, front ends) have been available to control peripheral equipment which is usually first assigned to an individual host machine.

2.2.3 Requirements in class 1 networks

As soon as components of the computer (still a single machine) are relocated (Figure 2.6) the following consequences follow:

- The implementation of objects and operations on them decomposes into bounded or boundable parts which may be located in different places.

- The control over the implementation and its correctness must follow the same path, since certain components may now be hidden. Every relocated element of the data processing installation is assigned at least one control element, which controls the local actions of the device and monitors and provides basic assistance for communication (at least with the elements of the data processing installation which the device serves or is served by).

- An entity is required to coordinate the actions of the distributed control elements and provide assistance when these get stuck.

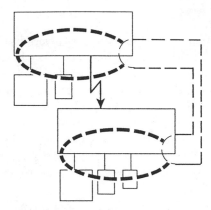

Figure 2.6   Computer with relocated components.

In what follows, we shall call the above entity the control manager. The control manager has two groups of interfaces:

- Interfaces 'downwards' to the individual control elements of the relocated parts of the data processing installation.

- Interfaces 'upwards' to the highest control components of the operating system and if necessary to the user surface (operator).

The control manager guarantees the necessary transparency for the operating system as a whole and supports it in the execution of its tasks.

Here is a small example. In an SNA network with only one domain, the front ends and the cluster controllers are relocated. The front-end control component is the *Network Control Program* (NCP). The control manager resides, together with the operating system (for example, OS/MVS), in the host (for example, /370) and is called a *System Services Control Point* (SSCP). It monitors the NCPs and their interplay with the access methods (for example, ACF/VTAM) together with the execution of protection requests.

We shall not discuss further details of the implementation of a control manager here.

The management of such a system is now a well-known task, and one which is to a large extent resolved. In his book (Terplan, 1987), Terplan describes in great depth the four areas of responsibility of the management of classical communication networks: operational control, administration, analysis and tuning and capacity planning. These areas are largely characterized by different reaction-time requirements.

On closer consideration, many of these tasks are the same as those of a standalone operating system; in other tasks, the network plays a role.

2.2.4 Additional problems in class 2 networks

Class 2 networks may have very different orders of magnitude. In small networks, the main management problems are associated with the organization of the file-server hard disks and the specification of access rights.

More recent PC LAN software packages take this point into account in a more appropriate way than before. The PC LAN program 1.3 from IBM, the LAN Manager from Microsoft and NetWare 2.1 from Novell provide a set of additional mechanisms for management of the user hordes.

We shall consider three typical examples: management functions in Novell's NetWare; the Extended Services of the IBM PC LANP 1.3 for logical control of the client/server environment and the IBM Token Ring LAN Manager; and the trace and performance tool for obtaining statistical data from the Token Ring network. This will give the reader a feeling for different task areas which result from the separation of the logical and the physical network.

2.2.4.1 Management functions in NetWare

We assume a knowledge of the basic structure of Novell's NetWare, the market leader amongst PC LAN operating systems; otherwise, see (Kauffels, 1990).

Menu-driven service programs facilitate the maintenance and control of the network for the system manager. System administrators may use them to organize the network in such a way that normal users do not require any prior knowledge of DOS or the Novell software. File structures which they require for their work are automatically made accessible to them.

Most noteworthy is the facility for accounting for services in the network, which was only previously known on mainframes. A value can be placed on every individual service (for example, access to a file on a server). The individual user is now allocated accounting points with which to account for the services used. If a user exceeds a value prescribed for him, only the system administrator can then renew his access to the system by increasing his accounting points.

The time of network access may also be controlled. For example, in periods of particularly heavy use, such as between 11.00 and 12.00, access to certain servers or services may only be granted to a few authorized users. This means that particularly important tasks may be executed with priority.

The network load may be controlled at all times. For this, spot recordings of the network load are made in the LAN. Longer term indicators of the network load and the load behaviour in the network can only be obtained using add-on products from other companies.

We shall not discuss the exact descriptions of the individual service programs and utilities and Novell NetWare here. These are described in detail in the product descriptions and manuals.

The most important functions and facilities are summarized briefly below:

Network management:

- Addition, modification or deletion of users and user groups.
- Execution of console operations ('virtual consoles') by every PC in the network, for example:
  - Display of various statistics.
  - Control of the file server (for example, taking down). Checking of data locks.
  - Final deletion of files.
  - Changes of printers and selection of various print formats.
  - Queue protocols for print, archiving and batch-job servers.

Accounting:

- Facilities available to the supervisor:
  - Specification of a credit limit for each user.
  - Monitoring of the state of accounts of individual users.
  - Generation of a test path for system use.
  - Variation of tariffs according to the time of day and the day of the week.
- Criteria on which accounting may be based:
  - Duration of connection.
  - Number of blocks written to and/or read from disk.
  - Area occupied on storage disk.

Network security:

- Locking of user accounts, specification of an expiry date.
- Password encryption, regular changes of passwords, minimum password lengths, etc.

- Restriction of user log-in times and of workstations on which it is possible to log in.

- Access rights which specify the directories which the user may access and control the access to individual files using file attributes.

Management in the broader sense also includes the sensible management of data and the provision of replacement resources to alleviate the consequences of breakdown.

The operating system *System Fault Tolerant* (SFT) NetWare in version 2.x increases the reliability of local area networks with a facility for duplication of particularly sensitive parts such as, for example, the server disk or the system controller. In case of a disk error, the breakdown of a disk drive or a controller or a power failure, the data integrity of the LAN is preserved. All system fault tolerance functions of SFT NetWare work automatically and do not interfere with the normal operation of the network. There may even be slight performance improvements in read access to data, since the software accesses the disk with head at the next data position.

SFT NetWare 2.1 incorporates the connection facilities of Advanced NetWare and contains all the functions which are built into SFT NetWare Level I and Level II. SFT generates two file assignment tables (FATs) and directory entries for each disk and stores them on different disk cylinders. This guarantees the availability of a backup copy of the important disk management data. In every write procedure, the data is again read and compared with the content of the main memory. In the case of error, the defective block is marked as unusable and a replacement block on the disk is automatically used. If required, disks may be shadowed. All information is automatically stored twice and compared. If there is a read error on one disk, an automatic switchover to the other disk occurs without the need for the work to be interrupted.

In addition, SFT provides for the duplication of controllers, disk drives, and host interfaces. When one of these devices breaks down, switchover and logging follow automatically.

Data areas that are frequently accessed are held in the file server RAM (file caching). The number of directory accesses is halved because all directories are also held in the RAM (directory caching). A fast search procedure is also used to find entries in large directories (directory hashing). The read/write heads are only ever moved in one direction until they reach the disk boundary. This means that file access does not depend on the sequence of requests but on the sequence of the files found (elevator seeking).

In addition to increases in performance, the version NetWare 3.1 /386 is characterized by a revised file system and by various network management improvements intended to make the use of the new NetWare more pleasant. The improvements include simplified and faster installation, extended data security, dynamic resource configurability and improved support for the printer service.

One very nice feature of NetWare 386 V.3.0 is that files on the hard disk are not deleted when the delete command is issued, but only when the hard disk is full and the system needs more space. Deleted files retain their security parameters until they are completely removed from the system. This means that only authorized users may regenerate files deleted in error and process them further. Today we can conjecture that it will soon be possible to use these options together with a magnetic tape drive to expand the file space almost *ad infinitum*. NetWare 386 V.3.0 also has all the fault tolerance characteristics of SFT NetWare 2.15, including disk shadowing, duplicated disk controllers and transaction tracking.

A facility for duplication of whole servers is expected soon.

2.2.4.2 Management functions in the IBM PC LAN program

The IBM PC LAN program creates a client/server environment with a classical structure based on a Token Ring network or a baseband or broadband IBM PC LAN. It is intended for management of the logical LAN. Management of the physical LAN is via the LAN Manager, the IBM product for Token Ring network management, not to be confused with its namesake, the LAN Manager from Microsoft or with the trace and performance tool described in the next subsection.

Every server can take on network management functions in a certain area. The only central network manager is an add-on product in the form of one dedicated PC per Token Ring.

The functions of the network server are:

- Allocation of resources to network subscribers.
- Allocation of priorities for the use of resources on the server to the network subscribers.
- Allocation of names and passwords to workstations and users.
- Provision of a small number of error statistics.
- Provision of so-called public resources, such as spool areas, etc.

IBM offers the Token Ring network manager program for monitoring the Token Ring LAN. This program may be used to log and analyze errors in the network. Another possibility is the PC network analysis program. This contains several programs which can execute monitor and trace functions.

The main features of the PC network program include:

(1) Symbolic station names. Every station within the network must be allocated a name.
(2) Symbolic subdirectory names for uniform access to the network.
(3) Communication between stations based on logical links.

(4)   Menu-driven operator dialogue or DOS-like command language.

The menu-driven nature of the network control makes it easier for the users to learn the network commands; in many cases, it even makes knowledge of these commands superfluous, since the menus cover almost all functions needed to control the network.

   In addition to the base services which correspond to the functions of the PC LAN program V.1.2, the more recent versions from V.1.3 contain extensions called Extended Services (ES). Using the base services within the LAN, programs and units may, as usual, be used simultaneously by several systems. Performance improvements against the earlier versions have not been determined. The cache memory, which may be used to optimize access, may now be transferred to the Extended Memory Store (EMS), which is supported, as standard from DOS 4.0.

   The following extensions of the PC LAN program are incorporated in the extended services:

- Dialogue-driven assistance to the control and operation of the system and 'on-line reference'.
- Menus to manage and access resources of the server PCs.
- Introduction of the domain concept and the system administrator function.
- Introduction of user numbers and password protection.
- Definition of 'file sets'.
- Introduction of an 'application selector' according to the pattern of OS/2.
- Use of Remote Initial Program Loaded (RIPL) to improve the network transparency and to integrate so-called diskless workstations into the LAN.

As in SNA, the concept of domains is new, although it has a different sense here.

   A domain consists of one or more ES servers in a LAN. Here, a server is responsible for the management of the domain. This must be the first system generated when a new LAN is constructed. Only the system administrator has direct access to the so-called domain controller. This permits the management and definition of the resources of various servers as one. The system administrator defines the resources within a domain and the users who may access them.

   Several domains may be defined in a LAN. Thus, the names allocated in a domain must be unique in the LAN as a whole. The names of the domain and the domain controller must agree. For the users, the resources which are available within the domain appear as a 'single system image'.

A domain includes the various servers and the given users but no workstations.

The system administrator is responsible for the management of the domain. He is responsible for the installation of the programs on the servers and for the definition of the domain and its management, including:

- Definition of the users and the resources which they may use.
- Definition of the ES servers.
- Definition of RIPL stations.
- Allocation of user IDs and passwords.
- Allocation of user rights for file sets.

The system administrator may manage the domain from any ES station. Only users with the privileges of a system administrator may log in to an ES server.

The user numbers are allocated by the system administrator. Users may log in to the system with their user numbers, and with their passwords if necessary.

The login must take place directly when the system is switched on. This means that machines can only be used when the user has a valid user number.

The system automatically constructs an environment for the user which is specified by the system administrator.

The user is presented with a menu, the application selector, from which he may select the desired application. The basic menu prescribed by the system administrator contains several statements which the user may use to call his standard applications together with DOS and LAN functions. He may extend this menu according to his requirements.

User access to all the resources available in the domain is usually from a workstation. The system administrator is responsible for the configuration of these stations.

Internal resources are defined, managed and used within the domain. Amongst other things, these include programs, data files or printers. External resources may be either defined within a domain and used from outside it or made available outside and used by users within the domain. These include resources which are made available on another server, on another domain controller or ES server or in another compatible network. All externally-usable resources are identified as such in a special file (external.bat) and thus may also be reached by users of the base services.

A file set is a directory on an ES-server disk, including all files and subdirectories. The system administrator defines the name, the content and the location of a file set. Additionally, he also specifies which users may access it and the various access rights. A home file set is a directory on the domain controller which is set up for each user by the system. Users have read/write access to their home file set.

The security concept allows for a user to log in to a domain once only. When the system administrator assigns the user a password, this may be changed at will by the user. If he forgets his password, only the system administrator can assign him a new password. If a user tries three times to log in under the same user number but with an invalid password, the workstation is automatically blocked and can only be used again when it is brought up completely from new.

2.2.4.3 IBM network management facilities in Token Ring networks

IBM has two different programs for monitoring the Token Ring, namely the trace and performance monitor and the LAN Manager. The programs, which are normally installed on a dedicated PC in the ring, monitor the ring for hardware and software errors and provide facilities for controlling the throughput in the ring. Errors are notified to the operator together with advice on how to recover from them.

It is possible to monitor individual LANs and several LANs linked by bridges. Errors are recorded with the date and time on a diskette or disk. Stations may be logically removed from the ring in order to analyze errors in more detail. Here, other management tools, such as those from Proteon are advantageous, since they also permit the physical removal of a station from the ring. In the case of logical (protocol controlled) connection establishment, the user of this station can immediately attempt to access the ring again; if the port is locked, as with Proteon and Ungermann Bass, this is not possible.

IBM LAN Manager   The LAN Manager is primarily used to record and analyze errors. Modifications of the ring configuration may be logged for security reasons. In a DOS environment, it is also linked to NetView/PC. NetView/PC uses the LAN-Manager error messages to generate the typical alerts in IBM environments, which are then forwarded via SNA networks to the main system. System programmers may then carry out the error analysis centrally at the mainframe network-management console. As a prerequisite, either a dedicated DOS PC with a real-time coprocessor interface card, which is connected to the central manager PC over a switched line for access to its data, or an OS/2 PC with a suitable adapter (not necessarily dedicated) is required.

The monitoring functions may be executed in other subnetworks which are connected via a bridge.

When several Token Ring LANs are installed in a company or a concern, central control of the Token Ring manager DOS PCs using NetView/PC (respectively, the OS/2 EE PCs using the LAN Manager from V.2, when NetView/PC is not needed) is often the only organizationally sensible way of monitoring the network.

From version 2, the LAN Manager is able to forward the error messages to the host NetView via the normal Token Ring link without having to establish an additional line. However, this version requires OS/2 EE as operating system while the other version can run under DOS. This variant also has little to recommend it since errors in the Token Ring in the area of the gateway to the host are detected but cannot be communicated onwards.

For small networks, it is sensible to install the LAN manager on the OS/2 server so as not to increase the cost of the overall system unnecessarily.

The error analysis uses menu-driven evaluation programs. The individual stations may be assigned symbolic names which are stored in a special name file. Access to this program may be restricted by password entry. Permanent errors are recorded directly. Support functions in the program facilitate debugging. Temporary errors are only logged when a predefined threshold is exceeded; thus, the error statistics remain readable. Alterations to the Token Ring configuration may also be logged.

The control mechanisms for data protection in the new versions of the LAN Manager are also important. It is possible to record exactly who has worked at what time in which segment of the LAN and which LAN workstation was used. Unauthorized or inadvertent access may be automatically prevented by appropriate programming.

The LAN Manager may also be used centrally from the NetView operating station or from the station on which the LAN Manager is installed to monitor and configure all IBM source routing bridges in the LAN. In particular, for every ring a record is made of the number of broadcast and non-broadcast frames transmitted into each other ring. If frames could not be forwarded, the reason for this and the frequency of this error are recorded. Entries such as the bridge number, the maximum frame size, symbolic names or the hop counter, which determines the maximum number of bridges over which a message may be forwarded, may be altered via the LAN Manager.

Trace and performance program   Only dedicated use of the IBM trace and performance program is possible and a special trace and performance adapter is required. This adapter may also be used in the normal operation of a station in the Token Ring, but contains an EPROM with extra commands which are used for trace and monitor functions.

If the PC is operated in monitor mode, the load pattern in the LAN is recorded over a long period. If desired, the results can also be prepared in graphical form. This is only sensible when firstly an IBM-compatible printer is available and secondly when the recording time is at least several hours. The instantaneous load is shown directly on the PC screen in the form of a bar chart. Here, the average token waiting time of a station, which again depends on the overall load in the LAN, is also of interest.

Trace functions of this type, with extensions and additions (mostly connected with the analysis of other protocols such as TCP/IP or IPX/SPX

(Novell)), are offered by several other manufacturers (for example, the Sniffer from Spider and the LAN Analyser from Excelan) as alternatives to the IBM product.

In general, we note that, even in a simple homogeneous small-system environment such as the IBM Token Ring, there are three different non-integrated management tools, namely the logical client/server program PC LANP, the LAN Manager and the trace and performance program. The Token Ring clearly shows how little thought has been given to management. For, in practice, these three tools have to be supplemented by two others: a physical cable tester and logic analyzer for error management at the lowest level and a configuration and inventory database. There are also special programs for data protection.

Until now, we have assumed that the Token Ring does not depend on the host, which it normally does. In this case, there is also interaction with the host-based management tools, as we discover in the next chapter.

It should now be clear where the problems lie. Every management product has its own surface which one must learn; this does nothing to increase productivity.

There are comparable products for the Ethernet world.

The LAN Manager will not exist for much longer in the form described above, since its functions are not integrated to any great extent and since there is no LAN-software-independent user management. The solution, which has already been announced, is called the LAN Network Manager and has a fundamentally different structure which leads to considerably-extended functions. We discuss this in a later chapter.

2.2.4.4 LAN management according to IEEE 802

As the LAN standardization body, the IEEE 802 panel is required to promote the unified management of local area networks via appropriate proposals. It can be said, in the author's opinion, to have failed until now.

IEEE 802 assumes that the network is constructed according to the guidelines of the ISO reference model. As far as the management is concerned, this only presupposes that the lower layers are implemented exactly according to the standard; there are no other prerequisites for the upper layers. This is largely due to the fact that ISO itself only thought of considering the management at a very late stage.

The functional requirements on local area networks according to IEEE 802 specify the following LAN network management functions:

- Guaranteed compatibility between devices from different manu-facturers.

- Specifications for the installation of common protocols and interfaces for local area networks.

- The management should be defined to correspond as closely as possible to the previous layering of the ISO reference model.

- There must be mechanisms to manage and allocate shared network resources.

- The end users of different service classes should be able to manage their own address space, completely or in part.

- There must be a mechanism for simultaneous access to several, alternate layer-3 protocol units and/or network management units and/or layer management units.

- It must be possible to restart following transient errors.

- Features to facilitate network maintenance, diagnosis and repair must be present.

- The functions must be defined according to existing standards and those in preparation.

- The functions must be such that relatively simple interfaces to other networks or common carrier equipment can be constructed.

The administrative aspects of network management must also be seen in the context of the control and management of a complete distributed system. When we consider these aspects, we note that they represent nothing more than a certain form of application with a system-oriented purpose, where the users carry out a well-defined set of management and control activities.

Thus, it is reasonable to execute (or permit the execution of) the activities on special workstations distributed across the whole system in a structure comparable to that in which applications are normally distributed across the workplace. The workstations communicate over the same routes as the application processes. For each node, there must be at least one node-management workstation and/or one node-management process group.

A node-management process group alone is not capable of providing the required services. It must be supported by the lower layers. Thus, the following approach to node management is taken:

- The level-management part of each layer of the architecture delivers status messages and receives control messages from the local node management.

- In every local node, node-management entities coordinate local administrative activities; they report status information and receive control messages from global monitoring positions, suitably distributed across the network.

- Administrative interfaces supply assistance to a number of administrative staff for the purpose of interaction with the workstations involved. These staff then become part of the control process.

The following concepts form a basis for the LAN network management:

- There exists a hierarchy of management levels within the model:
    - Global (over connected networks).
    - Network (a single element of a series).
    - Node (a single end system in the network).
    - Layer (a single architectural layer).
- In the context of the management of the resources of the open system, end-to-end protocols are used to exchange current information between peers.
- Every layer has management capabilities.
- Layer-management service requests and responses are viewed as being generated and terminated in each layer.
- A single node may have several management units within a layer.
- There are mechanisms to identify layer-management end products.
- Management facilities within a layer communicate with remote peer management facilities of the appropriate layer via the layer below.
- Management facilities of the same layer within a node communicate directly.

IEEE 802 has not finally agreed on the release of the proposals. However, the following functions may be assumed fixed:

Initialization and termination of activities

- Network and protocol configurations.
- Restriction of parameters.

Monitoring and statistics

- Immediate.
- Cumulative.

Provision of assistance during normal operations

- Access controls.
- Parameter changes.
- Addressing.

Handling of abnormal operations

- Error detection.
- Restarting.
- Diagnosis.

In the author's opinion, the IEEE 802's most interesting proposal is the hierarchy of management levels, which takes considerably greater account of the reality than other approaches.

The demands which LAN systems impose on daily management work are very different from those of, for example, SNA tree cabling. Often the practical problem of documentation is neglected.

2.2.4.5 On-line communication systems

Many users are aware of the problems of communication systems which have grown over the years; these include confused cable systems, unknown routing plans and errors which can only be located at great expense. Until now, this situation was restricted to star-shaped old systems (SNA, terminal networks, telephone). With the use of local area networks, the effects of this situation on operating costs and availability are increasing noticeably.

Local area networks are dynamic infrastructures. Large numbers of new connections (up to 100% per year) and a high rate of staff movement lead to major, permanent modifications. Moreover, local area networks are noted for their simultaneous use of the cable system and for the heterogeneity of their protocols and manufacturer-base. If the overview is lost, the operational costs of help-desk facilities, modification of the network structure and debugging increase sharply. In addition, the personnel costs are enormous (studies by the company ComConsult speak of 100% additional costs) and there is a danger of considerable breakdown costs or losses of productivity. An investigation by the company Infonetics illustrates this danger. The growth of our networks may lead to breakdowns caused by unstructured extensions and network interconnections, with consequent losses of up to 1% of the company's annual turnover. The personnel requirement increases with costs an order of magnitude greater than the capital expenditure.

The solution of this problem requires the development of an operating concept. This covers the deployment of personnel, the description of their qualifications and the allocation of the activities to be carried out. The centre point of an operating concept is usually the on-line management which is responsible both for the on-line documentation and for controlling and monitoring the work to be executed.

An on-line management forms the basis for the operation of every network over a given size (over 100 intelligent stations connected). Based on an associated, object-oriented CAD/database system all the important network information (passive components, active components, configuration parameters, error statistics and history, user information, end-device descriptions, etc.) is collected and simultaneously made available to several user groups. Typical user groups include network managers, planners, engineers and user-support groups. The system supports all the activities of day-to-day operation (change planning, moves, new connections, user advice, debugging, etc.) and maintains an awareness of the current network situation. It must be supplemented above by the so-called monitor management. The main advantages of an on-line documentation system are that it provides for fast reaction to errors and changes, preserves the overview of the network and reduces the number of operations staff required (since many of the day-to-day activities can now be supported and optimized).

When bringing a network into operation it is advisable to have ready-made on-line documentation on hand for installation. This may help to avoid lavish and sometimes very expensive later documentation and the operation of the network will then be supported from day one.

An on-line database for network management must be provided with intelligent functions which support all the phases in the life-cycle of a communication solution. Particularly important here is the support for activities designed to reduce operational and breakdown costs. The high proportion of personnel costs for the operation of the network is a background factor. Particular attention should be paid to the hidden personnel costs of, for example, engineers or staff not fully assigned to the running of the network.

An on-line management system can and should be used to good effect even in planning. Extensive product, component and object libraries lead to planning with a high level of network know-how. The associated assessment operations to check the plausibility, analyze errors, review the costs, generate component lists and produce advice for operation and installation provide for error-free, cost-effective network design.

Network managers, those involved in user support, field engineers and planners all gain from the implementation of on-line management as part of the network operation. This supports the operational tasks of the various user groups. The use of on-line management with appropriate operational modules now guarantees the optimal cost-effectiveness of a network. With the optimal use of personnel, it is possible to monitor all operational situations and to introduce any necessary measures in the shortest possible time. This minimizes the typically hidden personnel costs of network operation. Typical operation modules include: object report, user report, physical connection report, logical connection report and inventory management.

Changes to the network structure occur every day; they may involve moves, an extension, a new connection or a device change. Until now the associated hidden operational costs have been enormous. With an on-line management system, the typical work associated with changes is optimized. With the optimal use of personnel, changes may be made with minimum danger of error. Typical components of the change module include: change planning, operational advice, plausibility controls and cost analysis.

Let us consider a specific example.

The prerequisites for an on-line management system are:

- Multi-user capability
- Networked system
- CAD/database coupling in both directions.

Currently, management systems with very different origins and very varied functionality are being marketed. Examples of the different origins and functionality include:

- Telephone management (Steinmeyr, Safenet LAN)
- Architecture/facility management (Isicad, Command)
- Network management (ComConsult, Communication Manager)

To illustrate the structure of an on-line management system, in the following we describe the structure of the ComConsult Communication Manager, since this is the only system on offer which was specially developed for this purpose.

The ComConsult Communication Manager is a modular system the modules of which may be combined in an application-specific manner. One of its strengths is the detailed database which contains nearly all the required objects, complete with attributes. The main modules of the Communication Manager are:

- On-line management
  - Cable management with distribution management and automatic relocation and connection functions,
  - Ground plan management,
  - Configuration management of all active and passive components,
  - User management,
  - History management,
  - Plausibility/consistency monitoring.
- Help-desk support
  - Problem management with system management and problem assessment,

- — Error message registration, distribution and tracking,
- — Consideration of degrees of urgency,
- — Storage and retrieval of solutions of recurring problems (and the like).

- Change management
  - — Control and monitoring of all changes to be made in the network,
  - — Comparative planning,
  - — Production of technical operational advice.

- Facility management
  - — Inventory management of all network components and end devices,
  - — Location management,
  - — Management of contract data for purchase, loan, leasing and maintenance contracts.

The above modules of the Communication Manager may be supplemented by architecture, electrical planning and DP system-engineering modules.

The structure of the Communication Manager, which is typical of that of all management systems of this type, involves a system technology with a client/server solution based on a network.

A central server implements the database system (here, ORACLE, supplemented by object orientation) and the image archive. Any workstations may access this server over a network (Ethernet or Token Ring). AutoCAD is used as a CAD system on graphics-based workstations. AutoCAD and ORACLE are so closely interlinked that both database queries using CAD operations and image selection using database operations are possible. Thus, despite its powerful functions, the user surface is kept simple; this also guarantees its acceptance in the field.

2.2.5 A model of the management in open systems

In the context of the standardization of open systems, ISO has also been concerned with the problems of system and thus also network management. In order to standardize network-management components and protocols a conceptual model for the management must be generated to match the ISO/OSI layer model (Figure 2.7).

We only touch on this problem briefly here and devote Chapter 5 to the most recent status of these developments. In the specification of management tasks by OSI there has been a clear change of perspectives over the last five years, which the author will not keep from the reader.

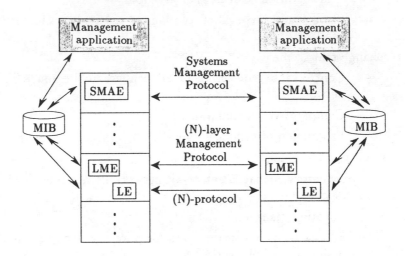

Figure 2.7 OSI management architecture.

In the first formulations, the management together with the information processing was considered to be the facility for planning, organizing and controlling the resources available to meet the users' information-engineering needs.

The needs of the users were covered by the relevant active and passive components and objects. The physical implementations of the components were not apparent to the users. Conceptually, resources are viewed as OSI resources, which are abstract objects on which certain operations are specified.

Corresponding to these operations, in most cases there exist boundary conditions which are described by the protocols of the OSI layer containing the resource (usually, this is layer 7, the application layer).

An incarnation of an OSI resource is an object. A sequence of parameterized operations on an object is a management function.

As far as the ISO reference model is concerned there are three management layers: application management, system management and layer management.

The application management includes the control of the application-layer application process groups managing the individual tasks.

Application management includes the following tasks:

- Process control, such as initialization, suspension and termination of application processes.

- Allocation and release of resources.
- Control of concurrency and detection of bottle-necks.
- Control of restarts after errors.
- Security controls such as maintenance of keys or passwords.
- Journaling.

The application management is a component of the application layer.
The system management has tasks such as:

- Identification of a system as a network system.
- Activation and deactivation of participation in the network.
- Maintenance of system parameters.
- Reconfiguration after system errors.

The system management is usually also implemented using processes of layer 7. Both of the above management groups obtain their information from dedicated parts of the underlying layers, the layer management services, the tasks of which include:

- Collection of statistics and journaling.
- Recording and notification of errors which cannot be immediately removed.
- Entry, deletion, allocation and release of communications resources on behalf of the system management.
- Reconfiguration under abnormal conditions.

In contrast to the otherwise strongly-hierarchical procedures, the management entities of layer 7 communicate directly with the level management entities. This is important when, for example, implementations of the middle layers have broken down completely and one wishes to find out about the state of the network as a whole.

The ISO working groups propose that the ultimate responsibility for the overall functionality should lie in the hands of people. The activities and intercommunication of such people cannot be the subject of OSI standardization, although a number of their activities could be viewed as connected with OSI management functions and the interactions of these.

Here too, a number of functions are envisaged which ultimately belong to the narrow tasks of an operating system.

We consider this problem again in more detail in Chapter 5. Firstly however, we consider the comprehensive class of distributed systems.

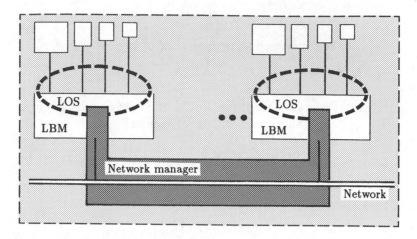

LBM: local base machine, node
LOS: local operating system, node OS

Figure 2.8   Distributed system.

2.2.6 Special requirements of distributed systems

In this section, we move directly to class 4 networks, since we expect the strongest requirements here.

Pure class 2 networks are not particularly interesting from the management point of view, since, in any case, they only represent a transitional stage towards distributed systems.

The management of class 3 networks is heavily dependent on the individual nodes. Since class 3 networks are, almost without exception, constructed according to the guidelines of the ISO reference model, we shall discuss their management in the next chapter in the context of the corresponding ISO recommendations.

A distributed system (Figure 2.8) consists of two groups of components: nodes or points (which are computers in the above analysis), and a message network which connects the spatially-separated nodes.

The message network may be composed of several message networks. In the same way that the nature and the work of nodes may vary over a broad spectrum, there are also many different message networks with very different structures and roles.

The operating system of a distributed system (this operating system is usually also called a distributed system) carries out exactly the same tasks on behalf of its users (now spatially distributed) as the operating system of a dedicated machine.

However, in this case, the prerequisites for the execution of the necessary tasks are less favourable:

- The network environment implies various control points which are distributed across the whole system.

- The operating system has to manage global and local resources; the latter are visible, the former are only visible and accessible indirectly.

- The local managerial operating system components reside in the nodes for which they are responsible, the global managerial operating system components are distributed across several or all nodes.

- The existence of shared, physically uniform, secure storage cannot be assumed.

- The nodes are distributed and accordingly, not every node has full sight of the overall plan.

- Particular attention must be paid to the message systems.

Solutions may be found to most of these problems. These solutions are always greatly simplified, if we can assume, without having to worry about the details of the message network, that noise-free communication between two objects at different points in space is possible at any time.

Under normal circumstances, this can be achieved and there exist proposals which also take account of the abstraction from real transport systems and transmission equipment.

However, the case in which the message network breaks down, completely or in part, temporarily or over a long period should not be neglected.

This requires another component, the network manager. Its tasks may be characterized as extending the tasks of the control manager, as follows:

- Support for the correct functioning of the distributed system as a whole by ensuring the correct functioning of the message transport system and the node components correlated with it.

- Notification and recording of the use of the network resources.

- Query and modification of the states of network units.

- Provision and coordination of the use of network resources.

- Support for the implementation of a security policy.

The network manager represents the logical link between distributed operating system components. It coordinates the actions of the distributed control elements and provides transparency.

At the same time, it may be used to provide the users with additional information which is not visible to the local stations.

This perspective of the distributed system omits all purely operational aspects, such as the accounting for services.

Thus, incorporation of the most important aspects of a class 1 system does no harm to a distributed system.

In the above sense, the network manager is a program which, in the ideal case, runs without external intervention and implements all the internal management functions. The external functions are of course the responsibility of people.

The case of fully-automatic network management outlined here is a vision of the future, which may perhaps become a reality within the next decade. Until then, we are on a journey which began twenty years ago, when telephone lines on which data was transmitted were monitored and repaired with practically no assistance from data systems technology.

The distributed system (in the sense of an operating system of a set of networked nodes) is as it were the end of the journey for the conventional isolated operating system with its communication-utilities software, and the new beginning of a completely different generation of systems for which spatial distributiveness is as natural and problem-free as the presence of internal buses in PCs today.

We commend the digression into distributed systems in Section 2.3 to readers who wish to know more about this. For other readers, OSI network management is considered further in Chapter 3.

2.3 Digression: distributed systems

The basic idea of distributed (operating) systems (which we shall denote by DS in what follows) is the combination of computers and message transport systems under a uniform view. It is not possible to give a unique definition of a DS since in the literature there are a number of meanings.

2.3.1 Definition and delimitation of distributed systems

In the remainder of this chapter we consider a complete information-processing system of the following form:

- The system consists of a number of computers (points) each of which has its own storage and peripherals and a computational capability. With an appropriate operating system, each of these computers is able to execute information-processing tasks. As far as the performance of the computers is concerned, it is only assumed that in parallel to the processing of one or more application tasks, they are also able to execute infrastructural and system-related programs.

- All these computers are suitably interconnected.

Appropriate here means that there exists a message transport system between the computers, which permits the exchange of messages between the cooperating points in such a way that transparency of a transaction is not violated. For a user, the transparency of a transaction consists of the fact that there is no noticeable difference between the reaction speeds when a transaction is executed on a physically-near or a physically-remote station.

In order not to restrict the generality unnecessarily, no more assumptions should be made about the node machines. The node machines are generally apparent through their command sets and the functions associated with these. The requirement for elementary multi-programmability is largely based on the fact that in parallel to the execution of a communications-related program, in addition to the execution of the program, it is also necessary to implement and monitor a logical communications link. Continual switching between applications and the communications programs leads to unacceptable performance.

From the user's point of view, a DS looks like a normal operating system on a conventional individual machine; however, it is a program which controls and manages the resources of several, possibly-heterogeneous, independent computing systems and makes a uniform interface available to the user (Tanenbaum and Renesse, 1985).

There are two main characteristics:

- A variety of components due to the inclusion of heterogeneous computers and various message networks in a single environment.
- Transparency as a result of appropriate abstraction of the system components; to the user, the distributed environment looks like a virtual single processor system.

The transparency provides an adequate means of distinguishing DS from network operating systems. In the latter, the user must usually get to know where the resources or services he requires reside and how these may be applied for his purposes.

From the user's point of view, transparency is characterized by the fact that the user does not need to know on which computer he is working (logically), where his programs are executed and where the necessary data and files are located. This may lead to further subdivisions within the concept of transparency (name transparency, location transparency).

As experiences with specific systems show (Popek and Walker, 1985), transparency cannot be rigidly maintained in all cases. In such instances, distinction must be made between the users and the operators of the computing environment.

Other restrictions on this concept derive directly from the above requirements. They differ mainly according to whether or not real DS are considered.

The variety of the components has the following effects:

- A variety of functions from the various computer systems.
- Many processors.
- Qualitative and quantitative parallel processing.
- Spatial distributiveness without narrow boundaries.

The 'multiprocessor' characteristic may be used as another distinguishing factor (Peterson and Silberschatz, 1985). The processors in a DS are loosely coupled since each processor has its own storage and the processors communicate via a message network. On the other hand, multiprocessor systems are tightly coupled, share storage and clock pulses and are connected to each other via the storage or via a highly-parallel connection network. However, this distinction is controversial. Many resource management strategies apply both to multiprocessor systems and to DS (examples in (Popescu-Zeletin, Le Lann and Kim, 1987)). In fact, the variety of components should also permit a multiprocessor system to be a processor component in the DS. This is also possible with appropriate abstraction.

The qualitative and quantitative parallel processing emphasizes the fact that multiprogramming and multitasking are of course implemented in a DS. As a result of the many processors, a higher degree of parallelism is obtained in the processing of independent problems. In the same way, it is also desirable to implement integrated services by the tight logical coupling of processors (invisibly to the user) to process coherent, costly problems. This places considerably higher demands on the resource management.

The transparency requirement implies a requirement for integration of all components into one unit:

- A DS is a system-wide operating system.
- A DS provides abstract system components and in the most favourable cases is itself based on these.
- A DS implements distributed control according to the principle of cooperative autonomy.
- There is a distributed description of the system.

The DS is system wide and uniform. In practice, it may be necessary for a DS to permit cooperation with machines which are connected to the same transport system (for example, machines controlled by the DS) but which run under their own autonomous operating systems.

Because of the transparency requirement, the use of components must be independent of the location at which they are implemented at a given time. Their provision and use may be viewed as abstract characteristics. The conception of the already very abstract local base machines in (Kröger, 1984) provides a very useful simplification of the construction of a DS. The local base machines are then clearly a combination of hardware and a local operating system kernel. This approach leads automatically to a discussion of the use of existing operating system kernels. Another possibility is to bring up the DS from scratch using corresponding machine drivers. For conceptual reasons and on portability grounds, both cases result in a kernel interface relatively close to the hardware, on which the higher DS components sit.

The principle of cooperative autonomy says that all points involved have an equal share in decision-taking processes which affect them as a whole. One important aspect here is the guarantee that such decision processes terminate. One advantage of this principle is that the decision only involves those points concerned while the remaining points are not loaded with overheads which are unnecessary from their point of view. Thus, seen from an individual point, cooperative autonomous decision processes may be of an altogether higher complexity than comparable hierarchically-centralistic decision processes. The thesis is that experiences of systems with a long history, in particular of natural systems, teaches us that the principle of cooperation is more successful in the long-term than the principle of perfection.

The distributed description of the system complicates the structure of the DS considerably, since it must be clearly demonstrated which states may be seen as inconsistent and how reality should be evaluated or guaranteed. The decisions in a DS need not in all cases affect all points of the message system.

Semantic consistency is another important aspect, and means that system services, supporting directories, frequently-used application programs, etc. must have the same effect regardless of where they are executed. This is particularly important when it is possible to reallocate programs and parts of the memory, which is also critical from the point of view of reliability and availability. Semantic consistency is important for software maintenance. A considerable maintenance problem arises if different software versions are used, to compensate for local environmental differences.

Unfortunately, the goal of semantic consistency conflicts with goals of local autonomy, since it greatly restricts the possibilities for installing software at individual points and for adapting the software to the user.

2.3.2 Further delimitation of network operating systems

Since transparency is the most important characteristic feature of the DS, it also provides the basis for distinguishing between DS and network operating systems (which may also be used to support the cooperation of spatially-separated computer systems).

In a network operating system every node or computer has its own operating system which is supplemented by the corresponding network components. In a DS, on the other hand, parts of a uniform global and system-wide operating system run in each node. This global, system-wide operating system may fall back locally upon homogeneous or heterogeneous node operating systems, which are then integrated into a unified system at the component level.

The activities of each user are essentially executed locally in a network operating system, extended by remote login facilities which permit the use of services on remote nodes. In contrast, the allocation and relocation of the activities in a distributed system is transparent, being realized by a dynamic allocation of processes to each relevant node (process migration).

As far as file transfer is concerned, a distributed system provides a system-wide common name space, so that here too, the location of the file is hidden to the user.

In a network operating system, access to remote files requires an explicit file transfer.

One major aspect which distinguishes distributed systems from network operating systems is fault tolerance, which, in the case of the distributed system, may be supported by a variety of measures, but which is only possible with difficulty in the network operating system because of its autonomy and diversity.

From the point of view of the network operating system, a protection problem arises at the point where users wish to access files on remote computers and the user authorization must be checked.

In the simplest case a remote login is required, whereby the user identifies himself on the remote computer. The allocation of user authorizations on all required computers is then a prerequisite.

Simpler intermediate solutions which may reduce the management costs include combining external users into a class of guests or an appropriate mapping of user identifications onto one another.

For a DS, it is essential that system-global unique identifiers are allocated, managed and used for protection purposes.

The following aspects serve to distinguish a network operating system, consisting for example, of several independent personal computers with a print server and a file server, from a distributed system:

(1)   Every computer runs its own complete operating system and not part of a common distributed operating system.

(2)   The execution of activities on remote computers is implemented via explicit remote login to these computers and not with the aid of the process management of the distributed operating system.

(3) Work with remote files involves an explicit file transfer where the user must know the location of the files and the addressing is not carried out for him by the operating system.

(4) The facilities for fault tolerance are quite poor, because when a computer breaks down, its functionality is completely lost and the loss cannot be translated into a degradation of the service.

2.3.3 The most important functions of a distributed system

A DS has the following basic functions:

- Interprocess communication. Support for interprocess communication over the network, using the facilities of the message exchange system. This involves the use of the transport protocol to establish the service level protocol.

- Management and allocation of resources. Allocation of resources to users, decisions about where a request is executed, possible generation of new resources from the existing system resources, installation of new resources in the network, support for the replication of resources to increase reliability, provision of mechanisms for concurrency control and synchronization.

- Name management. Linking of names to resources and their network addresses, generation and management of directories, support for name servers, localization of resources for servers/users, support for transparency (for example, by observing the principle that names should not be linked to locations and that no location names should be incorporated).

- Restart after failure. Fault tolerance in various layers of the system architecture.

According to (Tripathi, 1987), these are possible functions of a DS. A DS does not necessarily comprise all these functions. Most other sources name at least one other important group of functions:

- Protection functions. Specification of user rights and their implementation, security policy, protection against attacks from outside (unauthorized users penetrating over the network).

The users of a DS move in a space of abstract objects and operations on these, which are chosen as practically as possible for the solution of their problem.
    Requirements from the user's point of view include:

- Provision of adequate aids to problem solving. In the past, neither purely-central nor purely-decentralized DP systems have proved universally useful for all applications. Only the networking of computers with different structures and different functions will permit the provision of a broad, general spectrum of aids to problem solving. The combination of various types of systems and their customization will play an ever-increasing role in the future. In addition to distributed systems, concepts such as SAA are fundamentally appropriate in this respect.

- Minimization of the cost of accessing resources in the distributed framework. The current situation for an average user, when a network operating system is used, may be roughly characterized by the fact that he must know a lot in order to solve a problem using the available data-system resources, but his knowledge may have nothing to do with the problem in hand. The success of the personal computer may be traced back to its minimization of the overheads needed in problem processing. This should be maintained if possible. Transparency and virtualization are methods which take these aspects into account.

- Maximization and simplification of the facilities for communication with other users or programs. The variety of possible communications interfaces which mostly contain a combination of technical-physical and logical elements should be replaced by one (or at least fewer) logical interface(s) which is (are) in particular independent of device characteristics.

- Broad provision of functions with emphasis on the following:

  - Functionality: extensible by the user, functions usable system wide and appropriate to problems, system-wide uniform system language.
  - Reactions: at least sufficient to maintain transparency, ideally also for time-sensitive applications.
  - Reliability: measures to increase it, possibly using system-wide redundancy.
  - Security: specification of a security policy and its implementation.
  - Extensibility by problem-free integration of new hardware and software resources using existing aids (for example, configuration changes in the network management context).
  - Coherence by implementation of a uniform view for all resources and protocols for their use. Hiding of location-specific properties and system-wide naming together with similar use of resources system wide.
  - Comprehensive portability.

In this digression, we cannot go any further into implementation-related approaches to problems in distributed systems. The digression is based on Chapter 4 of (Kauffels, 1990) and on a series of articles on distributed systems written by the author in 1988 for DATACOM.

2.3.4 Examples of distributed systems

In this chapter, we have already mentioned the names of distributed systems on several occasions. We would now like to provide a brief systematic summary of two very important and closely-related examples.

A coarse distinction may be made between the following classes of distributed systems:

- DS kernels with minimal functionality.
- Integrated systems.
- Object-oriented systems.
- Systems based on a server-pool model.

A real system may belong to several classes, for example it may be both based on a server-pool model and object-oriented.

DS kernels provide an almost minimal set of primitives for process management, memory management, message exchange and the management of backup memory media. Examples here include ACCENT and MACH from the Carnegie Mellon University ((Fitzgerald and Rashid, 1985) and (Rashid and Robertson, 1981)) together with the V KERNEL from Stanford University.

Integrated systems allow one to run a broadly-configurable complete standard software on any machine, which provides the machine with all the aids it requires. Today's systems are based on the UNIX operating system and run on UNIX machines. They also make available some of the previous UNIX functions, thereby guaranteeing a certain compatibility for older programs. Examples include LOCUS which was originally developed at the University of California in Los Angeles and is now produced by LOCUS Inc. (Popek and Walker, 1985), D-UNIX from the Bell Laboratories, Birlix from GMD ((Härtig *et al*, 1986) and (Härtig and Kühnhauser, 1986)), the Cambridge Distributed Operating System (Needham and Herbert, 1982) and SAGUARO from the University of Arizona.

Object-oriented systems view applications as abstract objects on which they execute abstract operations. Examples include ARGUS from MIT, EDEN from the University of Washington (Almes *et al.*, 1985) and AMOEBA from the Vrije Universiteit Amsterdam (Mullender and Tanenbaum, 1986).

Systems based on a server-pool model make a pool of servers with the required services available to each user. The Cambridge Distributed Operating System is a simple system of this class.

Here, we shall consider LOCUS and its important IBM implementation AIX-TCF.

2.3.4.1 LOCUS

The LOCUS operating system is a distributed version of the UNIX operating system and has additional properties for the distributed mode of operation and the support of high reliability and availability.

The system allows one to use a set of networked computers like an individual computer by providing a large number of supporting functions for the underlying network so that this is invisible to users and programs. This transparency drastically reduces the costs of software development and maintenance and produces a marked improvement in user behaviour. Other features of the system include additional system flexibility, diskless workstations, full duplex mode, I/O to mainframes, transparent shared peripheral resources and incremental growth over a large configuration area without the need for software modifications.

Transparency is supported by a heterogeneous network with many different computers. Program sections for specialized machines may be relocated to and executed on appropriate computers without users noticing.

LOCUS also supports the correspondence with other networked machines which do not run LOCUS and with conventional gateways. In this way, with some parameter alterations, existing application programs may also be made available in the network environment. LOCUS provides a number of facilities for re-finding resources in distributed systems.

Reliability and availability are two other goals of LOCUS. Various applications in the database and office area make high reliability and availability an absolute necessity. In addition, the distributed environment may bring new problems which are more difficult to overcome than in the conventional case.

One of the main components of LOCUS is a reliable file system which, under all circumstances, reliably stores a consistent version of files (COMMIT mechanism).

The following behaviour is desirable in a distributed system: access to local resources should function as though the remote access mechanism were not there. A program which uses only local resources should behave as it would on a local UNIX system.

Remote access, which is naturally somewhat slower, should be reasonably similar to local access. If this goal is achieved, many placement problems associated with the optimal placement of resources will disappear. LOCUS attains both these goals and is thus currently unique in its kind.

2.3.4.2 IBM's AIX-TCF

In addition to its traditional SNA/SAA products, IBM is also concentrating on the AIX line with a view to its use in the technical and scientific area. The system /6000 introduced at the beginning of 1990 certainly makes life harder for conventional workstation suppliers such as Sun. The cooperation with LOCUS has resulted in something interesting as far as distributed systems are concerned: TCF in the AIX framework is a partial implementation of the LOCUS concept.

This section is not intended to provide a basic introduction to the IBM AIX operating system. IBM offers the following AIX products:

- IBM Advanced Interactive Executive/370 as an operating system for medium to large processors (IBM 9370, 4381 and 3090). AIX /370 is the most powerful link in the AIX chain.
- IBM AIX/RT for the RT PC 6150.
- IBM AIX PS/2 for the PS/2 family from model 55SX with 80386 processor.
- IBM AIX V.3 for the POWER computer of the /6000 series.

If not otherwise noted, all subsequent statements refer to the most powerful version, AIX/370. AIX/370 supports AT&T's UNIX System V Interface definition and, according to IBM, is functionally equivalent to UNIX System V Rel. 2. It is also functionally equivalent to Rel. 4.3 of the Berkeley Software Distribution (UNIX 4.3BSD). Some System V commands have been replaced by BSD commands with more facilities. Experience shows that the functional equivalence should be treated with caution. IBM has also announced that it will support the IEEE 1003.1 standard (POSIX) as soon as it is officially released.

The most important system extensions over and above System V or BSD are:

- Transparent Computing Facility (TCF) for a computer cluster (mixed system /370, RT or PS/2) based on Token Ring or Ethernet.
- LAN support: TCP/IP on Ethernet or Token Ring.
- Interworking with DOS-PS/2 using 'AIX Access for DOS Users'.
- Interworking (mail, file transfer) with other /370 operating systems.
- Full screen editor (in addition to the UNIX editor vi)
- CMS commands callable from an AIX/370 workstation.

The interworking with other /370 operating systems is simplified for AIX/370 by the fact that it itself only runs as a guest under the VM operating system. A VM machine provides virtual processors and resources which may be managed, for example, under CMS, MVS or VSE and also under AIX/370.

In this way, it is possible to generate several virtual AIX machines in a single mainframe. Since AIX/370 manages most of its resources for paging, spooling and scheduling itself, no negative effects on the overall performance need be feared.

AIX/370 has two different modes of operation with different operating system kernels:

- The XA mode for VM/XA SP with 31-bit addressing, 1 Gbyte address space and 768 Mbyte for each user process.

- The 370 mode for VM/SP with 24-bit addressing, 16 Mbyte address space and 8 Mbyte for each user process.

The VM file transfer support enables AIX/370 users to exchange files with other users in an (SNA) network of VM machines. Here, interworking between AIX/370 users, VM/CMS users and MVS/TSO users is possible. The conversion from ASCII to EBCDIC is carried out automatically.

For AIX/370, the LAN connections are implemented either via the 8232 LAN channel station or directly for the 9370. Smaller computers are directly attached to Ethernet or Token Ring.

IBM's TCF allows up to 31 processors to be combined into a cluster. The processors may be a confused mixture of PS/2 models (70 and 80), /6000 systems and some /370 models. The PS/2s must run AIX PS/2 TCF, the other computers must run AIX/370. TCF needs a LAN (Ethernet or Token Ring) or a channel-to-channel adapter (CTCA). TCF interworks directly with the LAN. The logical link at the process level is synchronized by a token protocol which is based on the Internet Protocol (IP) of TCP/IP. Neither TCP nor UDP is used. This type of process coupling uses the LAN optimally, since the delay times of the logical link control may be taken for granted.

To the users, the cluster has the appearance of a single uniform system. The set of networked computers is really connected together at the process level.

Neither users nor application programs need to know why the systems are connected together or the details of where the data is located. A user who logs in to any TCF AIX system has access to all resources of all computers in the cluster. Thus, the cluster appears like a system to him.

User processes run on any processor in the system, regardless of where the user is logged in. The controls for this may be executed automatically or by the user. In addition, with appropriate programming, it is possible to split up processes between the processors. An editing procedure may, for example, be relocated to a PS/2 system, while a complicated calculation is run on the host (process transparency).

An administrator may even relocate a running process from one system to another. This is carried out in such a way that a process which is initially running on a source machine is then started at the same time on the target machine, the processes run in parallel up to a synchronization point, stop and then only the process on the target machine runs on.

All computers and devices in the cluster behave like a single machine. All resources are given a standard name with which they are referenced from all points (name transparency). Objects may change machines without any changes to the user's perspective (location transparency). Commands and options always have the same effect regardless of where they are called (semantic transparency).

In contrast to the general objective in distributed systems the load is not automatically balanced across the network. Instead, load-balancing commands are provided. For example, the 'on' command permits the explicit entry of a desired target machine, the 'fast' command places the process on the fastest free machine. The machine profiles are defined at the start. If most machines are PS/2s and there is only one /370, the /370 machine is automatically the sink for everything, unless its performance parameters are set to be the same as those of the PS/2s. This may, for example, be sensible if one does not want the main work on the /370 (for example a database) to be hindered by too great a load from the PS/2s.

The management of the AIX cluster is extremely simple. Computers may be added or removed as required. TCF always tries to keep as many resources as possible available. This is above all ideal for operations which require a certain reliability. TCF can, for example, provide for a minimum performance.

The fact that AIX TCF can easily store files several times (under the same name) and manage them contributes to the increase in the reliability. This may be used for backup purposes. Moreover, the file system is very stable, since the physical media are not used in order but staggered according to a certain key. Taken together with the multiple storage of files, this means that part of the cluster may peacefully fail at times. A total loss of data is very unlikely.

The updating is as for a distributed database using a 'commit' command.

Of course, TCF also provides for distributed file and record locking.

The professional aggressiveness of the AIX venture can scarcely be outdone: concepts which until now lay in the academic workstation corner have been transferred to the main stream of commercial DP. Now it depends on the application programs as to whether anything comes of it.

2.4 Summary of network and system management requirements

In the previous sections, we described various classes of networks and derived the network-management requirements for each class. Today, most networks are relatively isolated, in other words, there are class 1 terminal networks and class 2 PC LANs but the gap between what is technically possible and what is installed by users is steadily increasing.

Integration, for example, in the sense of a PC–host coupling via LANs, in which a class 2 network jointly takes on the logic of a class 1 network, will at first be slow and relatively cautious. From the point of view of the network management, such a cautious process is welcome since means of integrating the control of the various system worlds are slow in reaching product maturity (see also Chapter 7).

Instead, the means currently available are used to control the subnetworks and the remaining problems associated with network integration are left untouched. It is possible to do this for a while, however, the basic problem must be faced at some stage. Moreover, this does not simply amount to integrating a cable tester for LANs with a line tester for SDLC connections.

Usually, overall plans for network and system management completely forget certain aspects, such as, for example, planning and budgeting for an on-line documentation system to replace the little flags on the cables in large installations or a plan for user training.

The author cannot guarantee that the following list of possible approaches to global network management functions is in any way complete. He only wishes to show that a purely technically-oriented 'management software' or 'distributed system' approach does not provide adequate coverage of all aspects.

The functions may usefully be subdivided into three dimensions: the user dimension, the network dimension and the technology security dimension.

We now discuss these dimensions individually.

2.4.1 The network dimension

We begin with the network dimension. The main functions of the extended network and system management are listed below.

2.4.1.1 Documentation

This comprises documentation of the installed system in full detail, including the cables, plugs and sockets, the cable routing in the buildings, the properties of the attached devices (adapter cards), the values to be associated with these devices (parameters), the installed software and its properties, the values to be associated with these properties, components for redundancy, plans for alternate circuits in the broadest sense and the structure of the logical network if this structure is not covered by another tool. The documentation must also cover structural facts and the location of the cable conduits together with their present contents and electrical characteristics, including, for example, the distribution of sockets, their protection, the network power supply and the protection against leakage.

2.4.1.2 Installation of components

The conditions laid out during planning (see the technology-security dimension) provide for the purchase of components. These must be suitably procured and installed and the company or organization must provide guidelines on how to handle different devices and on which devices may be used at all. A number of additional new conditions should be observed when installing hardware components. For example, it is not advisable to install servers, gateways, bridges or other devices with infrastructural functions in PC LANs in the immediate end-user areas; these should be installed in the technical areas to which only authorized personnel have access. The components must be installed in accordance with the conditions of the manufacturers' guarantees and not as happens to seem appropriate. These same comments apply to software components, which are not discussed further here. Finally, every step of the installation must be documented in the documentation system.

2.4.1.3 Configuration of components

Configuration planning is always said to form a major part of network and system management. Components and their software and firmware must be installed in such a way that they fit harmoniously into the existing data-processing environment. Such an installation is not trivial and in most cases leads to modification of the existing configuration parameters. All such modifications must be adequately documented. Here too, the documentation tool would be a suitable solution. Mostly, however, it cannot carry out this task, and the configuration software is stored with other software, namely the configuration management of the existing management software. It would of course be sensible if all these different applications could use the same documentation database. New concepts such as Open View, EMA or SystemView provide for this.

2.4.1.4 Status monitoring

The state of the physical and logical units must be permanently monitored (in practice the monitoring takes place over short intervals), since otherwise there would be no information about the state of the network or system. The length of the monitoring intervals naturally depends on the units in question. For the elements of classical terminal networks corresponding tools from various manufacturers have been in existence for a long time and have been successfully used. In the case of LANs, there are also corresponding monitors and tools for the physical network and for extensions of the network software for the logical network. Finally, new operating systems such as UNIX have facilities, for example, to produce a running log of protocol-stack implementations. Status monitoring is a central point of all standardization efforts.

2.4.1.5 Load measurement

In order to make reliable statements about the operational state of a network or system, we need to observe not only static states, but also dynamic processes. This observation is the goal of load measurement. Thus, load measurement is critical because, given a route between two logical or physical units with n subroutes there are $(n^{(n+1)})/2$ possible ways of considering subroutes singly or in combinations (only fully connected subroutes). This quadratic complexity determines one's choice. One normally learns too late whether one has made the right choice. Moreover, as a result of multiplexing or channel access algorithms, many different virtual connections usually run over a physical route. Here again, it is now a question of the aspects one wishes to consider. In the case of a connection between two applications, it is this virtual connection which is of interest. However, if one follows the path of an application in an operating system via, for example, a LAN PC adapter card, the internal memory there, the queues and the processing in this card, through the LLC, the MAC, the PHY and the cable, through gateways, routers or other networks to the destination application, there are a number of obstacles which have a negative effect on the virtual connection. Many of these obstacles are associated with the interworking of the adapter card and the internal PC bus. Load measurements can sometimes lead to completely misleading results. If a Token Ring trace and performance tool records only a load of a few percent, this does not necessarily mean that the number of connected devices could be increased by a factor of ten, because even ten times the load would still be a small percentage. In many cases, this actually only means that the handshaking between the PC, the server and the application on the one hand and the adapter card on the other hand is poor. Often, the operator can do nothing about this, in other cases he can. The objective of load measurement to reflect the dynamic behaviour of the network can only be attained if one gives careful consideration to what one wants to measure.

2.4.1.6 Maintenance/tests

By the time it comes to errors and expensive standstills, it is too late. Only proper and careful maintenance of all components is the long-term guarantee of as few errors as possible. This is true not only for all physical components but also for the logical components of a network. Defective power supply is as much a cause of crashes as bad software. Software maintenance is a critical problem, particularly for those working with PCs. In the author's opinion, no networked workstation in the end-user area should have more than one diskette drive, since it is relatively easy to use the drive to take data out of the company and also to introduce virus-infected programs into the network. Regular tests of all components are part of the maintenance.

Such tests are frequently provided for in the case of complex structures but regular tests of cable systems are rare in practice.

2.4.1.7 Error prevention and recovery

The primary task of fault management is error prevention, to which all the measures described above contribute. However, at some time, even with the most diverse of measures, errors do occur. These errors may be coarsely divided into well-behaved and badly-behaved errors. In practice, the former do not cause interruption of work and are limited and easy to eliminate. One example might be a broken-down workstation, without any worthwhile data of its own, which can be replaced by a workstation from the spares store within a few minutes while the station worker has a coffee. Badly-behaved errors lack some of the properties of well-behaved errors, these include, for example a crashed server disk (not everyone has NetWare SFT III with duplicated servers) or a local or remote controller which has for several hours produced blank screens. The tools, methods and replacement techniques used to recover from errors depend on the extent to which the work of a company or an organization relies on DP, since this largely determines the cost of a standstill. However, we may assume that this dependency is ever-increasing. The 1989/90 study by Infonetics of the statistics of standstill times and the availability of large networks is sometimes alarming.

For internal edification, we give a quotation relating to errors essentially due to Murphy (the serious reader may skip this paragraph). Murphy's law states that 'if something can go wrong, then it will go wrong'. The first digital corollary says 'Murphy's law is optimized by computers'. The second digital corollary is even more explosive 'everything goes wrong once'. The first electronic application tells us that 'nothing is inconceivable for computers, even the impossible – except what is desirable'. As far as errors in networks are concerned, we may deduce the following:

- You can never avoid a major breakdown by producing a small one.
- In the best case, the small breakdown joins the large one in order to give it support.
- There are no cheap breakdowns.
- If a breakdown was once cheap its true cause was not determined.

2.4.2 The user dimension

The role of users in computer networks and integrated systems has already been discussed in Chapter 1, where certain negative development aspects were described. The author hopes that his views on this (described in part above) are wrong. However when a network and system management solution is sought, the following aspects of the user dimension must be taken into accounted and acted on.

2.4.2.1 Access rights, user profiles

It is impossible to manage the logical network without a detailed description of what, when, where, who, why and how one wishes to manage. Basic considerations tell us that no network in which the use of all resources is free of restrictions can work properly. The specification of access rights in the framework of the generation of user profiles is the basis for any more extensive security policy. The user profiles themselves provide information about the nature and size of the required resources and about associated quality requirements. Many software packages (including both application and system software) now no longer work at all without the entry of user profiles and access rights, unless one is able to repeal the built-in security mechanism. Much has been written (even in this book) about the available types of access rights and how to use them. All those with planning responsibilities should analyze this point carefully. One should do nothing more with the network before the question of the user profiles and the associated requirements is clarified. However, it is not sufficient to maintain the *status quo*. From the start, care must be taken to ensure that proper consideration is given to each extension of the network and its capabilities on the one hand and to the users and their wishes on the other hand. Otherwise one ends up with the common and rightly feared 'lending of rights'.

2.4.2.2 Installation of new services

When installing a network, in order to reach a stable initial operational state, one begins with a basic set of urgently required services and extends their provisions to the users as required in the user profiles, once the users have been suitably installed. This is enough to begin with. Soon, however, there will be demands for new services, which is a good sign that the network has been accepted. If new services are installed, they should first be tested by selected users, preferably in an independent experimental network in which new hardware can also be tested. After this, a training phase must be prepared, planned and smoothly executed to prepare the users concerned and get them used to the new service. In parallel, the service may be installed in the network and tested (initially it should not be available to normal users). The author realizes that some readers now have their heads in their hands because they find this way of introducing a new service too complicated and unrealistic. However, the fact is that deviation from this procedure carries considerable organizational and security risks. Anyone who wants to accept these risks for a speedy and economical installation must carry the responsibility himself.

2.4.2.3 Evaluation of log files

Most management systems generate log files during their operation; these provide information about user behaviour. These log files should be statistically evaluated at various intervals to obtain information about the distribution of the use of resources and services. This data is very important for further planning. Sometimes log files show the areas in which operator errors are common. Further training is clearly appropriate here. Finally, log files also provide information about frequent failed attempts to access devices, data or services. Capacity planning is called for here; however, some data may point to errors or to the occurrence of errors in the near future. It should be noted that log files may also provide personal data about individual users. The checks mentioned here may be suitably combined so as, for example, to support the collection of performance data about individual user profiles. Log files should only be evaluated by particularly well-educated and trustworthy staff. Neither log files nor their evaluations should fall into the hands of end users; they should be regarded as data to be particularly protected. In any case, observation of the legal rules regarding the protection of personal data and consultation with the company-internal authorities responsible for these areas (for example the works committee) is recommended. Only acceptance by all sides is a sure psychological basis for network and system management.

2.4.2.4 Server configuration

We have already discussed this point implicitly. When configuring server machines in the framework of a multilevel company-internal computer philosophy, one must take care to meet the subsidiary conditions arising from the user profiles and the security requirements. In addition, for PC LAN servers in particular, sufficient thought should be given to data security and data integrity. This includes both the provision of automatic backup facilities and the use of software utilities for disk security (including disk shadowing, duplicated disk subsystems or whole server machines and the use of uninterrupted power supplies). All this naturally involves appropriate configuration planning. The results of the configuration should be documented.

The user dimension is, so-to-speak, infinite. Attention should be paid, at least in large organizations, to the construction of a user service centre. This user service centre is the centre for all DP problems. Here, we must distinguish between a large organization which mainly operates a terminal network and an organization which mainly operates distributed PCs and mini-networks. One example of the first case is that of a large bank (Büker, 1990). Here 200–600 calls per day come in, in peak periods more than one call per minute. The user service is divided into two levels. The first level accepts all calls and tries to determine whether the problem is simple (after the hundredth call about a blank screen, you have already known for thirty minutes that a controller has crashed or that the screen is blank because there is a plug out) and can be resolved immediately by the first level or whether it has to be handled by the second level. The latter deals with all difficult problems. In this example, six people are required for the user service, two of them at the first level. So as not to place unnecessary psychological demands on these two, the first level positions are rotated amongst all the workers in the service centre. The service centre uses a facility which, after very rapid entry of an identification character from a database over the telephone, fetches the most important information about the terminal, its linkage into the system, the software which it uses and other components. Such a system must of course be well cared for.

A user service centre in the LAN area appears somewhat different. In modern LAN system-software groups of users are looked after by so-called group administrators. An administrator is responsible not only for the user problems but also for the execution of simple server-configuration tasks, the installation of new workstations and the provision of paper, etc. He is supported by local LAN-oriented management software, such as, for example, the new IBM LAN Network Manager, which helps him to implement security requirements and to document the configuration. Naturally other manufacturers will soon provide something comparable. The group administrator is a representative of the lowest level of an administrative hierarchy, the highest level of which comprises the administrators in the computer centre or failing that in a service centre. They have facilities for remote monitoring of all networks and subnetworks and may intervene in error situations. This structure also means that the management centre may obtain relatively one-sided information from the subnetworks while the execution of the controlling operations falls largely to the local group administrators. In many companies, the basis for such a structure already exists. One only has to use it.

With the general development of computer systems, the above examples of purely-central and purely-decentralized data processing are increasingly rare in practice. Distributed data processing over PCs, minis and mainframes is increasingly common. Here, the two alternatives must be suitably combined. The increasing number of tussles over competence between mainframe people, PC freaks and mini-fans serve little purpose and are certainly not defused when each group tries to blame the other for errors.

Thus we come to the last (for the time being, in this edition) dimension, technology security.

2.4.3 The technology-security dimension

Practically no articles or books about network or system management deal with the important topic of technology security. This is usually left to corporate consultancies, thus this section largely consists of the author's subjective recommendations.

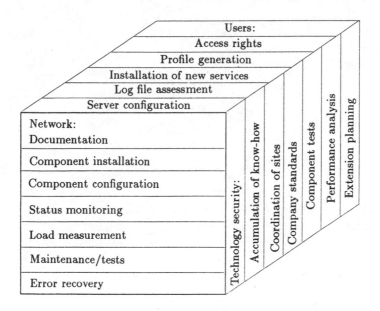

Figure 2.9 Approaches to a solution: functions.

2.4.3.1 Accumulation of know-how

Often companies and organizations become far too dependent on consultants, who, even though they are professionals, may be wrong. It is possible to think through, plan, construct and get a network off the ground with consultants. All extensions and alterations may be discussed with them. Consultants also help to bridge rifts in companies and to bring about discussion. However, the permanent monitoring and control of an operational network is not a matter for consultants. It is useful to build up and maintain ones own know-how for all stages of a network from its conception to its taking out of service. Solid knowledge on the client's part also usually helps towards a satisfactory outcome of a consultancy contract. It is a matter of giving appropriate consideration to long-standing company-internal matters, which it is impossible for the consultant to understand in full, and to their consequences for the network. Large companies usually have their own network centre-of-competence. Companies whose size only allows for one competent person are comparatively unfortunate. Dependence on a single competent person should in principle be rejected because of the company's vulnerability to blackmail with its ever increasing dependence on the network solution itself. Thus, it is also the job of a serious consultant to help to increase know-how.

Only appropriate individual know-how guarantees a fast reaction in

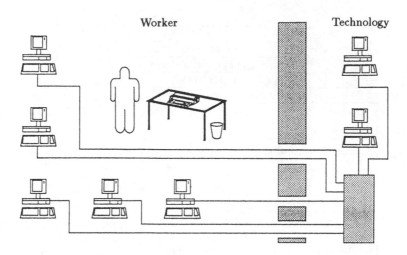

Figure 2.10   Basic security: structural measures in the PC area.

case of error and long-term secure operation of the network. This enthusiasm for further education should be promoted in order that the total know-how is not limited to a knowledge of the current installation but alters with it. This causes difficulties as far as new planning is concerned.

2.4.3.2 Coordination of sites

Large companies or organizations with several geographical locations often have the problem of local DP culture. In particular, when something is done at each location, strivings for independence are soon seen amongst those in charge at the individual sites. In the past, this was not a problem for relatively large sites with completely isolated data processing environments. However, advances in communications technology now result in high-performance company-wide networks and the necessity, because of the pressure of competition within a branch or because of the EC market, for greater integration of sites. As mentioned above, different factions usually exist even within a site. They must be made to agree amongst themselves and embedded in a company-wide concept. There can be no company-wide network or system management solution without this. There may also be cases in which this is actually not desirable.

2.4.3.3 Company standards

The coordination of sites is a part of the process of creating company standards. In the days of purely-central data processing, it was relatively

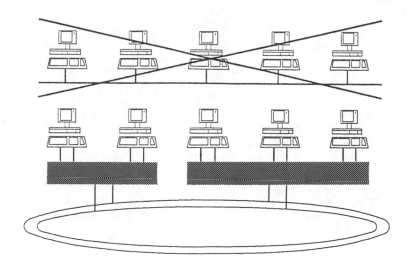

Figure 2.11   Basic security: concept of the redundant PC LAN.

which should not, once the basic choice of a manufacturer had been made. In many companies and organizations, the increasing heterogeneity of data processing, falling hardware and software prices and the spread of personal computers have led to a turning away from this clear line. Frequently, departments buy departmental computers, large numbers of PC networks and all their PCs by mail order. There is then no one there who knows the devices and there is no more money for training, maintenance or upkeep. These systems soldier on for a while, until one day problems do arise, at the latest when one wants to connect them to a computer centre to access the data there. The computer centre staff are then angry with the simple-minded department and the department's single PC freak gets together with others like himself to find a broader basis for action. This leads to trench warfare. Acquisition by the simple-minded is a problem which must be assigned to the past, since in the future such procedures will be increasingly harmful for a company. This is because of the ever increasing demands and capabilities of the hardware and the software on the one hand and the immense market on the other hand. Company standards in the form of mandatory guidelines for purchasing should be issued and checked from time to time. For example, a procedure which only allows the purchase of three basic types of PCs with standard fixtures makes service and support much easier. Above a certain number of workstations it is thoroughly economic to undertake all maintenance oneself, in the form of total exchange, so that everyone always has a functioning workstation. Under certain additional conditions, this

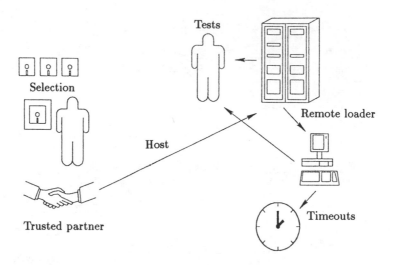

Figure 2.12 Basic security (certified software).

procedure is also applicable to networks. One must agree on the network type, one or two protocol stacks, basic fixtures for servers, etc. Of course, this model may be criticized for being too inflexible and taking too little account of changes in the technology. This is not the case. On the contrary, in the author's opinion, of recent years, the permanent fluttering between versions, especially as far as PC networks and software are concerned, is very damaging, since every version (for example, software) brings new training requirements and all-too-frequent modifications of the resources which cripple productivity. Experience shows that an average typist takes on average 4–6 weeks to become familiar with a word processing system to the extent that he can achieve an average standard of work using it on his own and can tackle more exacting work with the help of colleagues. If he is supplied with a new version every year, he would require at least two weeks of training, which would be unacceptable. A company may also have several different word processing systems and simply replacing the typist may have to be paid for by another 4–6 weeks of training. The same applies to all staff who come into contact with DP and have no marked natural talent. In addition, company standards help the company to achieve greater production and better discounts.

2.4.3.4 Component tests

All components must be tested before they are installed or brought into operation and from time to time again after that. Unfortunately, as far

	WP			MF		NORT
	prv	all	exe	prv	exe	exe
Major	rwed	rw	r	rwed	r	
Miller 1	rwed	rw	r	rwed	r	
Miller 2	rwed	rw	r			
Sims	rwed	rw	r			
King	rwed	rwed	r	rwed	r	
Admin		rw	rwed		rwed	r

Figure 2.13   Basic security: security policy.

as communication protocols are concerned, one cannot rely on upwards compatibility and the interaction between hardware, communication software and application software must always be checked whenever a change is made (for example, an update). In extreme cases, for PC LANs, a software change may necessitate hardware modifications. For example, NetWare 3.x does not support as many different network adapter cards as NetWare 2.x although it also supports others, etc. Conversion of a server to the new version may also make it necessary to change the adapter card. We shall not give any more examples of this wide field. From cables to application software, on-going tests are a prerequisite for long-term certainty of operation of the network.

2.4.3.5 Performance analysis

We have already discussed a similar problem in the paragraph on load measurement. Load measurements may be used to derive performance information which must be appropriately correlated for planning purposes. Mathematical analytic techniques are also used for this for telephone and trunk networks. For LANs, because of the high complexity, these various techniques are often misleading and require specialized mathematical knowledge. For the average user, use of the manufacture-provided tools (which are often tailored to that manufacturer's environment) is recommended.

2.4.3.6 Extension planning

Many of the measures discussed above are also used to plan extensions. This must be an on-going process if the planning team is not to be suddenly taken by surprise by additional requirements. Equally, extension planning covers the whole spectrum from cables to applications. Planning must be complete. What use are free logical places in an SNA system in which it is desired to operate logical links, if on the other side, there are no more facilities for simple and fast attachment of end devices?

All the above measures are used to ensure that the network project runs as smoothly as possible, that the network operation corresponds as closely as possible to the wishes of the operators and the users and finally that the 'standstill' times of the network and the attached systems are minimized. It will sometimes be difficult to obtain staff, money and devices for all these measures, since in practice, not all tasks provide immediately visible contributions to increases in productivity. However, this is a short-sighted attitude. It is very difficult to support a network solution with economic arguments and one cannot contrast it with the case in which there was no network at all, since the data processing with and without a network would take very different forms (Suppan, 1990). The costs of a network standstill are easy to calculate, for example, in the form of the idleness of the staff involved in the management structure or in the form of the loss of manufacturing production. All managers in a company or organization should get a feel for the problem and the costs of its solution; the arguments of the first two chapter of this book should help in this.

2.5 Summary

We have seen that network-management requirements depend on a large number of factors and that one cannot talk about *the* network management. In the next chapters, we describe the most important theoretical and practical models, mechanisms and procedures for network management together with planning requirements (also for management) and various other problems.

We begin with the classical network management of IBM (SNA–CNM, Chapter 3), DEC and Siemens (Chapter 4).

Chapter 3

Network management in the IBM area: SNA-NMA, NetView and SystemView

- Introduction

- The development of the area of SNA/SAA network management

- The Network Management Architecture and its core product, NetView

- The future perspective: SystemView, IBM's comprehensive management strategy

- Summary

IBM is an almost unchallenged leader in the large-systems area. Through the use of local area networks (mainly Token Rings) and the creation of long-successful industry standards for the personal computer, IBM's plan is opening towards distributed data processing. The medium-system area is also well served, recently even with AIX systems which also take account of non-IBM standards.

IBM was the first company to tackle the problem of providing clients with management tools for large-system environments. That these tools satisfy narrow internal protocols and specifications is understandable, for the problem of controlling large SNA networks arose more than a decade before management was even thought of in the context of the OSI reference model, or other communications standards.

The change in the structure of data processing (first of all without the heterogenization aspect) has caused IBM some considerable worries; indeed, the hierarchical structure which the SNA network had from the outset was destroyed. The discovery of 'intelligence outside the host' has resulted in some rethinking.

With the introduction of basic architectural logic units with graded reaction capabilities in a still purely-centrally-controlled network management, the *Network Management Architecture* (NMA) concept (also called Computer Network Management (CNM)) saw a first opening up of the IBM world even to other manufacturers. NetView, the core product of this strategy was a collection and reorganization of existing management tools, but was further developed over various versions and releases. It is now very widespread as a host product. However, its counterpart, NetView/PC has not left the starting line, since its facilities for the management of autonomous units (PCs) in, for example, LAN environments, are viewed as too minor in comparison with the cost.

Thus, IBM has developed new products for special environments, for example the LAN Manager or the trace and performance tool, described in Chapter 2, for control of Token Rings. These were initially standalone products but have increasingly become interfaces to NetView.

All these products are now successfully used, although clients do not view them as part of their medium- or long-term strategy. SystemView is IBM's new concept for integrated network management (including that of heterogeneous environments). At present, SystemView is just a set of empty shells, since there are only a very few products. Like old wine in new bottles, NetView is once more paraded as the core product of the strategy. There are still many uncertainties surrounding SystemView; however, it should be as important as SAA was four or five years ago.

In this chapter we use examples to present the problem and, above all, illustrate the evolution of the associated area as far as IBM network management is concerned. We then introduce CNM and NetView. At the end of the chapter we describe new developments such as SystemView and the extended LAN Manager.

3.1 Introduction

As is already clear from Chapter 2, there are additional requirements on a management system, on top of the basic tasks of network management, comprising the planning, implementation and control of the various physical and logical elements of a network.

These relate above all to the interplay between information from the system and the decision takers, the network administrators. The latter must receive the appropriate data delivered, formatted and represented. They need a facility to exchange information amongst themselves and with the whole system. We may assume that the administrators are spatially separated from each other.

The processing and distribution of the information should be as available and fast as possible.

Today, the management of larger networks requires more than the administrator's intuition, in particular in the case of IBM SNA networks.

Next, we consider the changes in the SNA area over the course of time.

3.2 The development of the area of SNA/SAA network management

SNA together with its extensions in the framework of the System Applications Architecture (SAA) may be taken as an example of the development of a family of network hardware, software and firmware for terminal control into a basis for the implementation of distributed applications in a multi-faceted environment of machines, from workstations to mainframes. First we consider the classical environment, then we come to the changes which accompanied SAA and consider the communication facilities of the system /6000 and the ESCON architecture as contrasting examples of the further development of the communication area.

3.2.1 The classical area

The basic structure of a traditional SNA network is a class 1 network. The overall power of control lies with the *System Services Control Point* (SSCP, also abbreviated to CP). All interaction between terminals and application programs is controlled by the access methods, the database software and the communications software in the host. The control elements are in part logically broken down as far as the host is concerned into cluster controllers and communications controllers (see also Figure 3.1).

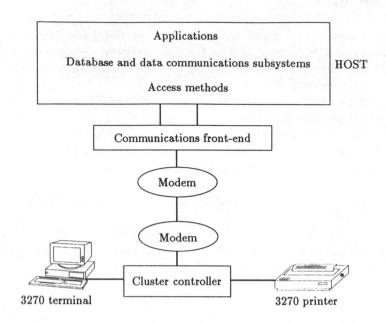

Figure 3.1   Basic structure of a traditional SNA network.

Every message flow relates to the host. Thus, message sizes, the overall message envelopes and intermediate arrival distributions may be very safely predicted. The intermediate arrival time is the time between the beginning of the transmission of one message and the beginning of the transmission of the next message. If the average message length (for example, in units of time; a message field of 12000 bytes on a 9600 bauds communications channel has a length of approximately 10 seconds) and the distribution of the intermediate arrival times are known, it is easy to calculate the average load and the average empty time and much more (according to the mathematical structure). This is a great help in planning, as one might imagine.

Because of its restricted scope and area of influence and also because of its largely predictable behaviour, an IBM network of the old class 1 structure is very easy to manage.

3.2.2 The effects of SAA: the modern SNA network

SAA provides uniform applications, user, development and communications support for PS/2 models, /3X and AS/400 systems and mainframes of the /370 series.

The integration aspect is not solely restricted to the communications engineering, but also provides for a common approach to the conception of databases.

In order to achieve this, in the context of communications support, it was necessary to extend the previously exclusively-synchronous SNA architecture and to structure the highest SNA functional layer (layer 7) with the aim of generating, transmitting and processing an electronic document composed of several independent parts on every reachable node in the network. We shall not discuss SNA itself any further here, see (Kauffels, 1989) and (Kauffels, 1990).

In particular, SNA was extended by:

- APPC (Advanced Program to Program Communication).
- SNADS (SNA Distribution Services).
- DIA (Document Interchange Architecture).
- DCA (Document Contents Architecture).

Thus, applications may exchange data in large networks with other applications in the network, regardless of whether the application is installed on a central mainframe or a network processor. The necessary prerequisites for a transmission between applications are covered by the APPC interface.

The introduction of the APPC concept, which is also known as PU 2.1/LU 6.2 after the SNA components which support it physically and logically (physical unit of type 2.1, logical unit of type 6.2), provides a convenient interface for the communication of transaction programs. So-called 'verbs', which appear similar to a high-level programming language construct, are used as communications objects. Every node in the SNA network which implements this interface may, regardless of its complexity, communicate with another node having this interface, via a logical link (conversation).

The type 2.1 node is also called an SNA low entry networking (LEN) node and supports a peer-to-peer connection. A network of such nodes permits multiple and parallel connections between the nodes.

The APPC interface is supported not only by IBM but also by many other manufacturers and thus provides an appropriate basis for the communication of transaction-oriented application programs in a heterogeneous networked environment. An ISO working group includes APPC in the OSI standardization as a transaction processing element.

SNADS specifies how data and documents are transmitted from one network node to the next until they reach the destination; for this, it uses the services of APPC. DIA is responsible for monitoring the distribution of data or documents. DCA goes a step further and describes the significance, the form and the contents of a document.

The document form and exchange specifications will have to hold their own ground against the ODA/ODIF models defined in the context of the OSI endeavours.

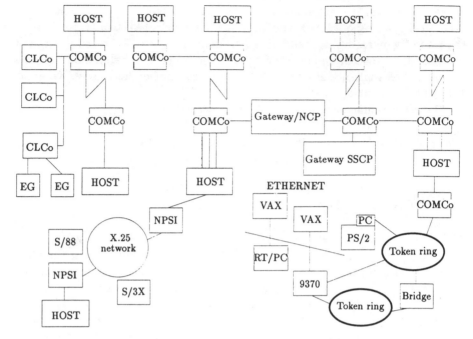

Figure 3.2   Modern multi-domain network.

The further development of SNA is characterized by two main streams:

- Construction of the basic architecture, with regard to a high transparency in the sense of SAA.

- Opening of the architecture in the interests of heterogeneous communication and international standards.

Figure 3.2 shows an example of a highly ramified, complicated, multidomain SNA network consisting of several subnetworks, with products from various manufacturers. The upper half of the figure shows an SNA Network Interconnection (SNI). Here, two multi-domain SNA networks are connected together via the gateway SSCP and the gateway network control program (gateway NCP).

A CP controls the functions of the resources of a node. Every SNA host is locally or remotely attached to various communications and cluster controllers, point-to-point and multidropped connections being found in similar numbers.

Moreover, hosts may be connected together via packet-switching WANs, PBXs, or Token Ring networks. Finally, in many cases, connections between non-IBM subnetworks (for example, from DEC, HP, Tandem, Wang or Siemens) are created using SNA networks. This is largely because, while the range of networking products meeting the ISO standards remains extremely thin, SNA is today one of the very few common denominators between different subnetworks. 'Everything can have a little SNA' from the PC to the host.

The management of a modern SNA network today corresponds to navigation through a complex of logical and hybrid networked environments.

Lower down on Figure 3.2 there is a typical SNA host and cluster-controller subnetwork. The IBM system /36 subnetwork is characterized by the Advanced Peer-to-Peer Networking feature (APPN) which is based on the physical node type 2.1 LEN. APPN generates distributed dynamic directories and executes special functions for intermediate nodes. The subnetworks of third-party manufacturers, on the other hand, in most cases indulge in central control and usually appear to the SNA hosts as PU 2.0 cluster controllers.

In the context of the extensive adaptation of IBM's APPC standard by the other manufacturers, this picture will be subject to ongoing change over the next five to ten years, so that hosts from other manufacturers will be able to communicate with SNA hosts at logically-higher levels.

We now restrict ourselves to the *status quo*. SNA is responsible for the management of logical end-to-end connections in the session layer and the physical management of routes in the network and of data links. This was relatively easy in the original environment of a class 1 network. In a distributed environment, this is a good deal harder:

- In a distributed environment, message sizes and envelopes, together with the times of arrival of some messages in some buffers, are not as predictable as in classical terminal networks.

- Small systems such as PCs, PS/2s, /36, AS/400 and /6000 may operate as standalone information-processing units and emulate 3270 terminals or transfer files. In so doing, they create even more unpredictable traffic volumes and thus additional uncertainty factors as far as the network load is concerned.

- The traces of LU–LU end-to-end sessions, which are used for diagnosis and other purposes, must run over gateways if necessary. Whether this operation is sensible, successful and efficient depends on the extent to which the administrators of various subnetworks and user organizations are willing to cooperate.

- The performance of a packet-switching WAN cannot normally be controlled by the external users.

- The management of the host domains and controller subareas is usually carried out on the PU 2.0 node type.

- Non-IBM devices and environments may collect (possibly locally) a great deal of current management information. However, this information is not necessarily comprehensible to the SNA host, if indeed the latter receives it at all.

The present control systems for SNA/SAA networks, portrayed by NMA or CNM, are currently sufficient if, for specific environments (for example, LANs), they are supplemented by other components. Even in the near future they will certainly no longer suffice, since IBM is opening its OSI communications architecture via OSI/CS and its TCP/IP communications architecture via support for the DoD protocols in the main operating systems. However, this is not enough. In addition to new solutions, the ESCON architecture will certainly produce new problems. In order to clarify these currents within IBM for the reader, we consider the (relatively harmless) example of the system /6000 and the (relatively exotic) ESCON architecture.

3.2.3 Examples of new IBM communications facilities

There are scarcely two other such dissimilar components in a company- or organization-wide network than the open AIX/UNIX system /6000 and the ESCON architecture for connection of host systems and peripherals. There is scarcely a better way of characterizing the breadth of IBM's networking capabilities.

3.2.3.1 The communications facilities of the system /6000

The spread of UNIX has increased disproportionately over the years 1989–1991. There are various reasons for this. It is now very difficult to determine those applications which no longer function sensibly with DOS and Windows and those for which a UNIX solution is still expensive. Such examples would be candidates for OS/2.

In addition to the functional aspects, it is mainly psychological factors which speak for or against the longer-term association with any given operating system. In Germany, unlike in the USA, there is a tendency towards fundamentalism. For example, an IBM client normally uses OS/2, not because he actually needs it, but because it comes from IBM. It would be wrong to trace this back to technical immaturity. In fact, in most cases, it is a question of preserving immense investments in information technology for the future.

Were IBM to couple LAN servers with a communications manager and a database manager so that, for example, OS/2 workstations could interrogate DB2-SQL databases, this solution would be very well received in conservative user circles (and these are in the majority: banks, insurance

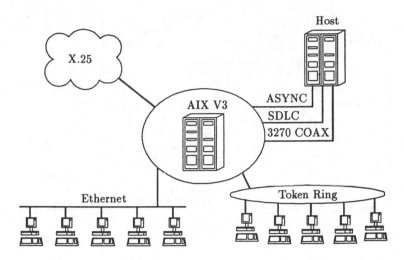

Figure 3.3   System /6000 (AIX communication facilities).

companies, administrations, ...), even though this solution might no longer take IMS databases into account and/or be much too expensive. Often the feeling that one has bought something with a secure future also counts.

However, with the new version of AIX and the system /6000 which was introduced in 1990, IBM has given even conservative user groups a clear sign as far as UNIX is concerned. These new IBM products may be expected to give a major impetus to the UNIX market as a whole. Neither should we forget the public area where in many cases, in the context of tenders, use of UNIX is made mandatory by corresponding guidelines.

Since the system /6000 (Figures 3.3, 3.4) also provides an excellent server platform for larger PC LANs, by way of example, we shall now distinguish this system from its UNIX version.

Predecessors of the new IBM AIX version 3 include AIX/RT (1986) which derives from UNIX System V, AIX for the PS/2 and AIX/370 which, as a guest operating under the VM operating system on the /370, can manage a virtual machine.

The main standards in the UNIX area come from the international manufacturer-oriented X/Open group and the OSF. Under the X/Open trademark, the X/Open group wishes to create a uniform application environment and specify things such as a system-interface specification, portable, standardized versions of programming languages such as Pascal, Ada, C, Cobol and Fortran, data management under ISAM and SQL, X-Windows technology and the X/Open transport interface (briefly mentioned

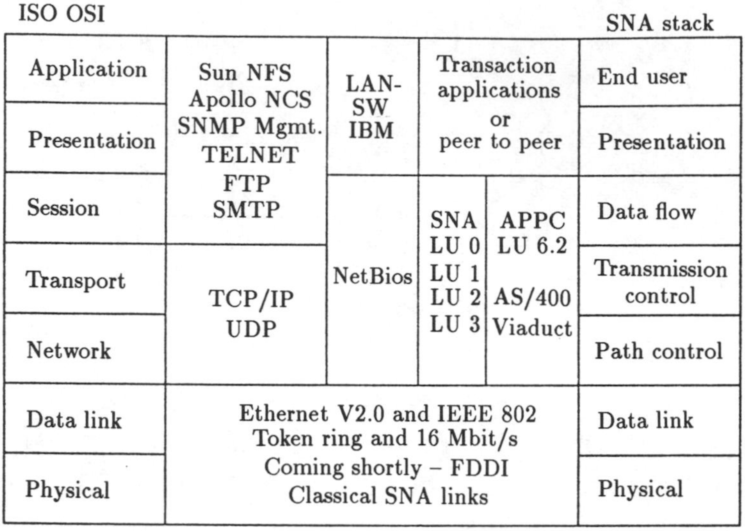

ISO OSI   SNA stack

Application	Sun NFS Apollo NCS	LAN- SW	Transaction applications	End user
Presentation	SNMP Mgmt. TELNET	IBM	or peer to peer	Presentation
Session	FTP SMTP		SNA | APPC LU 0 | LU 6.2	Data flow
Transport	TCP/IP	NetBios	LU 1 LU 2 | AS/400	Transmission control
Network	UDP		LU 3 | Viaduct	Path control
Data link	Ethernet V2.0 and IEEE 802 Token ring and 16 Mbit/s			Data link
Physical	Coming shortly – FDDI Classical SNA links			Physical

Figure 3.4   System /6000 and AIX protocol structure.

above) in the so-called X/Open Portability Guide (XPG3). The OSF wishes to implement a uniform operating system (OSF/1) with the following properties:

- Compatibility with the basic versions UNIX System V and Berkeley UNIX.

- Security level B1 of the security guidelines of the National Computer Security Center (NCSC).

- Integration of technology from different manufacturers
    — Core based on IBM AIX 3.1
    — File system based on UNIX BSD 4.4 VFS
    — TCP/IP communication protocols
    — Sun's NFS
    — AT&T's Network Computing System (NCS).

Other important bodies as far as UNIX standardization is concerned are the IEEE's POSIX, AT&T's Unix International and, of course, ISO. Regardless of the fact that these bodies are always in disagreement, we may now assume that many UNIX systems are broadly compatible and capable of interworking in an integrated communications network. As far as internetworking is concerned, the aspect of software portability is initially less interesting.

AIX version 3 has the following properties as far as the standardization and history of UNIX are concerned. It covers the 1988 IEEE POSIX 1003.1 standard and the X/Open Common Applications Environment. It has 'base level compliance' (an original IBM term, but no one knows what it means) with X/Open XPG3, conforms with UNIX System V.2 and V.3 and BSD 4.3 and has source-code compatibility with AIX/RT 2.2.1.

The virtual address space of AIX consists of 4^{10} bytes, a maximum of 4^{10} bytes per process. In the disk-management framework, a logical volume manager allows a logical volume to be distributed across several physical ones. In addition, whole file systems may be shadowed. As far as networking is concerned, NFS, NCS, the Newcastle connection and file transfer are poorly supported.

The user surfaces comprise the well-known UNIX shells and the graphical AIX Windows based on OSF/Motif and X-Windows (the latter are SAA surfaces).

As far as protection mechanisms are concerned, the target is class C2 of the NCSC Orange Book which allows for very refined access-control lists.

Networking of AIX computers is provided for by the functions mentioned at the beginning of the chapter, where additional extensions relating to the embedding into the SNA/SAA environment are made. The technical aspects of networking are covered by Token Ring, Ethernet, SDLC, X.25 and asynchronous connections which are supported in AIX by interfaces to the appropriate link protocols. In addition to the software support for TCP/IP, NFS and NCS, which is found in all modern UNIX systems, AIX also has:

- SNA services /6000 for SNA support with logical units 0, 1, 2, 3, 6.2 and physical units 2.1.

- 3270 host connection program /6000 and 3278/79 emulation /6000 with screen emulation, file transfer and character conversion.

- X.25 file transfer and network management.

- AIX VIADUCT AS/400 with AS/400 access to SQL databases.

- Network management /6000 integration in SNA systems with support from NetView and SNMP (management system for TCP/IP environments).

- DOS integration
    - Personal computer simulator /6000 with simulation of DOS 3.3 and integration of DOS files
    - DOS servers

— X-Windows for DOS
- IBM NetBios on Token Ring.
- OSI support with X.400 electronic mail, FTAM data transfer and gateway from OSI to TCP/IP.

General alternative communications configurations of the system /6000 are shown in Figures 3.3 and 3.4. In addition to the communication facilities which are targeted directly at the SNA world, there are many new alternatives which are certainly not available with the previous tools. To summarize, one might hope that with the system /6000 IBM wishes to deliver complete heterogeneous systems.

3.2.3.2 The Enterprise Systems Connection Architecture

With the announcement of the system /390 at the end of 1990, IBM announced a new group of data switches and controllers which enable the new computers to establish dynamic channel connections amongst themselves, to peripheral devices, and to older computers. This involves a (very) local, very-high-speed network based on fibre-optic connections in a star topology. The products are the hardware basis of the new *Enterprise Systems Connection Architecture* (ESCON). ESCON channel connections are faster than before, run over greater distances and require less connections than before. Some existing devices such as the 3174 communications front-end can reach not just one host, but up to eight hosts simultaneously over ESCON connections. ESCON is not a general-purpose LAN in the sense of Ethernet, Token Ring or FDDI, but is reminiscent of DEC's VAX cluster architecture. Its area of influence extends beyond hosts and their immediate environment, its goal is the narrower communication of these components, with a view to the use of a distributed operating system. Other LANs or WANs are reached by intermediate computers which are attached to the host channels via ESCON.

ESCON offers considerable improvements over the previous channel connections. This is not surprising since the previous solutions stem from the early sixties. The distance between the devices may now be up to nine kilometres, instead of the previous 100–150 m. However, the transmission speed is only increased by a factor of 2.2 from 4.5 Mbyte/s to 10 Mbyte/s, which is the net rate of extended FDDI systems. Thus, the connections correspond to the technological state of the art.

ESCON switches may be used for dynamic switching and reconfiguration of connections without the need for the devices involved to be restarted. This considerably simplifies, for example, backup configurations. The cabling is also simplified since the ESCON fibre optic cable is almost only a thousandth of the weight of the copper cable for the previous channel connections.

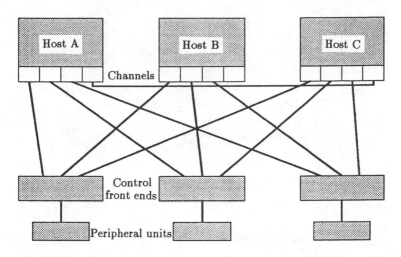

Figure 3.5   Conventional channel connections (point-to-point connections).

The ESCON fibres are the same as those released by IBM for the 16 Mbit/s Token Ring and for FDDI, namely multimode gradient index profile 50/125 or 62.5/125 micron fibres or monomode 9/125 micron fibres.

ESCON connections may be direct point-to-point connections between two devices, or indirect connections via the ESCON director. The ESCON director is the centre point of a star topology. Its use can drastically reduce the number of channel connections. There are two directors, the model 9032 and the model 9033. 9032 may have between 28 and 60 ports, in multiples of four ports. A maximum of 30 ports may be simultaneously active. 9033 has 8, 12 or 16 ports. The 16-port switch supports up to eight connections simultaneously. ESCON controllers (in practice the network adapter cards) can be delivered for most 3090 computers. Computers for which there is no controller must be upgraded to the next highest machine for which a controller does exist. The controllers are compatible on a computer with controllers for the parallel I/O channel interface. Finally, the ESCON converter allows existing devices with 'old' connections to be integrated into the ESCON architecture by converting the parallel I/O channel protocols into ESCON protocols. The converter is connected to the existing copper cable on one side and to the ESCON fibres on the other side.

There are also two types of converters, namely the 9034 which supports practically all IBM peripherals and mainframes, and the 9035 which may be used to connect IBM 3990 mass storage devices which already have an ESCON connection on the working side, to parallel I/O channels.

However, there are restrictions which must be taken into account

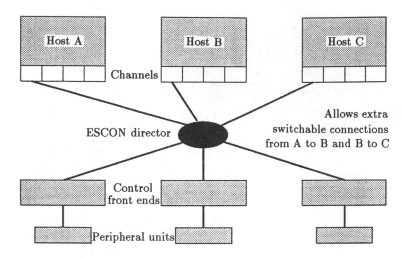

Figure 3.6   ESCON channel connections (use of the director).

at the planning stage. The much-loved 3174 controllers can be connected to ESCON devices and hosts using the 9034. But, the 3174 is built in such a way that it can only communicate with one host at once. Although the ESCON director will permit simultaneous connection to various hosts, logical connections can only be established with a single host. The newly-announced models, 3174 12L and 22L, have a completely different structure and can make full use of the ESCON architecture in that they can be simultaneously addressed from up to eight hosts. However, the older models have scarcely been updated, even the concurrent communications adapter feature, which permits connection to at least two hosts, is not a suitable replacement with its maximum data rate of 64 kbit/s.

The 3745 front ends are compatible with ESCON. The next models will probably be equipped with integrated ESCON support so that converters will no longer be needed. IBM has announced ESCON support for the 3172 and system /6000. AS/400 links have not been talked about for some time.

Because of the many possible configurations, the planning of ESCON networks requires accurate traffic analysis, since a network which is only optimized with respect to its cable cannot in certain circumstances achieve sufficient throughput. Thus, for example, two computers may be linked via the director over a cable to a peripheral device, although the bandwidth of this same cable may not be sufficient for the high data rate needed to support both computers.

ESCON does not just permit simple stars. Directors may be switched together so that further cable can be saved. But the construction only allows one director to be used as a switching centre, the other supports only one fixed connection between the first director and a selected device. According to experts, this restriction is a result of deficiencies in the ESCON management-and-configuration software.

There are a number of products which are useful at the design stage and when operating ESCON systems. The ESCON analyzer is a software package for PS/2 systems which collects statistics about error situations on ESCON connections. How do PS/2s come into ESCON? It is assumed that ESCON will contain a number of control PS/2s. All these control PS/2s will be connected over a Token Ring with a central PS/2 system which functions as the main console. This Token Ring also runs in all ESCON control processors, in mainframes and peripheral devices, in order to fetch appropriate information. The Token Ring cannot be used for other connections but is exclusively reserved for ESCON control so as to increase reliability.

However, this is not the only extra network. A so-called ESCON monitor requires extra cabling over an EIA 232 connection. This may be used to switch ESCON units on and off.

Are three different networks enough? No! The Sysplex timer also needs its own cable, which is the same as that of ESCON itself. Because of the real-time requirements, it cannot be left to run on the other cables. Unlike the VAX cluster, the communication software of which already contains a number of tools and functions (such as automatic backup), ESCON is a comparatively bare transport vehicle. Application-oriented functions must be taken care of by infrastructural software such as the DB2 database system. ESCON only supports auxiliary functions such as the 9037 Sysplex timer (Sysplex stands for system complex) which synchronizes the internal clocks of the systems attached to ESCON and thus provides the basic prerequisite for the concurrent execution of parallel programs on several computers and for unique time stamps (for example, in a database program).

As if this is not enough, there is also the ESCON manager. This comprises host software for configuring a director. It can establish and release connections between ports, establish fixed links between ports and support communication between specific ports and the establishment of dynamic connections to specific ports. The manager actually uses the ESCON connections themselves. Even when a host does not have an active connection to a director, the manager can interconnect with the director. The manager software should normally be stored in each host. The manager is reached via a 3270 terminal.

Many of the communications and teleprocessing programs which were announced at the same time as ESCON are simply old programs which now support ESCON. This means, for example, that all programs which use VTAM will run unchanged under ESCON, provided one chooses the VTAM version appropriate to ESCON.

3.3 The Network Management Architecture and its core product, NetView

In current (classical) IBM installations, the *Network Management Architecture* (NMA) specifies the management services which are needed to plan, organize and control the functions within an SNA network.

NetView is the product which goes with NMA. Installed on the host, it has a relatively-complete knowledge of the processes in the logical and physical network. The new version 2 of NetView was announced at the end of 1990.

3.3.1 The Network Management Architecture

Table 3.1 shows the most important components and elements of NMA.

Problem management is the process of handling problems in the network, from determination to solution. As far as problem determination is concerned, problems in the hardware, software or firmware are detected by an automatic process or by hand. Diagnosis determines the cause of the problem. In many cases, it will not be possible to eliminate the cause of the problem immediately and initially attempts must be made to simply bypass the problem and to recover from any errors resulting from the problem. The solution of the problem consists of corrective measures which settle the problem for good. In many cases we will not be dealing with isolated or isolatable problems, but with chains of problems which must be resolved one by one. Moreover, often, an internal problem may be hidden by an external superficial effect. In the end, tracking is an important conclusive procedure: it records the history of the problem, from its inception to its solution. The inclusion of tracking is particularly important for the solution of problems which may be related. If one is thinking of using knowledge-based systems in the future for network management, one must also recognize the particular importance of tracking in the generation of the knowledge base.

Performance and accounting management is that part of NMA which quantifies, records, controls and balances the use of network components. The monitoring of response-time measurements involves the generation of problem messages when predefined thresholds are exceeded. The recording of the load and availability of network resources and servers, together with the measurement of the delay in network components, may involve the generation of corresponding alarms when predefined values are exceeded or fallen below. Performance tuning involves the modification of critical network performance parameters in order to increase the overall performance. This also involves tracking and monitoring with messages issued at fixed values. Accounting is concerned with deriving a proper, adequate and use-dependent distribution of the overall costs over the units in use.

Table 3.1   SNA computer network management.

SNA NMA			
Problem management	*Performance and costs*	*Configuration management*	*Change management*
Problem determination	Monitoring of response times	Determination of relationships between physical resources	Software modification
Problem diagnosis	Monitoring of availability	Determination of relationships between logical resources	Microcode modification
Problem bypass	Monitoring of load	Relationships	Hardware modification
Restart	Monitoring of delays		
Problem solution	Performance tuning		
Problem tracking	Performance tracking		
Problem control	Performance control		
	Accounting		

Configuration management controls the information which is needed to identify networked resources and their dependencies and interactions at any given time. This applies both to physical and logical network resources such as hosts, communications front ends, cluster controllers, modems, multiplexers, concentrators and protocol converters and to their software and firmware. Resources are identified according to their line types, serial numbers, inventory numbers, telephone numbers, real and virtual memory allocations and program numbers. Logical resources are characterized by the information generated by the operating system, such as SSCP, LU or PU names, addresses, domains and capabilities. The resource relationship identification is the process of identifying and recording the physical and logical configuration of the network resource topologies.

Change management is the process of planning and controlling changes (introduction, removal and modification of networked hardware, microcode and software). Software change control looks after software updates, including the installation, removal and modification of modules

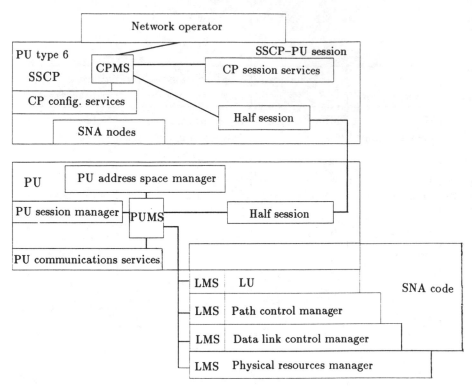

Figure 3.7 Interplay of SNA network management components.

which are only installed temporarily. The microcode and hardware change controls are responsible for journaling installation, removal and structural, functional or other modifications of the microcode or the hardware, respectively.

The four main elements of NMA are executed by a network operator. This may be a program or a person. In this way, IBM is keeping open the shift in the development of management structures towards artificial intelligence. The operator must have access to an SNA node, the Control Point Management Services (CPMS) and the Physical Unit Management Services (PUMS).

In order to further clarify the functional description, we assume that CPMS resides in a PU5 host. Then it manages all Physical Units (PUs) of its domain via SSCP–PU control sessions. CPMS forwards inquiries from the network operator to the PUs to determine their status. CPMS sets parameters and tests remote resources. It requests management service data such as test results, response times and error and performance statistics. In addition, spontaneous messages such as alarms on physical and logical units are collected and recorded. This data is preprocessed for further processing in the four main areas of NMA.

Table 3.2 NMA. Architectural units.

Focal point	Performs central network management control
•	NetView
•	NetView distribution manager
•	NetView performance manager
•	NetView file transfer program
•	NetView network billing system
•	NetView traffic engineering line optimization system
•	NetView tariff database
•	Information management
Entry point	Performs management services for itself and attached units.
•	System /36
•	System /38
•	System /88
•	Series /1
•	3174/3274 cluster controllers
•	3710 network controller
•	3708 network conversation unit
•	3220/3725 communication controllers
Service point	Supports the network management of third-party devices and non-SNA devices and environments
•	NetView/PC
•	Token Ring network
•	ROLM CBXII, 9750, 8750
•	OEM PBX
•	OEM SNA and non-SNA devices
•	non-IBM devices

CPMS interworks with the 'operator', 'configuration-services', 'session-services' and 'half-session-services' (for CPMS–PUMS and SSCP–PU half sessions) components of SSCP, within the framework of the CPMS protocol restrictions arising from its area of influence within a domain.

The PUMS is resident inside a PU. It provides management services at node level. PUMS receives management service Request Units (RUs) from the CPMS via an SSCP–PU control session and converts them into internal requests adapted to the given implementation. It forwards these requests to the internal functional units involved and sends CPMS the data it requested, together with certain spontaneous alarms or events. This all happens in SSCP–PU sessions. In addition, PUMS interworks with local-management-services (LMS) components of the nodes which control the LU half session resources.

PUMS interworks with PU components including the PU address space manager, the PU configuration services, the PU session manager and the corresponding half sessions. In addition, within the boundaries of its area of influence, PUMS interworks with the LMS physical resources manager, the LMS link control manager, the LMS path control manager and the LMS LU.

Management service data is sent over the logical connections in identifiable packets.

NMA makes a constructive distinction between focal points, entry points and service points. This is shown in Table 3.2. Usually, the focal point resides in a system /370 host. It makes processed and sanitized network-management data available to central network-management applications. Entry points are points which make network-management services available to themselves and to the SNA resources and devices connected to them. Service points provide management services to support access by non-SNA units (manufactured by IBM or not) to SNA.

Service points are, so-to-speak, network-management servers: they collect network-management data from non-SNA units, convert this data into SNA network-management service data and forward the information to a focal point. The communications between the non-SNA resources and the service points are not managed by SNA protocols.

NetView Rel. 1, which was announced in mid-1986, is the strategic implementation of a focal point within SNA. It combined elements of IBM's previous most important network-management products. In mid-1987 came Rel. 2 for the most important /370 operating systems MVS/XA, MVS/370, VM and VSE. Rel. 3 of 1989 incorporates further elements of the IBM network environment such as Token Ring subsystems and LEN.

3.3.2 The host perspective

NMA pieces the scattered elements of SNA together. It specifies the management services which are needed to plan, organize and control functions in SNA networks. However, NMA also has drawbacks. Most NMA products are host and cluster-controller based and reflect the philosophy of central control; but this philosophy contributes to the overheads and reduces the throughput. Moreover, the standstill of a critical network-management host may cripple the network management and thus also the recovery process. What is more with central control, the process of restart after errors may disrupt data traffic which is not involved (for example, resulting in considerable slowing down of sessions or lost or modified data).

NetView, the current base incarnation of NMA implementations belongs primarily to the system /370. It is powerful in its field, but has clear limitations. It is not oriented towards fundamental requirements such as are commonly found in small-system environments networked with SNA. Although gateways to subnetworks with small systems such as a system /36 are possible, these subnetworks do not possess any management facilities which would be independent of a system /370.

Perhaps IBM will one day define a set of management facilities for these systems based on the LEN functions. Until such time, /36 and /38 support a communications-and-system-management feature which implements change management and distribution together with problem determination and management.

Problem management and the support for problem determination are today compatible with the NetView command facility and the hardware monitor. Change management and configuration support are provided by the system /36 distributed systems node executive, the system /38 distributed system services and the system /38 SNA alert support, which are all compatible with the NetView distribution manager. The new announcements of ACF/NCP V.5 Rev. 2 and ACF/VTAM V.3 Rel. 3 in 1988 already lead the LEN architecture into a subfield of SNA.

Current NMA products are largely interdependent and highly interrelated during their operation. This is not a problem in a homogeneous environment. In a heterogeneous environment, non-IBM oriented subnetworks are usually under a local management which monitors them and collects statistics about their work. At present, it is not usually possible to connect this local management with NetView in an integrated manner. However, IBM has developed and issued a number of interfaces which could solve this problem. However, in addition to general SNA compatibility, this requires third-party manufacturers to develop a network management which is fully compatible with NMA.

3.3.3 NetView version 1

NetView (Figure 3.8) currently represents the core of the IBM network management products. The basic component in NetView is the command facility. It is descended from the Network Communications Control Facility (NCCF). In practice, NCCF was extended by the facilities to interwork

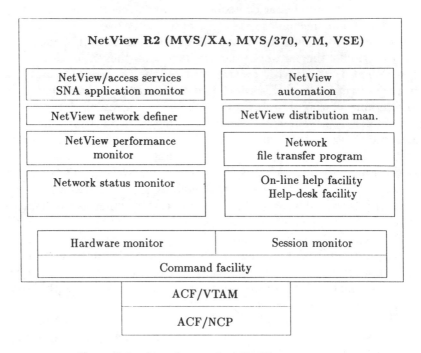

Figure 3.8   Overview: various NetView components.

with other new NetView components and to support new network products such as IBM 586X/38XX modems, 3710 network controllers and Token Ring networks. One element of the command facility, the Terminal Access Facility (TAF) supports various terminal screen sizes from 1920 to 65025 characters per screen page. The command facility helps in configuration (for example, of modems) and in load balancing.

The network hardware monitor is an extension of the Network Problem Determination Application (NPDA) and runs under the command facility. It checks whether preset thresholds have been exceeded or fallen below and generates corresponding alarms to the network operator (a person or a program). Alarms may be sent dynamically to selected operator stations. They relate to the problem areas previously described. Statistics about alarms and events are continuously extrapolated.

The Link Problem Determination Aid (LPDA) is used in conjunction with the hardware monitor TEST command to test local and remote IBM terminals. The LPDA tests include a test of the remote DTE interface and of the state of the connection and the execution of a self-diagnosis on remote modems. The signal-to-noise ratio of a connection and the state of a connection to a modem may also be tested. Lastly, a send/receive test

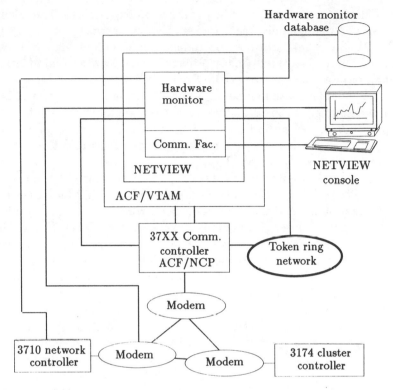

Figure 3.9   NetView alarms: interplay of the components.

requires modems to send themselves predefined bit patterns and report the results of a comparison.

In addition, the hardware monitor is able to monitor Token Ring networks connected via controllers such as the 3725. For this controller, the Token Ring connection is via the line attachment base type C using ACF/NCP V.4 Rel. 2 or higher. The 3745 controller is designed to support all levels of version 5 of the NCP. The NCP Token Ring interface (NTRI) interprets and records unresolved alarms, events on lines and problem determination statistics. Figure 3.9 shows examples of this.

Another important core component of NetView is the session monitor. Like almost all other important components, it is also a further development of an existing product, namely the Network Logical Data Manager (NLDM). It also runs under the command facility. The session monitor is designed to implement software problem determination, and configuration and performance management (using monitoring and recording mechanisms) for SNA LU–LU connections. The monitor observes sessions, both in isolated SNA networks and through gateways.

The configuration data of the NetView session monitor includes the names of the primary or secondary half sessions, subarea and element addresses, a domain name, the name of the subnetwork, the node type (SSCP, PU, LU, link, cluster controller), node names and addresses, together with node identifiers (many objects in SNA have several identifiers, depending on how they are viewed). Other configuration data for a session includes: the virtual route number, a number representing the transmission priority, the number of the explicit route, the number of the explicit route in the opposite direction, an indication of the operational status of the route in the opposite direction, the name of the service class and the log-mode name which is issued by the SSCP.

The session monitor generates a status for the Virtual Route (VR), consisting of the following elements: domain name, network identifier, name of the VR and of the end-point PU, subarea address of the end-point PU, PU type, VR pool counter, VR pool limit, VR status, buffer status, smallest, largest and current VR window sizes, sequence numbers of the last packets exchanged, system time, description of the VR status (for example, VR active, route busy, VR blocked due to various known conditions, unexpected blockage of VR, VR permanently blocked).

Only when the reader compares the goals and the notions of network management described in Chapters 1 and 2 with this collection of individual messages, does the size of the task of systematic achievement of the previous goals become truly apparent. In order to perform its tasks, the session monitor must carry out extensive further data processing. Currently, however, the complicated interworking of its internal components (and this is a criticism of many NetView users) occasionally generates a totally unrepresentative variety of results, the automatic reappraisal of which still leaves much to be desired.

The NetView status monitor STATMON is an extension of the VTAM Node Control Application (VNCA). It returns the status of the domain and a hierarchical view of the network resources and enables the network control to control the resources. It also permits occasional updating of the domain status indicator field, skimming of the NetView log and an automatic reactivation of network components when they become available after breakdown. In addition, STATMON has a filter for critical messages which are forwarded immediately from the command facility by the hardware monitor, VTAM or TAF to the operators (usually people).

The NetView on-line help and help-desk facilities are an extension of the Network Management Productivity Facility, (NMPF).

The on-line help facility simplifies the installation of the command facility and of the hardware, session and status monitors, and their adaptation to the client. This facility is augmented by tutorials, a full screen editor to read network-specific description files and command lists (CLISTs) to automate frequently-used operator and network functions. CLISTs are high-level execution statements which cause the execution of a number of statements in a high-level language or assembler in order to accomplish a specific task (or a number of tasks). It is also possible to incorporate the results of tests that have just been executed together with other conditions.

The help-desk is an online driver through procedures for diagnosing network faults. It helps one to detect and (if necessary) reactivate non-operational terminals, transactions or applications, to notice slow reaction times, to deal with problems detected by the monitor and to process system messages.

The performance monitor R3 is a VTAM application which monitors, records and graphically illustrates the network performance and load. It runs under the MVS and VM operating systems and is activated from the operator console via TAF under the command facility.

The NetView performance monitor R3 supports the extended accounting mechanisms which were provided in NCP 5.2 on 3745/3720 machines and in NCP 4.3 on the 3725 on a per session basis. When primaries in the context of a LU 6.2/PU 2.1 run on a peripheral node, accounting data which was previously mainly generated in host-based applications is provided for such node combinations and is forwarded to the performance monitor in the host. This data and the corresponding control information include, for example:

- Session accounting for primary, secondary or all LUs.

- Immediate or delayed collection of the accounting data.

- Thresholds for data entered group-wise.

- The presence of back-up sessions.

- The number of half sessions to which the session accounting applies.

The NetView file transfer program for MVS is a VTAM application which is a strategic product for the transmission of bulk data in a /370 MVS, VM/SP or VSE system environment. NetView FTP MVS is delivered as a base product and as a product with additional facilities (Advanced Function Feature, AFF). Both variants support the previous product FTP version 2.2 MVS which provides the following basic functions:

- Direct file transfer without spooling.

- File handlers for various file-system access methods such as VSAM or QSAM.

- Checkpoint/restart.

- Data compression.

The NetView FTP MVS base product has various extensions, such as queue management, server mechanisms, parallel transmission, operator console commands and the identification of remote NetView FTPs. AFF refines these facilities further.

The network definer runs under VM/SP and is used for interactive creation and updating of the definition tables for VM-based SNA networks, including the 9370. Its configuration management is based on ACF/VTAM definitions which support locally connected SNA and non-SNA devices and an integrated communications adapter for fixed and switched connections. In addition, it can handle X.25 adapters, channel connections, connected Token Ring networks and SNI connections. In the light of the more recent extensions with TCP/IP it is certain that this protocol suite together with the 9370 connections will likewise also be supported soon.

The configuration definition is used by the NetView command facility, the hardware, session and status monitors and the operators.

The NetView distribution manager for MVS/XA, MVS/370 and VM/SP operating systems provides functions for change management within the framework of centrally-controlled distribution of data and software in the SNA network. For this, it implements the VM end-node support, system /36 intermediate node support APPN, and PC-DOS end-node support (provided these are connected via S/36), together with system /36, VSE, 4680, series/1, system /88, 8100 and other directly-connected end nodes.

According to the environment, the SNA change management is supported by SNADS, DDM or AIX; it will surely also soon be supported by OS/2 EE.

NetView access services for MVS permits simultaneous access to several VTAM applications from a single screen via parallel sessions. It automates logon/logoff procedures based on user profiles and implements an interface to SAMON, the SNA application monitor which reports the status of all active VTAM applications, and links terminals to a VTAM application.

The NetView automaton is a subsystem which automates various key functions in NetView under MVS, VSE or VM. We see three basic areas of this automaton: the message table, the task and the hardware monitor alert. Essentially, the automaton on its own activates CLISTs (which were previously activated manually) according to prescribed conditions.

The message table allows one to specify criteria which imply the automatic CLIST activation. The task links NetView responses to the operating system or a subsystem together with NetView messages to the corresponding sinks, without the need for manual intervention. The hardware monitor alert extends the facilities of the NetView hardware monitor. It starts an automatic scenario by activating predefined CLISTs after it has been notified of alarms or network events. In the framework of the NetView Inter-System Control Facility (ISCF) application and ISCF/PC, the automaton provides automated console operations, which allow it to control and monitor target operating systems and hardware control consoles and also to execute initial program loads and initial warm starts from a focal point.

The NetView automaton is not a knowledge-based or self-learning system, but simply an automaton with very restricted capabilities and facilities. Nevertheless, it clearly characterizes further developments in this direction and the functions which will be implemented by corresponding systems in the first instance.

NetView Rel. 3 forms the basis for the handling of all network alarms in VM/SP, VM/XA, MVS/370 and MVS/ESA environments. It allows a focal point to record alarms of its own or any connected domain. Rel. 3 provides language support for PL/1, C and interfaces to knowledge-processing tools. The IBM LAN Manager which is responsible for management tasks in a Token Ring environment is also supported. NetView Rel. 3 command lists may be formulated in the SAA-compatible, high-level procedural language REXX.

NetView version 2 is discussed in Subsection 3.3.6

3.3.4 NetView/PC

NetView/PC is a strategic NMA service-point implementation. It is an extension of the NetView services and is designed to extend the NetView network management over IBM LANs and ROLM PBXs (perhaps also soon Siemens PBXs) and over non-SNA and non-IBM communications equipment. In Token Rings NetView/PC may, for example, connect a LAN to NetView over a gateway PC.

NetView/PC was issued prematurely and is above all designed to enable third-party manufacturers to implement their products with communications monitoring parts which communicate with the entry point to which they are attached.

NetView/PC is defined by base system services, which are an extension of DOS. These include a help facility, initialization aids, a session manager, a dialogue manager and a remote console facility which allows NetView/PC stations to control one another.

The Token Ring network manager (LAN Manager) is a NetView PC LAN application. The LAN Manager informs NetView of faults in the Token Ring, the exceeding of error limits, the self-healing of the Token Ring and other events. The IBM LAN Manager also supports PC LAN broadband installations and the bridge program assists in the management of interconnected LANs.

NetView/PC accepts service point commands from NetView and forwards them to the corresponding application.

However, there is much criticism of NetView/PC, which is directed against its lack of performance under DOS, its lack of sufficient features and the fact that its interfaces are difficult to program. NetView/PC should open the IBM SNA world to third-party manufacturers, as far as management is concerned. However, because of the construction, all the actions of NetView/PC hang at the service point and it is some time before the focal point NetView does anything, if at all. Thus, many manufacturers are now working on a direct focal point linkage.

IBM itself complains that the interface has often been misunderstood. The OS/2 EE version of NetView/PC was intended to overcome the performance bottle-necks. However, this seems not to be the case, since users are already complaining.

In its performance and development, NetView/PC is far behind NetView. NetView is used in more than 2000 large US host environments. According to a market evaluation by IDC, NetView/PC has only made it to 30–50 installations. Third-party developers who have relied on the NetView/PC specifications are particularly affected by this.

The original purpose of NetView/PC included, for example, the control of remote LANs. In the meantime, the manufacturers of LAN operating software, such as Novell, Microsoft and 3Com, have designed better utilities for the management of autonomous LAN subsystems.

3.3.5 Some criticisms of NetView and alternatives

NetView is an important tool for the control of large networks. Its centralistic approach is appropriate to the structure of a modern SNA network, provided there are enough components which may be correspondingly relocated.

In addition to basic functions, it also contains a collection of utilities. The possible uses of these are strongly moulded by each host environment. In the end, this leads to a confusing variety of systems.

NetView will surely develop further in the direction of distributed processing and gain an appropriate place even in the SAA spectrum.

One current problem is that NetView generates too much information which cannot be sensibly evaluated by the normal set of operators. The development of the system must involve a further automation of all the functions if it is to have a chance of succeeding.

According to the application, there are alternatives to NetView, of which we shall name only a few.

Net/Master from Cincom works directly with VTAM, so that neither NetView nor NCCF is used. According to experts and users, Net/Master has two major advantages over NetView: easier management of resources and a fourth generation language as user interface. Net/Master is described in more detail in (Melchard, 1990), so that we shall not concern ourselves with it further.

Other products, such as Net/Center from USWest, refine the surface of NetView.

All in all, the use of alternatives is always associated with a certain risk, which affects the reaction to extensions of the IBM SNA concept.

3.3.6 The new NetView version 2

Simultaneously with many new announcements regarding a new family of mainframe computers, at the end of 1990, IBM introduced a new version of NetView and the future management strategy, SystemView. We shall discuss SystemView later.

NetView version 2 introduces a number of mainly architectural improvements on its predecessor. The practical effects of these improvements include better use of the system resources, an uncomplicated exchange of alarms with IBM and non-IBM devices and more effective interworking with devices on local area networks.

The most important and long-awaited architectural extension is the facility to communicate with NetView over the APPC/LU 6.2 interface. This high-quality, transaction-oriented interface can be implemented on practically all devices from the PC upwards and there are already many implementations for many different operating systems outside the IBM world. The delivery date for NetView version 2, release 2, for MVS has been given as the end of 1991. The use of this interface is a reasonable alternative to the unloved NetView which, however, will still be supported by IBM. The APPC interface allows for much more elegant tailoring of the information exchange with NetView, since this interface requires applications wishing to communicate with NetView (most want to deliver data to NetView) to do this with only a few commands. For communication via NetView/PC, applications must first be ported to an SAA-compatible operating system, which, for example, makes communication with UNIX systems other than AIX considerably more difficult.

The user interface of the new NetView is the GMF (NetView Graphic Monitor Facility) graphical interface which is based on OS/2 EE and the presentation manager. GMF provides a multicoloured representation of the network, parts of network or LAN segments and attributes a coloured status to devices or parts of the network. Depending on this, certain other actions are possible. GMF is based on SAA's Common User Access Model; there is nothing else exciting about it because all other manufacturers of network management products use similar representations. One might ask oneself if, in practice, the representation is sufficiently fine, when one compares the relatively crude solution of the presentation manager, which is mainly associated with the use of small screens, with products which, for example, use large-format screens based on Sun workstations as high-level solutions which, amongst other things, save the user from having to zoom in and out.

On the other hand, using 3270 terminal emulation, the GMF solution enables one to make GMF screens accessible and usable on terminals other than PCs. Moreover, an OS/2 EE system may access various networks using the multi-terminal ASCII emulator. But, as of today, GMF is unable to display logical units graphically. This is a major disadvantage since the management of the logical network is in fact an important part of the NetView functions and the LUs and the sessions between them are very necessary for this. These are shown as before in list form. Non-SNA units can only be displayed if they are attached via NetView/PC. This is increasingly less desirable for the future. IBM, in the author's opinion, should immediately develop GMF further, otherwise the trend towards alternative products (which is considerably stronger in the USA than here) will grow.

In the future, the degree of networking of PCs will increase further. IBM has also taken this into account since the connection between NetView and LANs has been further improved. On the LAN side, the LAN Network Manager (we discuss this below) together with the LAN Station Manager form a new core component. In short, the LAN Network Manager extends the functions of the previous LAN Manager by the facility to use a SQL database on a OS/2 EE system for LAN-environment configuration data. This data is so comprehensive that new functions to increase data protection and data security can in practice be executed in the link layer, completely independently of access-control functions (for example, of the LAN server). Moreover, it also has a graphical interface and the additional facility to monitor Ethernet segments.

On the network side, IBM has increased the automation table from 11 terms in NetView 1 Rel. 3 to 81 terms! These terms describe commands that are executed when alarms, warnings and other messages from an attached system or device arrive. The seventy new terms practically all relate to LAN management.

Finally, a number of related commands can now be executed by a single command.

The new NetView introduces improvements to the newest IBM controllers, such as the 3172. The 3172 may be used as a LAN gateway or as a VTAM remote channel-to-channel controller. In the first case, the 3172 Token Ring connects token bus and Ethernet networks directly with the I/O channels of /370 or /390 hosts and FDDI LANs with hosts equipped with the ESCON high-speed channel technology. As a remote channel-to-channel connector, the 3172 connects geographically-distributed computing centres via T1 or ESCON fibre-optic connections. Alarms and warnings from the 3172 are forwarded directly to NetView version 2. Thus, very different computer configurations may be centrally controlled; however, in the medium term distributed or redundant control centres may also be established at geographically separated locations.

3.4 The future perspective: SystemView, IBM's comprehensive management strategy

In the future, one must increasingly assume that IBM SNA networks will cooperate with or even contain (as subnetworks) networks which do not conform to the SNA guidelines.

The IBM network management approach, as shown by NetView, of opening certain interfaces by instruction, is clearly not generally good enough for the future. IBM clients will want to know how to control their company-wide information processing; one may also assume that these clients possess large computing centres mainly comprising systems from the new /390 range. This is no longer a question of pure network management; all the resources and the process of preparing the resources, from planning, through implementation, inventory taking, maintenance, upkeep and operation, to taking out of service, should also be executable in a heterogeneous environment.

SystemView is IBM's strategic answer to this question. The role of SystemView is analogous to that of SAA, namely to establish guidelines for structuring environments and products based on a fundamental approach as the basis for the design and implementation of corresponding products; assuming that a client uses and will continue to use mainly IBM devices and programs. As far as the real situation is concerned, this implies an opening in relation to international standards, since, without such an opening, further use of IBM equipment by clients can in many cases no longer be justified.

SystemView takes up existing product scenarios and describes their further development, based in the communications area on SNA (like SAA), in the database area on DB/2 and in other areas on existing products which are in the immediate stages prior to the delivery. Of course, this also means that there can be no complete SystemView solution in the forthcoming years, only a continuous development.

SystemView is basically a subelement of SAA. As with SAA, the introduction of SystemView also met with sharp criticism, which we describe in Section 3.4.3.

Firstly, we describe the structure of SystemView, the importance of SystemView for various system environments and the very first products.

3.4.1 The structure of SystemView

SystemView is based on the following principles:

- High user-friendliness with OS/2 EE-operated end user workstations, (IBM has a peculiar way of saying this, these are the workstations of the system managers or administrators).

- Use of a relational database technology.

- Integration and extension of NetView products.

- Increase in system-management productivity with increased room for automation.

- Protection of previous investments (which is naturally a considerable hindrance to the introduction of a completely new concept).

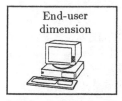
End-user
dimension

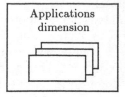
Applications
dimension

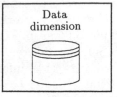
Data
dimension

- Integration of heterogeneous systems
- Further development of existing products
- Guidelines for new developments
- Strategic openness for clients and other manufacturers

Figure 3.10   IBM SystemView (basic structure).

Other (well-loved by decision takers) objectives of SystemView include an increase in cost-effectiveness and the promise to provide medium-term tools to improve the correlation with strategic company objectives.

In addition to the classical network management goals (as formulated, for example, for CNM) other objectives include the integration of products from different manufacturers and the control of heterogeneous networks (including those which integrate both data and speech). Finally, data protection also enters the wish list. SystemView should not be restricted to the management of central systems and centrally-controlled networks, but should also cover departmental and individual systems.

Every system management has its own applications, user interfaces and data. Currently, these things are typically haphazardly distributed, depending on the network, the location and the functions.

Today, if it is exchanged at all, management information is exchanged in peculiar forms. Nowhere is this exchange standardized, instead, two entities agree on a useful format which cannot in practice be used anywhere else.

In addition, the increasingly-required information about the overall state of the network (see Chapters 1 and 2) is practically unobtainable. Instead, whenever there is a breakdown there is a frantic search for its causes, during which time the interactions between the logical and physical system are often neglected since they cannot be recorded. ('The front-end processor stops. Thousands of IMS and TSO sessions are suddenly interrupted. The NetView operator is confronted with around 2000 messages in addition to the usual 100 per second. Most of these relate to the effects of the interruption, only some relate to its causes. Instructions are issued despairingly, the newly-appointed network operator telephones the shift leader. Costly minutes are lost and further analysis follows. After 1.5 hours the system is safe and sound and running again.' (Datacom, 1991)).

Business management: Stock management, financial management resource planning (personnel, facilities, data)
Change management: Planning and execution
Configuration management: Relationships between resources
Performance management: Performance and tuning
Operation management: Management of the usage of systems and resources with reference to company objectives

 – Unified application services
 – Generic system management processes

Figure 3.11   IBM SystemView (applications dimension).

Even if the requirement for knowledge of a system-wide overall state is dropped in favour of a restriction to knowledge of the system-wide state of individual services and applications, success is not always guaranteed, even with the best existing facilities.

Other problem dimensions include the increase in system and network management tools and the consequent increase (in quality and quantity) in personnel, (the best aids to LAN operation should also be used). Usually each tool has its own user interface, which scarcely helps to increase productivity.

Finally, during the operation of a system or network, there will be immense data sets which are firstly put together in completely different formats and are secondly not at all interrelated. Even if one assumes that almost all this data will not be used any more, a small percentage of this data from the past may be helpful for current problems. However, if this data is buried amongst the unused data, and if it is not stored in any generally comprehensible format and is not interrelated, it is of little value, since it usually takes too long to retrieve and assess.

In summary, from these facts IBM derives the following requirements on future network and system management:

- Productivity-increasing user interfaces with uniform syntax and semantics.

- Structured definition of the management processes as the basis for greater integration and automation, where these processes cover as many areas of system management as possible.

- A common data model for all system management functions to decrease redundancy and increase the level of the logical relationships between data.

This leads IBM to the requirement for a company-wide system management structure. Here, while IBM is banging on the general drum of possible heterogenization, it is striving, quite contrary to the OSI management framework, to take the leading role. An approach other than integration via hegemony would have been surprising. The reason for this is clear: the approach of managing not only networks but also systems goes far beyond the scope of the OSI network management framework. Since, according to IBM and amongst real clients IBM mainframes stand at the centre of data processing, it is clear that these tools to manage mainframe environments will be generalized. Moreover, since, in a no-nonsense view, a network is simply another way of getting data into and out of a computer, network management is clearly a part of system management, and not *vice-versa*.

Products conforming to the SystemView structure provide management functions and information relating to resources in the area of SAA systems, AIX systems, VSE systems and other IBM and non-IBM systems. The SystemView structure is based on open standards such as OSI, current architectures such as SNA and SAA and new architectural elements for network and system management.

The core of SystemView is a structure with three parts, comprising end-user, applications and data dimensions. The end-user dimension describes the equipment and guidelines which provide for a consistent user surface. The applications dimension is the environment in which the system management applications should be uniformly developed. Lastly, the data dimension describes the data definitions and the access mechanisms for the system management applications.

The definition of SystemView is relatively open at the moment, just as the definition of SAA was and still is. There is a SystemView consistency guide, in which the user interface is introduced in accordance with SAA/CUA. From the data model, it is certain that SQL will be taken into account.

The end-user dimension is an SAA-conforming user interface and should provide a consistent form of presentation for system management applications. It is based on Programmable Workstations (PWs) with OS/2 EE. IBM Germany found it too awkward to talk about PCs in the context of a PC strategy. US announcements speak of PS/2 systems under OS/2 EE, which clarifies the situation.

IBM lists the following properties which should contribute to increased productivity:

- Uniform user access. All system management functions obtainable via the same interface.

- Analogous execution of all applications (as far as possible) which should simplify the learning task.

- Object-oriented approach. Here, IBM only means that the colour pictures on the colour monitor (icons) are intuitively related to the functions specified by you. Nothing more can be read into this.

- Concentration on specialized knowledge rather than on product knowledge.

- Simplified development of applications by adherence to (IBM) standards and use of given basic functions.

In the favour of object orientation and by way of further explanation, we note that the idea of SAA Common User Access (CUA) is essentially to implement applications in the form of objects and operations on these objects. Within the interface a user can select an object and an action from a set of alternatives. Objects or functions with the same meaning are displayed in the same way, even when they occur in different applications. This eliminates a source of annoyance to users. The objects displayed correspond to the objects specified in the data model. This permits the achievement of a higher degree of integration. In different applications one always ends up with the same objects. Here is an example. A communications front-end occurs in several management applications. In the configuration management framework, the setting of parameters and the setting or influencing of relationships with other objects (such as a channel or an SDLC line) may be operations on these objects. Leaving the configuration application and moving, for example, to a problem-management application, the logical relationships of the communications front-end and how they are influenced are of interest. It is still the same front-end. If the processor is replaced by another model, in principle only a single change in the object database is needed, namely replacement of the object representing the old front-end by an object representing the new one. One would also like to do this within the OSI network management framework; here, the objects are called 'managed objects'. The path from the present structure to this is very long. However, new devices could be directly associated with an object file which is loaded into the database. A consistent data model is a prerequisite for this. It is annoying that here too, as above, the German description of SystemView is inadequate, while the US version on the other hand describes the objectives in a clear way.

The object-oriented nature of the end-user dimension implies serious structures for data and applications. It is not (as one might easily misunderstand) simply a question of measures to improve the structure of the user surface. We shall have to wait and see how far these declarations of intent become fact. However, since object orientation represents the state of the art of modern software technology, one should look calmly into the future here.

According to IBM statements, products which wish to conform with the end-user dimension must use PWs under OS/2 EE; they may conform with CUA if they use the dialogue manager, the presentation manager, IBM EASEL (a tool for developing presentation-manager applications) or the network graphic monitor facility.

As examples of products which will correspond to the end-user dimension, IBM cites the SAA asset manager/MVS (a database which allows users to store a data set concerning orders and settlements relating to their network); information/management; the SAA delivery manager (a program which forwards MVS or VM files to an OS/2 system); OPC/ESA (Operations Planning and Control/ESA analyzes the status of the defined production areas from a single point and looks after the processing of the controllable workload in accordance with the installation guidelines; it decreases the load on the operator by extensive automation); the NetView graphic monitor facility (an extension program for NetView which permits graphical representation of networks, subnetworks, components and events); the OS/400 systems management utility (which facilitates the central problem and change management, including for AS/400 systems); the workstation data safe facility (WDSF/VM) and the ESCON manager and analyzer (to manage the new ESCON host connections).

In time, the end-user dimension will contain an extended definition of the interface to SystemView and will provide a set of tools and services for use with SystemView applications.

In addition to a standard set of data definitions, the data dimension contains database services which can be used by system management applications. The data definitions represent the information-processing resources in the company and are specified in the SystemView data model. The data model includes the descriptions of the resources and their interrelationships and may be extended by IBM, software manufacturers and clients. A company-wide database which can be accessed via the SAA/SQL database interface is home to the data.

The SystemView data model is consistent with OSI standards ISO/IEC 10165-4 and ISO/IEC 10165-1 (see also Chapter 5).

According to IBM the aims and objects of the data dimension are:

- Shared access to data using a company-wide system-management database and a uniform data model.

- Improved data integrity by reduction of redundancy and standardization of data definitions.

- Simplification of changes by the explicit use of defined relationships between data.

- Support for management decisions based on current and easily-accessible data.

- Extension facilities.

- Avoidance of unnecessary manual entry of data which is already stored or can be derived.

Conformance to the data dimension implies use of the SystemView data model and implementation with the SAA SQL database interfaces. As examples of products which already satisfy these requirements, IBM cites the SAA asset manager, information/management and the OS/400 systems management utility.

The new IBM LAN Station Manager and the LAN Network Manager, which are discussed in Sections 3.4.4.2 and 3.4.4.3 (respectively), work with modified OSI managed objects. These new programs are clearly not consistent either with the data dimension or with the end-user dimension.

The applications dimension comprises a company's management applications. Two new areas have been added to the four accepted task areas of management. These areas are now called disciplines. The six SystemView disciplines are:

- **Business management** Stock management, financial management functions, planning of a company's resources such as staff, equipment and data.

- **Change management** Planning, execution and logging of changes.

- **Configuration management** Physical and logical links between resources.

- **Operations management** Management of the use of resources and systems in order to achieve company objectives.

- **Performance management** Collection of performance data, tuning, capacity planning.

- **Problem management** Problem chasing from the inception of a problem to its removal.

In general the objective of the applications dimension is to improve the support for automation of management functions. At the same time, IBM is thinking of generic system management processes which go beyond the boundaries of networks and operating systems (for example, a central problem management for a heterogeneous environment). There is also a search for greater closeness to standards such as OSI.

A narrower definition of interfaces and protocols for the applications dimension is still to come. Thus, there are as yet no complete guidelines for conformance. Of course, all IBM system management products have something to do with one or more applications-dimension disciplines and thus should also cross network or system boundaries. The interesting statement that the applications dimension will use existing ISO/IEC standards through the implementation of specifically-designed interfaces and protocols, such as CMIS/CMIP (see Chapter 5), was not visible in the German descriptions.

Current system-management applications are restricted to a specific type of resource, system environment or function. With the growth of applications-dimension products, interfaces will instead support generic managers and resource agents over heterogeneous systems, regardless of the network type.

3.4.2 Environments for SystemView

Environments for SystemView may begin with small LANs and extend to large multiprocessor systems which may be distributed in different places. The support for standards such as TCP/IP and OSI, and architectures such as SNA, extends the area of application. SystemView distinguishes between two classes of systems: managerial systems in which managerial applications (the so-called SystemView managers) provide interfaces for planning, management and control of resources, and managed systems in which agents use these interfaces. Managerial systems which exist in other contexts (for example, the OSI network management system) will be able to exchange information with SystemView managers and to undertake joint actions.

Next, we briefly discuss different environments and their relationship with SystemView.

3.4.2.1 SystemView and SAA

SystemView applications will be implemented across the whole of the SAA spectrum comprising the OS/2, OS/400, VM/ESA and MVS/ESA system platforms. The SystemView structure uses SAA to implement products with coherent interfaces, namely SAA CUA, SSA SQL CPI, SAA communications interfaces such as LU 6.2 and selected SAA communications services.

3.4.2.2 SystemView and AIX

The AIX network management environment contains basic elements for interoperability with the SystemView structure, namely connectivity to the SystemView network management function for problem alarms and operator commands using TCP/IP and OSI agents, access to AIX system-management functions for remote operation using the TCP/IP Telnet

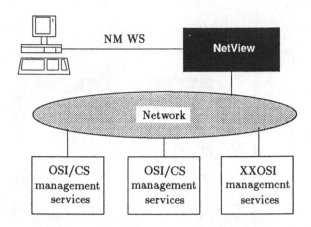

Figure 3.12   IBM SystemView OSI integration (current view).

function, receive facilities for remote login from the host using the host command facility and the facility to participate in the SystemView distribution of software and data via NetView distribution manager. Thus, in principle, complete remote control of AIX systems is possible. AIX systems which possess OSI software may also be addressed using the CMIP/CMIS contained in SystemView. IBM works openly with the OSF. Thus, SystemView products in an AIX environment will implement OSF management protocols as soon as these are defined; again we see an attempt to conform to OSI.

3.4.2.3 SystemView and OS/2

OS/2 has three roles as far as SystemView is concerned: it is a platform for the end-user dimension, a managerial system and a managed system. The SAA CUA elements of the end-user dimension are provided by the presentation manager and the dialogue manager. A managerial system consists of a set of so-called enablers (agents), tools, utilities, techniques, procedures and applications for managing standalone or distributed PS/2 systems running under OS/2 or PC-DOS. The support of the managerial system by a managed OS/2 system consists of system management enablers which are integrated in OS/2.

3.4.2.4 SystemView and AS/400

The system AS/400 supports the SystemView structure via system-management functions which, in OS/400 and other products, are integrated

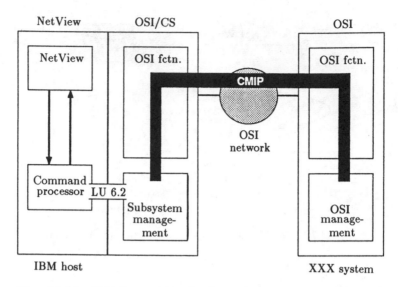

Figure 3.13 IBM SystemView (implementation of the OSI functions).

into AS/400. These functions are sufficient to control an AS/400 system and also to turn it into a managed system. The AS/400 system-management utilities licence program allows control of AS/400 through a central AS/400. The functions cover a wide area of the applications dimension and permit shared use of data, programs and processes within an AS/400 group. These functions will be increasingly adapted to the SystemView ground rules and extended.

3.4.2.5 SystemView and MVS/ESA and VM/ESA

MVS/ESA and VM/ESA are the most important MVS and VM environments for the implementation and support of interfaces and products based on the SystemView structure. MVS and VM system management aim to integrate and automate the management of individual systems or groups of systems. Here, particular value is placed on increasing the degree of automatic self-management, on providing uniform user interfaces and on uniform use of system-management data across system and product boundaries. MVS/ESA and VM/ESA may be both managerial or managed systems in SystemView. Products from the existing extensive range of products for management of hosts, networks, memory and database resources will be selected, partially revised or exchanged for new products so as to correspond to the SystemView guidelines. Immediate announcements were primarily aimed towards improvement of the operating system itself or towards improvement of the main management software. Here, the hardware naturally includes the new ESCON connection units, analyzers and above all the Sysplex (system complex) which turns several MVS systems into a logical unit; these are connected by hardware elements and corresponding software. OPC/ESA may be used to control various MVS/ESA systems from a single point.

It is planned to turn SystemView into a universal control element which, in addition to the network management itself (initially based on the further development of NetView), will also carry out memory management to improve the use of distributed or local DXC systems and database management in the framework of SAA.

In the course of the book we shall often return to IBM network management and so also to SystemView, namely in the comparison with the OSI-oriented schemes of other manufacturers and in the discussion of new LAN management proposals. Before these discussions and assessments, we must first be clear about the OSI network management framework.

3.4.3 Criticisms of SystemView

Next we come to the criticisms of SystemView which were raised immediately following its release. Critics believe that SystemView underlines how far away IBM now is from the development of a true integrated management solution. The confused tangle of the IBM product lines calls for a chaotic collection of various separate management tools. Many of these tools now run on expensive hosts and use a character-oriented 3270 terminal interface. In the future, they will also run on equally expensive PS/2 systems with the artificially-inflated, and in the author's opinion totally-inefficient, OS/2 EE operating system, thus with the communication manager, presentation manager, database manager ..., which are themselves coupled to the host environment. For the investment in 20 Mbyte memory space (OS/2 EE probably needs more memory space before the product is delivered) you get a colour monitor with a mouse to click. For this, other manufacturers provide nice UNIX computers with monitors if desired.

The vision of integrated company-wide management via SystemView is still quite vague and undefined. Even apparently clear concepts such as the universal object-orientation are interpreted quite differently in the various IBM divisions. At the moment, there is no unified management-data model underlying the current NetView or other management products. This means that even a brand-new 1991 or 1992 version of NetView will store the data in a format which it is highly likely that no one will be able to use later. Only very few IBM management products, such as the LAN Network Manager announced for 1991, actually use a relational database.

In general, there are uncertainties about the data model. Based on the information issued to date, it is similar to, but not integrated into the AD/cycle information model. AD/cycle is a range of IBM tools for application development in an SAA environment with VM, MVS, OS/2 and OS/400. IBM intends that AD/cycle tools should in time permit the development of integrated application programs which are portable over all SAA systems. At present AD/cycle is compatible with the host-based DB2 DBMS. The SystemView information model is also based on DB2. However, there is currently a difference between system management processes and network management processes as implemented by NetView. It is conjectured that the data model for the network management processes will soon be transformed into an AD/cycle product, which it will again be possible to use to address the repository manager. This may not be the case.

In choosing NetView, IBM has recycled an old system instead of developing a new one. This was not strictly necessary. NetView is the inelegant reality, SystemView is still a dream. Current IBM system management products are not in a position to control systems from other manufacturers. The only such facility is the ability to process messages and alarms if these are issued in the proper form.

In the face of the increasing popularity of network-management standards such as SNMP or CMIP, IBM has not managed to push through a proprietary management architecture, for experience shows that clients use IBM products only when there is no alternative, for example, to control the SNA backbone network. It is now possible to believe that IBM has learnt this and is orienting itself towards international standards. We shall address this theme again in connection with LAN management. However, the fact is that OSI has essentially been pushed away to a subsystem and that protocols such as SNMP or CMIP are, of course, only interchangeable transport and signalling mechanisms which one may or may not use. The structure hidden behind such mechanisms is considerable.

There is also the very widespread view that IBM's involvement in open standards is not credible. When one looks at the current implementation of OSI management functions in the framework of IBM products, it becomes clear why: OSI protocols are only used for communication within the OSI subsystems, everything else runs under APPC/LU 6.2.

According to Data Communications, the 1990 version of NetView is 'the answer to the problems of the nineties with the technology of the eighties'. It remains questionable whether SystemView will succeed in keeping hold of the users or whether it is a gigantic deception manoeuvre.

3.4.4 New impetus for LAN management in the shadow of SystemView

Three components from the LAN management area were announced in connection with SystemView. In order to put a little more life into

SystemView, we now introduce these as a low-end example of first products in the shadow of, rather than in framework of, SystemView. These components are:

- The 8230 controllable multi-station access unit.
- The LAN Network Management program.
- The LAN Station Management program.

Together, set against the alternatives described in Chapter 2, the trio form an almost revolutionary basis for the management of Token Ring networks with the following main properties:

- Access control at the physical level
- Conformance with OSI and IEEE management standards
- RJ-45 plugs, modularity.

The development of the complete management functions requires the new access unit, which we must therefore describe in brief.

3.4.4.1 The IBM 8230 controllable multi-station access unit

The IBM 8230 is a new modular controlled access unit for the Token Ring. It by far surpasses the performance and capabilities of the 8228.

The 8230 is a basic unit which may be extended using *Lobe Attachment Modules* (LAMs). It is switchable between 4 and 16 Mbit/s. It has its own control intelligence for interworking with the LAN Network Manager (described below) and full MAC access to both the main ring and the backup ring.

As standard, the unit is delivered with copper connections for the main ring but may also be adapted for fibre optics using changeover modules. Through active repeaters, unlike previously, the 8230 supports longer lobe lengths namely 145/375 m for type 1 data cable at 16/4 Mbit/s and 100 m at 4 Mbit/s for unshielded twisted pairs (UTP) of the type 3 cable specification. The plug-in LAMs allow up to 80 terminals to access one 8230. Each LAM has 20 connections. Against conventional 8228 access units, this represents a considerable simplification as far as drawing up network scenarios is concerned, since, for example, systematic cabling of office environments according to the four steps given in the standard (terminal area – storey – building – area) using an expandable 8230 is very much better supported than with the previous 8228 stock.

For its loyal clients, IBM has at last reacted to the fact that its competitors have already been producing cheaper multi-station access units for some time. This is also shown by the fact that in addition to the usual space-filling IBM cable-system hermaphrodites, the smaller, more practical

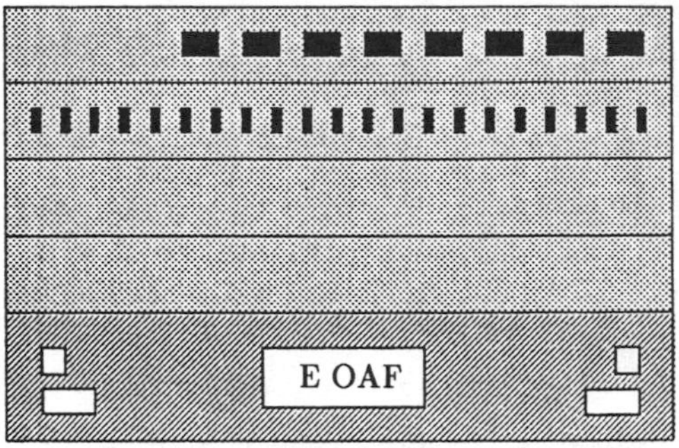

Maximum 80 devices connectable per unit

Hermaphrodite or
RJ 45 connection

Basic unit
Connection type 1 or fibre

Connection module
Maximum 4

E OAF

Figure 3.14   IBM 8230 Token Ring MSAU (network controlled access unit).

RJ-45 plug is now officially supported by corresponding LANs. However, this is not all that the competition can do more cheaply or more elegantly. The highlight is the close interworking with the LAN Network Manager, the further development of the Token Ring LAN Manager.

If a ring segment breaks down, the 8230 repairs it either on its own initiative or with the help of, and at the instigation of, the LAN Network Manager.

The LAN Network Manager's configuration table is supplied with information by the 8230, where the 8230 number (corresponds to an 8230 port) and the number burnt into the Token Ring adapter card form a three-level address which uniquely identifies the workstation regardless of the logical identification within a network program. In the case of errors, this identification is useful for statistical purposes; it is also used to forestall violations of the protection policy (penetration attempts).

The 8230 also supports (this is a unique feature at the moment) the disconnection of a port at the instigation of the LAN Network Manager. There are many reasons why this may occur and we shall discuss these later.

These new functions of the 8230 are in principle very welcome and were certainly unique at the time of their announcement. However, there are now reservations about the newly-won freedom for alternative hardware components of Token Ring networks, since the new functions could mean that indirectly, with adapter card address coding or port restrictions, compatible adapter cards may not even reach the ring.

The 8230 could coexist with the 8218, 8219, 8220 and 8228 on the same ring. However, for full exposure of its functions it is allocated to the LAN Network Manager.

3.4.4.2 The LAN Network Manager

The new LAN Network Manager is a program for controlling and monitoring IBM Token Ring networks, IBM broadband PC networks (which may each consist of several segments) together with IBM 8209 bridges linking Token Ring and Ethernet 802.3 or Ethernet V.2.0 systems. Like its predecessors, the IBM LAN Manager, not to be confused with the LAN Manager from Microsoft, is capable of central or decentralized and local or remote operation.

There are two fundamentally-different versions of the LAN Network Manager, namely the LAN Network Manager–entry which does not have its own user surface (instead it forms a NetView entry point which can only work with NetView version 2 Rel. 2 as focal point, when it runs as a task in an OS/2 EE system and communicates with NetView in the host system via the SNA gateway in the OS/2 EE communications manager) and the standalone IBM LAN Network Manager itself, which uses the SAA-conforming OS/2 EE presentation manager for communication with the user and the SQL-oriented database manager for construction of the LAN configuration file and corresponding management functions. There are also two versions of the latter, versions V.1.0 and V.1.1, with different functional scopes.

The LAN Network Manager extends the LAN monitoring and control functions of the IBM LAN Manager, mainly with the use of the database system with event files and configuration tables. The configuration table contains a large amount of station-specific information, most of which is generated and recorded by the LAN Station Manager. This data includes identification numbers, line-access-unit numbers, port numbers (this data comes from the 8230), room numbers, telephone numbers, etc., together with a description of the state (active, inactive, etc.). This data generates a precise profile of the physical network up to the logical link control.

The IBM LAN Network Manager provides a filter function for alerts, which may be used to ensure that only certain messages are passed to NetView. These filters may also be set from the NetView console.

Unlike its predecessors, the IBM LAN Network Manager can automatically accept a logical connection to a bridge as soon as the latter becomes operational, it also has more functions for automated network monitoring.

The LAN Manager–entry has basically the same functions but presently only for a single LAN segment.

Important features include the increased security functions and access control available for interworking between the 8230, the LAN Network Manager and the LAN Station Manager.

The management of the 8209 LAN bridge has been extended to enable the user to set and modify bridge parameters from the LAN Network Manager console. Additional statistics about delayed collisions, CRC and

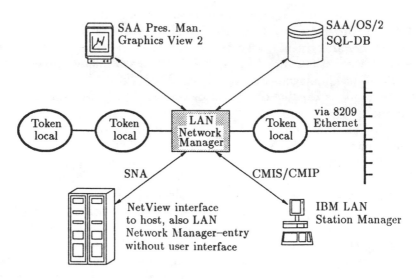

Figure 3.15 IBM LAN Network Manager.

frame errors in the 8209 Ethernet segment may be generated. It is even possible to define adapters conforming to IEEE 802.3 which support the 802.2 LLC as critical resources.

3.4.4.3 The LAN Station Manager

The IBM LAN Station Manager is the third element of the trio. It is a PC program under DOS or OS/2 which provides detailed information to the IBM LAN Network Manager, thus allowing the latter to generate a dynamic LAN topology, to centrally monitor the site of and changes in a specific station, to control the access to a station via the 8230 MSAU and to implement data protection and data security at the physical network level.

The LAN Station Manager runs on practically all PC and PS/2 systems and all fully-compatible computers; however, it needs an original IBM LAN adapter card for Token Ring or baseband or broadband PC networks. After installation, it only requires 15 kbyte although in DOS operation it needs the IBM support program 1.1 or 1.2 and in OS/2 operation it needs the extended edition communication manager.

3.4.4.4 Security functions/access controls

The trio permit layered access control to a Token Ring LAN segment at the physical level, according to the wishes of the client. This type of access

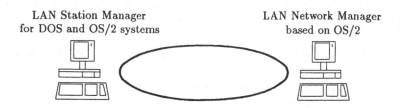

LAN Station Manager   LAN Network Manager
for DOS and OS/2 systems   based on OS/2

- The LAN Station Manager provides the LAN Network Manager with detailed system information in the form of OSI managed objects.
- OSI managed objects are specified in ASN.1.
- The information exchange is via OSI CMIP/CMIS.

Figure 3.16   IBM LAN Station Manager.

control is fully independent of control mechanisms at the logical level, as provided, for example, in the IBM PC LAN program, Novell's NetWare or version 2.0 of Microsoft's LAN Manager.

Access controls for a user station may be based on an adapter address, the 8230 identification number, the number of a line-access unit, the number of a port to a line-access unit or a time and a date. Thus, the LAN Network Manager configuration database may be used to make the network access rights of a particular station dependent on the adapter address, the time of day and the day of the week. The 8230 can provide for more detailed access rights. As soon as an adapter attached to an IBM 8230 switches on in the ring, the 8230 sends its own identification number and those of the line-access units involved, together with the number of the port at which the adapter is attached, either directly or via the LAN Station Manager to the IBM LAN Network Manager.

This information is compared with that already in the database. Further restrictions such as the time of day or the day of the week are used to decide whether to accept the connection request. If the values do not agree with the predefined values and fields a warning message is issued. The network operator can decide whether to logically remove the adapter from the network or even to deactivate access to the MSAU (with the consequence that the adapter at this connection can no longer be introduced into the network without management-operator intervention).

Thus, an unauthorized penetrator of the network must bring an authorized station under his control (by overthrowing it) at the right time, or reproduce all the physical parameters and withdraw the real authorized station unnoticed from circulation. Both these methods are considerable feats in comparison with the trivial tapping of Ethernet networks. In addition, the penetrator must possess certain information in the LAN Network Manager configuration database.

Other possibilities for unauthorized network access include conspiracy with the network administrator or possession of the network-management workstation.

Since the logical protection measures of PC LAN operating systems clearly overtax the patience and intelligence of average network administrators (as is easily seen from the inadequate use of these utilities which have already been available for some time), the author is pessimistic as to whether the Token Ring users will accept and use this additional security spectrum at the physical level.

It would be nice if the IBM trio were to represent the first incarnation of a new generation of management-friendly LAN components.

The LAN Station Manager describes objects according to IEEE 802.5/89, namely as managed objects in the sense of the OSI management framework. A managed object is characterized by its unique name, its parameters (the values of which are only fully fixed after its incarnation), its states (which describe the changes over time) and its relationships to other managed objects.

All station-specific information is represented by the managed objects. Thus, the configuration database in the IBM LAN Network Manager is a partial incarnation of the MIB relating to the LAN subsystem and the configuration management needs. Correspondingly, the management protocol between the IBM LAN Network Manager (version 1.1) and the IBM LAN Station Manager is based on (probably adapted) ISO Common Management Information Protocol (CMIP) specifications. The code used for communication is generated using the ISO/OSI Abstract Syntax Notation 1 (ASN.1). These adapted specifications were developed with 3Com. Criticisms of these specifications are given at the end of Chapter 7, since certain prerequisites for these criticisms have not yet been considered.

According to IBM the costs will be kept to scale. An 8230 with fibre-optic modules costs significantly less per connection than an 8228 with fibre-optic converters. The 8230 only becomes economical when all the connection points are used. The LAN Network Manager needs at least 8 Mbytes of main memory and an OS/2 EE 1.2 computer. The whole should be available in December 1991.

3.5 Summary

In this chapter, we have seen how the IBM environment is being developed further and how even the IBM product lines are being made increasingly heterogeneous. This includes facilities for communication with systems from other manufacturers (such as the OSI communications subsystem or TCP/IP support), which, unlike previously, IBM is now freely providing.

These developments necessarily have almost catastrophic effects on the overall structure of networks and of data processing itself so that new management routes must be found.

Whether the further development of NetView is such a route remains questionable. Too many elements of the purely-centrally-oriented data processing could hinder the creation of an integrated platform for network and system management.

SystemView is still a plan. Plans are surrounded with uncertainty. Thus, for example, SAA contains OS/2 as a strategic PC operating system. Four or five years ago IBM would almost certainly have been right to assume that OS/2 could become the designated successor to DOS. With the further development of DOS and Windows on the one hand and the increase in the user friendliness of UNIX on the other hand, it has reached the point where most users will only use OS/2 when forced to. Microsoft has in fact given up the further development of OS/2. This makes OS/2 an IBM-proprietary operating system.

How far elements of SystemView (like those of SAA) will be modified over time as a result of (justified) user resistance is very hard to assess.

Certainly, both the ongoing development of management standards in the OSI framework and the facilities which other manufacturers provide for network management will have a considerable influence on this.

Chapter 4

Classical network management: examples of DEC and Siemens

- Introduction

- DEC DNA and network management

- Siemens: SINEC and TRANSDATA

- Summary

The IBM concept of network management was described in detail in Chapter 3. Other manufacturers were also early to consider how they might supply their clients with tools to control, monitor, configure and extend communications or terminal networks. In this chapter we shall consider several classical approaches in the framework of TRANSDATA and SINEC networks from Siemens (now SNI) and DECnet from the Digital Equipment Corporation.

Both these manufacturers wish to orient themselves fully in the future towards the open communication standards of the OSI reference model. Therefore, manufacturer-specific protocols will stand side-by-side with the OSI protocols during a long transition phase. This is also advisable, since there are task areas, such as terminal control, which OSI does not touch.

Thus, we must now distinguish clearly between the management in manufacturer-bound classical environments and future-oriented plans for further managerial developments. This chapter contains a brief discussion of DEC DNA and classical DECnet management, while the DEC *Enterprise Management Architecture* (EMA) is described in Chapter 7, following the discussions of management in open systems. The same applies to the Siemens networks. The classical management which clients now have installed is described here, while Chapter 7 describes the latest OSI-oriented developments both of Siemens and of other manufacturers.

4.1 Introduction

Several years ago, one could not have predicted that SNA on the one hand and open systems communication according to the guidelines of the ISO/OSI reference model on the other hand, would be the main winners of the communications architecture race. Before communications architectures such as SNA, TRANSDATA or DECnet were developed, there were no PCs and no PC–host links, and distributed data processing had not been conceived of. Thus, today, many manufacturers are faced with the problem of extending their architectures designed to network terminals to host systems to accommodate the requirements of distributed data processing. Only IBM can take the view that most of the devices in question are in fact IBM or IBM-compatible devices. All other manufacturers must take a heterogeneous view.

Network management today is clearly suffering from this radical change; concepts for monitoring lines (etc.) do exist, but are no longer up-to-date. Neither is the functional basis, in the framework of the ISO/OSI recommendations, yet ready. In the most unfavourable cases clients may have three co-existent protocol stacks: the protocol stack of the manufacture-dependent architecture (not ISO or SNA); the SNA protocol stack and an ISO/OSI substack. All this runs on the most diverse local and remote networks with the most diverse application programs and functions. Perhaps a universal, integrated network management is too much to ask for. In the future, different network management schemes, protocols and technologies will also co-exist so long as there are clients with the different protocol stacks described above.

The main objective of OSI network management is the integration of these different management elements on the basis of standardized communication between the management installations.

Thus, basically, the management of network architectures and corresponding installations may take at least two forms: a management which is suited to old class 1 networks and which functions somehow or other and a management according to ISO/OSI, based on individual formulations and statements of intent. Thus, investment in existing network management will also be secure in the future. All manufacturers intend to integrate existing and future network management in an appropriate way.

Despite recent setbacks, DEC remains one of the largest and most important manufacturers. In TRANSDATA, Siemens has its own important, (at least in Germany), communications architecture, while SINEC is a *de facto* standard for manufacturing.

4.2 DEC DNA and network management

DEC long since announced the conversion of the Digital Network Architecture to ISO/OSI (DECnet Phase V/OSI). Consequently, even the network management has been redefined and is now called *Enterprise Management Architecture* (EMA). The transition to OSI has already been under way for some years, although it has been rather sluggish and recent OSI product announcements have disappointed users. Instead of the long-promoted absorption of the DECnet Phase IV core protocols into OSI protocols, there is now a transition to OSI protocols with the status of application programs *à la* OSI/CS from IBM. Moreover, the TCP/IP suite has been introduced as a further protocol stack.

Currently, most DEC users will have installed a classical DECnet; thus, at this point, we shall discuss DEC's previous approach to management.

4.2.1 DNA and DECnet up to phase IV

DECnet is a family of hardware and software products, which clients may use to permit their DEC computers and DEC operating systems to communicate without disregarding the bridges to the outside world (public networks, SNA).

A network consists of at least two nodes linked together by

communication paths. Every system in the network is called a *node*, a network decomposes into a maximum of 63 *areas* each containing at most 1023 nodes.

All more recent DEC systems with the most important operating systems (whence, with also the UNIX dialects) may be nodes in the network. Furthermore, IBM PCs and compatibles may be integrated into the DECnet.

In stark contrast to SNA, the nodes in the DECnet are peers and responsibility is distributed across the nodes. This has the advantage that, in principle, every node is open to user requests.

DECnet is based on the *Digital Network Architecture* (DNA), to which we shall return. DNA is considerably closer to the ISO model than is SNA, and DEC intends to make all DECnet products fully ISO compatible over the coming years.

When a DECnet is installed, the services available to the user include:

- Shared use of expensive peripherals.
- Free exchange of information in the system.
- Guarantee that files are up-to-date in the network.
- Remote job entry.
- Relocation of tasks to nodes which are equipped to deal with them.
- DECnet/SNA gateway.
- Reverse gateway.
- Access to TCP/IP under certain conditions.
- Access to OSI services such as X.400 or FTAM.
- Access to public networks.

The possibility of using different types of connections within a DECnet (for example, Ethernet, X.25 and twisted pair) is of interest.

DECnet has developed in phases, which have extended its facilities more and more. Today we are in Phase IV. For the last seven years, Phase V/OSI has been announced as being 'available in two years'.

DNA is the architecture towards which the construction of components must be oriented; it provides appropriate specifications.

We give a brief overview of the DNA layers (Figure 4.1).

4.2.1.1 User layer

This highest layer comprises user programs, user-level services which access the network, network services which provide direct support to users and to application tasks, and the global system management.

Architecture layers		
ISO		DNA
Application		User
		Network management
Presentation		Network application
Session		Session control
Transport		End-to-end communication
Network		Routing
Data link		Data link
Physical link		Physical link

Figure 4.1   ISO and DNA model.
Source: DEC.

4.2.1.2 Network management layer

This layer includes functions which are used to plan, supervise and maintain a network. It cooperates with all layers below it to obtain the necessary data and react in an appropriate way.

4.2.1.3 Network application layer

The basic functions of this layer are remote file access, file transfer, remote terminal capability, X.25 access with packet-switching interface (PSI) and access to SNA gateways. This layer is best compared with the current version of ISO layer 7, since in the ISO model, the user-oriented higher-level services and the overlying network management are not so strongly shaped.

4.2.1.4 Session control layer

This layer is responsible for the definition of system-dependent aspects of the interprocess communication, the conversion of symbolic names into addresses, the attaching of processes and access control.

4.2.1.5 End-to-end communication layer

This layer is responsible for the treatment of system-independent communications aspects such as connection management, flow control, end-to-end error control, and segmentation and rebuilding of user messages.

4.2.1.6 Routing layer

This layer is responsible for routing in the network.

4.2.1.7 Data link layer

This layer is responsible for securing connections.

4.2.1.8 Physical layer

This layer defines how device drivers and communications hardware should be implemented to enable data transfer through a medium. The functions of modules of this layer include monitoring of channel signals, synchronization on the channel, treatment of hardware interrupts and informing the layer above of the expiry of a connection.

Unlike SNA, the layers have a relatively strong hierarchy; thus, a module in a layer n may use the services of a lower layer $n-1$ to meet the requirements of a layer $n+1$.

4.2.2 DECnet user layer and network management

In DNA, the highest layer, the *user layer*, is defined to lie directly above the *network management layer* (DEC, 1985). These two layers together have approximately the same meaning as an ISO layer 7.

In DNA, there are no generally-applicable protocols for the user layer, since corresponding user profiles are created by the application programs using the facilities of the lower layers together with the appropriate access methods.

The capabilities and facilities of the network are best described in terms of various functions which a user or an application program may execute on the network.

Cooperating programs, which may be running in different operating systems or be written in different programming languages, are able to interchange data using corresponding programmable calls. Here, the technical execution of the data exchange, is carried out by communication modules in each node and involves the initiation, execution and termination of a virtual connection. The nature of the calls depends on the programming language used.

However, uniform messages, composed in a DECnet universal I/O language are used between the communication modules. The task traffic over virtual connections implies a large number of error and flow-control mechanisms.

Programs and users may access files resident on remote nodes. It is possible to exchange files between two nodes, to manipulate files and to transfer command files to a remote note to induce various actions there. The file actually exists on one and only one node. If a process wishes to access a remote file, it executes the appropriate commands which are directed at the so-called *File Access Listener* (FAL). This FAL is implemented on the node of the target file and channels all requests. This avoids many conflicts and guarantees that the contents of a file are up to date. A user never accesses the module which executes the communication directly, but always indirectly by external routines, which at the same time permit access control.

Every terminal in the network is in principle able to access all nodes in the network (virtual terminal). In practice, restrictions are placed on this facility. However, this also means that the terminals in the network are no longer assigned to individual computers but are arranged in clusters which then have a connection to the network.

Network managers may use DECnet commands to define and generate nodes and to isolate network problems. Network managers use loop tests, recording facilities and dump analyzers to monitor nodes. They also use a software package called Observer to maintain an awareness of the network performance so as to identify and resolve potential bottle-necks before they become critical (Figure 4.2).

Thus, users may count on the network always operating correctly. Network system management functions include:

- Planning of the node generation in order to tailor DECnet software to the particular application. This task should be viewed in conjunction with network-wide conventions.

- Generation of network software in order to construct an active node from the off-the-shelf elements.

- Definition and modification of network parameters in order to influence the various network parameters, the definitions of which determine the role of a node in a specific environment of a DECnet implementation.

- Operation of a node, including starting and stopping the node and its physical connections to the outside world.

- Monitoring of the node activity for performance analysis.

- Downline loading of system parts and tasks from executive nodes onto satellite nodes such as smaller computers or communication servers.

- Upline dumping.

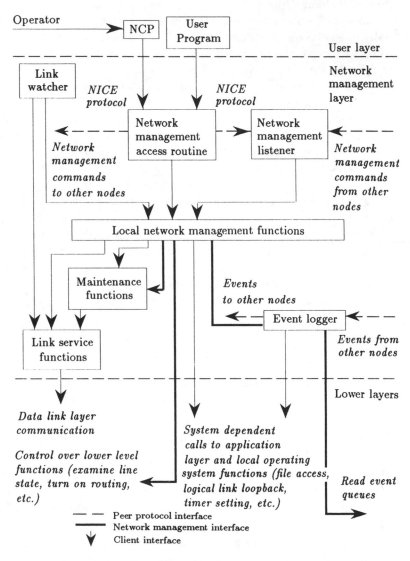

Figure 4.2   Relationships between network management components. *Source*: DEC.

The user layer of DNA contains the *Network Control Program* (NCP) which communicates with the entities in the layer below. The *Network Information and Control Protocol* (NICE) is used between entities in adjacent layers.

Various software tools help the system manager to monitor the network. The functions of the tools are, for example:

- Verification that communication between user-specified nodes is appropriate and correct.

- Tests of circuits, network components and lines.

- Tests of X.25 and IBM SNA gateways to check that they are functioning correctly and that the protocol conversion is properly executed.

- Initiation of memory dumps to indicate the reasons for network breakdowns.

In DEC-oriented networks, there is a central element, the network monitor. This maintains a network database which may be inspected by all users. In addition to the DECnet monitor, there are also a number of products which provide additions to the network operation. These include the Ethernim under VAX/VMS for testing Ethernet connections, the remote system manager for remote generation of nodes, the remote bridge software which manages bridges between LANs, the LAN traffic monitor which collects traffic and load data in Ethernet networks, the terminal server manager for downline loading of server parameters and the PBX manager.

DEC has provided an individual management product for every newly-introduced component since 1985 (for example, advanced Ethernets, protocol stacks such as TCP/IP, ...).

It is clear that the integration of these very different components must be one of the main tasks of the coming years.

4.3 Siemens: SINEC and TRANSDATA

The Siemens house, contains a number of different areas each concerned with a different aspect of networking.

Firstly there is the area which is concerned with PBXs. The ISDN system HICOM is certainly a sensible basis for the networking of, for example, PCs, in all cases where the message transmission speed is relatively unimportant.

In addition to HICOM, Siemens also favours networking with standard Ethernet components. The most interesting and most powerful IBM-compatible Siemens PCs of the PCD ranging up to the 486 processor may also be networked with IBM Token Ring products without problems. It is to be expected that Siemens will itself soon provide a Token Ring adapter for these PCs.

Another Siemens world concerns the TRANSDATA communications system for networking mainly BS 2000 based hosts with their peripheral devices.

Finally with SINEC, Siemens is an undisputed market leader for networking in the manufacturing area. Thus, we consider management of TRANSDATA systems and SINEC separately.

With the acquisition of Nixdorf and the founding of SNI, there is currently a general adjustment of product lines, where the ex-Nixdorf lines generally provide standard UNIX systems. This will probably not have a direct effect on the networks themselves.

The further development of TRANSDATA networks and their management is discussed in Chapter 7.

4.3.1 Management of SINEC systems

Many of the management functions in SINEC systems are heavily primed by the SINEC basic services such as file transfer; thus, in this discussion, we must also take into account the most important aspects of these products.

Siemens has developed the powerful and universally-implementable bus system SINEC H1, based on Ethernet for integrated manufacturing according to the CIM concept. It represents a flexible transport subsystem based on the international standards for layers 1–4 of the ISO reference model.

However, as far as industrial application is concerned, the standards for layers 5–7 of the ISO reference model are not stable enough for Siemens's clients to be offered operable implementations as solutions to their application problems.

The various automation systems on SINEC H1, which are optimally tailored to the tasks to be solved, require various communication-system functions.

To do justice to this variety of capabilities, Siemens has defined and developed the SINEC Automation Protocol (AP) and the SINEC File Transfer System (FTS).

In order to provide heterogeneous systems (with different automation components such as controls, personal computers and process computers for manufacturing automation), with an unrestricted ability to communicate, uniform standardized language tools are required. SINEC AP provides the common application-oriented language tools which automation systems within SINEC use to communicate (Figure 4.3).

SINEC AP defines all the rules governing the execution of a communication between two AP applications.

This protocol covers the possible forms of dialogue between two AP applications, the description of the reaction of a communication partner to a request from another application, the presentation of the information, the message structure and the communication semantics.

SINEC AP uses an application-oriented protocol based on the client/server principle, whereby, the AP application, as client, formulates and submits a request and the AP service supplier, as server, provides the

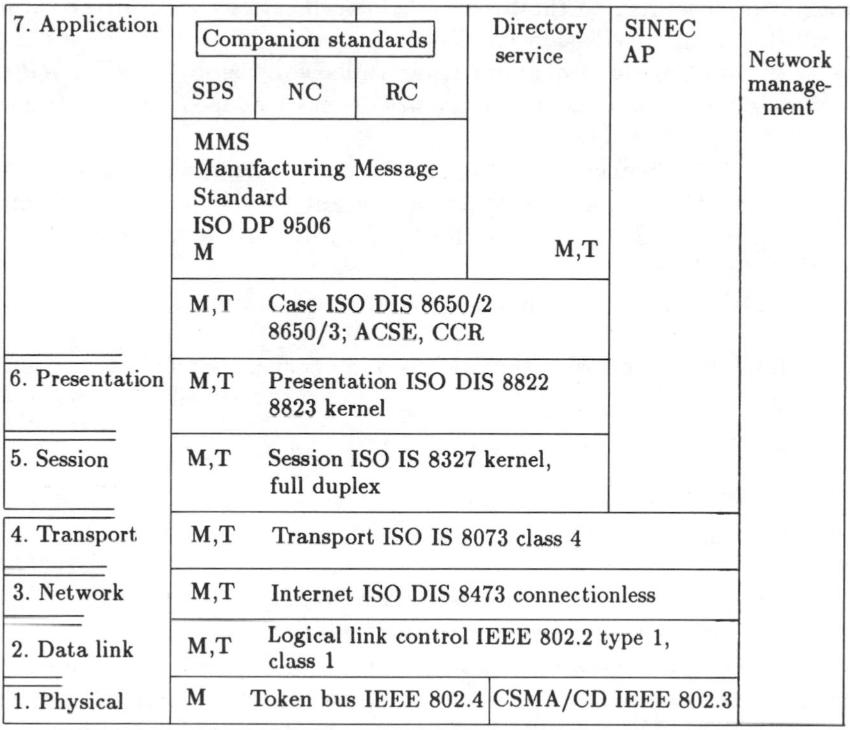

7. Application	Companion standards			Directory service	SINEC AP	Network management
	SPS	NC	RC			
	MMS Manufacturing Message Standard ISO DP 9506 M			M,T		
	M,T	Case ISO DIS 8650/2 8650/3; ACSE, CCR				
6. Presentation	M,T	Presentation ISO DIS 8822 8823 kernel				
5. Session	M,T	Session ISO IS 8327 kernel, full duplex				
4. Transport	M,T	Transport ISO IS 8073 class 4				
3. Network	M,T	Internet ISO DIS 8473 connectionless				
2. Data link	M,T	Logical link control IEEE 802.2 type 1, class 1				
1. Physical	M	Token bus IEEE 802.4	CSMA/CD IEEE 802.3			

M = MAP architecture

Figure 4.3 MAP and SINEC AP.
Source: Siemens AG.

service which the client expects of it. The server then sends the client an acknowledgement.

The function-oriented scheme again reflects the intention to implement a distributed automation system. It must be assumed that the AP application only has knowledge of the task allocated to it, which is to be executed as part of the process to be automated . This task decomposes into AP functions which must be requested or executed. The automation process as a whole determines how the functions are distributed across the resources.

SINEC AP incorporates functions such as serial message transfer, structured data transfer, time functions, commands, inquiries and signalling messages.

These system aspects also involve message transfer functions, such as multiplexing at layer 7, which permits multiple use of underlying resources or the transmission of information about the communication-system error states to layers 5–7. Connection of systems and components without network capabilities according to the SINEC AP specifications will, in the future, be possible using SINEC concentrators.

In addition to the automation tasks covered by SINEC AP, as previously mentioned, SINEC FTS has been developed for file transfer operations.

SINEC FTS may be used to exchange data identified by name (files) between host-oriented systems of the SINEC automation network. The main task of SINEC FTS is to transfer files and to initiate further processing in the corresponding system.

SINEC FTS covers the following areas of operation:

- Implementation of asynchronous and synchronous data transfer.
- Setting of checkpoints and restart after faults.
- Support for formatted text, directory and binary files.
- Post-processing.
- Specific data protection measures.

For portability of the FTS software to other systems, the SINEC FTS architecture has a modular structure.

The SINEC Network Management contains a number of elements which support the work of the persons responsible for planning, configuring and installing a network. SINEC NM assists developers of systems and application software and provides a means ensuring that the operation is as trouble-free as possible. The facilities of SINEC NM may be used by the persons responsible for the network or the system and by diagnostics specialists (either local or from a diagnostics centre) (Figure 4.4).

One major component involves the storage of data describing the network, the topology, the network nodes, the gateways from topological network elements, the transport and application end points and the relationships between nodes, transport end points and applications.

This description of the configuration management is generated from a generic network viewpoint. Corresponding parameter records are generated and modified using the profile management. This global database is used to generate local databases, which, together with the associated access functions, form the directory service.

Once the network has been brought up using the initialization management, it may be observed using network monitoring. Should intervention be required, this is the responsibility of the control management.

It is not possible to implement all these functions together with those previously described in brief, either at one time or at one place.

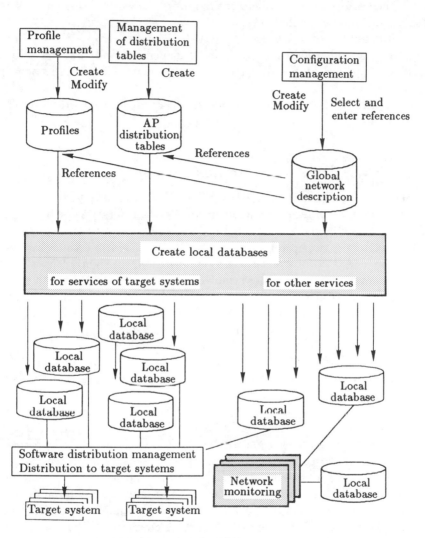

Figure 4.4   SINEC Network Management.
Source: Siemens AG.

One particularly economical approach is to distribute the functions to a console-station with high-level SINEC NM capabilities and to SINEC NM object-stations with basic capabilities.

The profiles and distribution tables, produced by the corresponding components during the design of an application solution, together with the global network description, are used to generate local databases which are distributed over the target systems by the software distribution management.

The performance management monitors the work of the network and helps to track down bottle-necks.

Functional tests are used to try to prevent errors. Should errors occur, they are identified by the fault management and may be fully or partially eliminated by the diagnostic management, either locally or using remote services.

Security and redundancy management round the architecture off.

4.3.2 TRANSDATA network management

The network management products for TRANSDATA have the same target objectives as those of other manufacturers of class 1 networks or in the case of SINIX networks, class 2 or mixed class 1/2 network systems.

An overall description of TRANSDATA is given in (Kauffels, 1989). The TRANSDATA protocol structure is illustrated in Figure 4.7.

However, the products are implemented in slightly different ways for the different operating systems; here, ACUT is a common central element for communications computers with PTN. Generally, as for TRANSDATA as a whole, the direction of march is towards ISO/OSI.

The liberal distribution of processing functions is supported by the extensive services of the TRANSDATA network management. This comprises functions to control and monitor computers and network components and to diagnose errors and faults.

These services also include the management of storage media and files on front-end processors together with a powerful file transfer facility. Importantly, these services are available locally on the front-end processor, but may also be used by another computer. This is a prerequisite for teleguided operation without a local operator. The network management entities in the processing computers (hosts) and the communications computers may interact in the network. Thus, a complete computer network may be administered from one TRANSDATA computer (Figure 4.7).

The most important qualitative features of ACUT are:

- Network-wide uniform man-machine language.
- Syntax checking and operator guidance.
- Logging in protocol stations or protocol files.
- Authorization checks using passwords, with three classes of authorization.
- Possibilities for automation using command sequences.
- Programmer interface for connection of programmed operators.

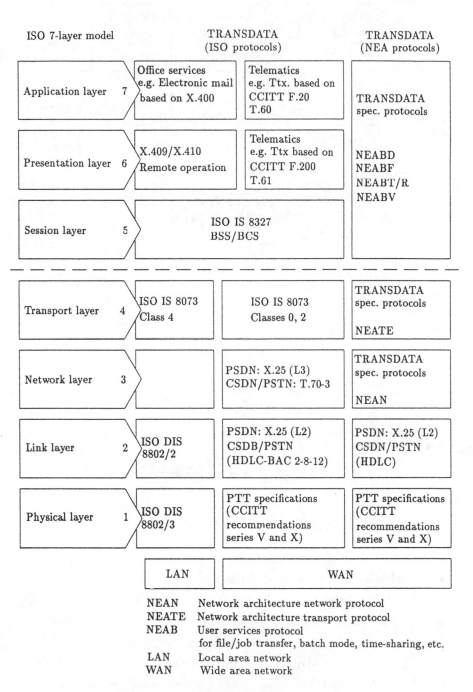

Figure 4.5   TRANSDATA protocol structure.

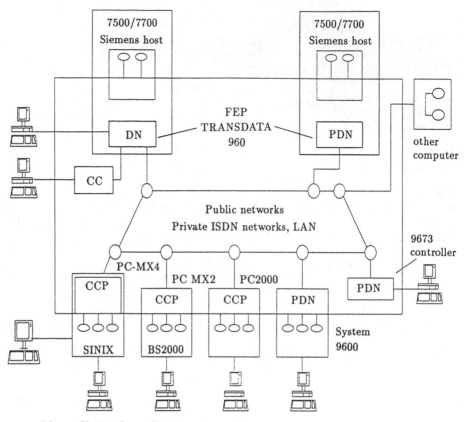

Figure 4.6   TRANSDATA communications components.

CC = Cluster Controller
CCP = Communication Control Program
FEP = Front End Processor

The network management functions of ACUT include:

- Commissioning/decommissioning of components.
- Activation/deactivation of DCE lines.
- Load and dump facility for the 9770 terminal station using BAM.
- Remote turn on/off of computers.
- Monitoring and control of local or remote computers.
- Signal messages about faults, breakdowns and changes of state.
- Inquiries regarding the state of network components and determination of measured values.

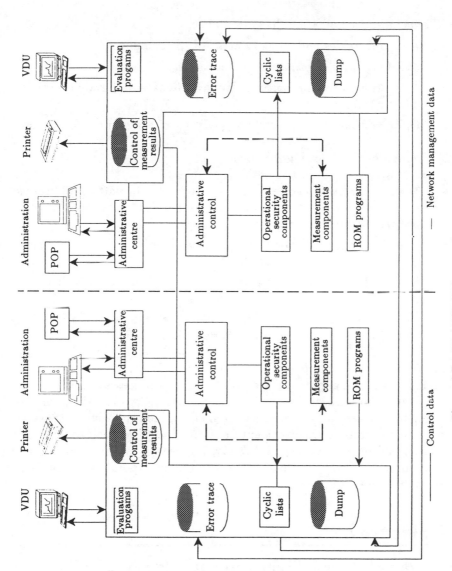

Figure 4.7 TRANSDATA network management.

- Activation of monitoring functions.
- Sending of short messages to administrators of the other computers.
- Program-controlled switching of the V.24 interface.
- Dynamic modification of operational parameters.

ACUT includes the following diagnostic aids:

- Access to tables and memory areas of the computer.
- Saving of error information and statistics.
- Activation of tracing routines, facilities to save and evaluate tracing information.
- Online or offline dump, including editing of the dump information.

ACUT provides the following services:

- Storage medium services (sign on, sign off, formatting of storage media, output of a storage-medium content directory, presetting for printers including code tables etc.).
- File services (initialization, compression, deletion of files, information about file characteristics etc.).
- Restartable file-transfer services (copying of files, library elements, etc.).
- Network-wide facilities to access RBAS, translators (APSYS, Cobol) and SPOOL 960 functions for unmanned operation.

For network-wide access to network-management functions, ACUT runs on a communications computer or with NTAC 2 on a processing computer.

With the inclusion of new devices and networks, the scope of the responsibilities of network management is continuously increasing. The Siemens network management is structurally related to the OSI network management framework. Today, Siemens is working on a closer approximation, which principally involves the incorporation of Siemens systems into an OSI context.

4.4 Summary

In the case of the manufacturer-linked architectures, classical network management covers the functional areas described by Terplan. A list of other products, which all do more or less the same thing, would not help the reader at this point. In the next chapter, we move from class 1 and class 2 environments to class 3 environments, namely open systems and OSI management.

Chapter 5

OSI network management

- General introduction to OSI management

- The OSI management framework

- OSI system management

- OSI layer management

- OSI protocol management

- Identification of OSI resources

- Summary

The environment for an OSI protocol world, and thus for the necessary management, is becoming increasingly specific. The various common and special application service elements (CASEs and SASEs) support a distributed system environment. For this, they use protocols and service elements of layers 1–6. In the lower layers there is a large choice of alternative transmission technologies which may be used to create subnetworks with varied qualities, transmission speeds and costs.

The OSI protocol environment provides for direct communication and supports distributed execution environments. Every protocol layer has the ability to monitor and control an individual instance of a communications link (in other words, the interworking of the entities involved in the logical link). In time, this will lead to a requirement for an extended mechanism, with the ability to observe, control and monitor all the OSI resources which provide the communication and execute auxiliary functions.

The OSI management framework is an ISO standards document (DIS 7498-4) which gives guidelines for the coordination of the further development of existing OSI management standards. It defines the terminology of OSI management and describes its basic concepts. This involves the use of an abstract model which indicates the goals and facilities of the OSI network management. Finally, the document describes the OSI management activities.

This topic was introduced in Chapter 2. The communications networks and the resulting overall systems were divided into classes. There are specific management requirements for each class. Parallels between the classes may also be drawn. In a real environment, it is highly likely that a network will consist of a mixture of subnetworks of the given classes. In this chapter, we discuss the state of international standardization and any relevant changes. In our classification, an OSI network falls in class 3.

5.1 General introduction to OSI management

Unlike in the case of previous proposals, the standardization bodies are now concentrating more specifically on the formulation of tasks and on the available aids.

Working Group X3T5.4 of the American Standards Committee (ASC) is charged by ISO with the responsibility for developing the OSI management standards. Corresponding activities in other standardization bodies are coordinated by X3T5.4.

The conceptual management framework has reached the first step of international standardization. Here, there are clear differences from the requirements and structures of older versions of the management framework.

Together with the information processing, the management is viewed as the facility to plan, organize and control the resources which the user has available to meet his information-engineering needs.

One problem with this perspective is that 'the user' is not defined in any greater detail. There are very different users. They should at least be provided with mechanisms which are sufficiently powerful for them to make structural modifications in an information-processing environment.

The needs of the users are covered by the appropriate active and passive components and objects and, if applicable, the networked system environment. Ideally, the physical implementations of the components are not apparent to the users and thus not liable to misuse or damage due to clumsiness.

In an OSI environment, a resource is also conceptually described as an OSI resource, which, at the end of the day, is an abstract object on which certain operations are specified. Examples of such resources include a generic electronic mailbox, a generic directory and a file description.

In most cases, these operations have additional conditions which are described by the protocols of the OSI layer containing the resource (this is usually layer 7, the application layer). One of the most important operations is the incarnation of a resource which, for example, generates a real system object, 'mailbox', tied to a user, from an abstract generic description of an electronic mailbox. It is understandable that this generation process is a management function, while the emptying of a mailbox is a function which is carried out by a single user (or by a small number of authorized users) and mailing to a mailbox may be carried out by almost any user.

An incarnation of an OSI resource is an object. In the OSI network management framework, it is a 'managed object'. Such incarnations are also called entities in the standards documents. As already mentioned, this is nothing mysterious. OSI resources are only templates from which deductions about 'reality' are made. Logical links may also be described in this way. A management function is a sequence of parameterized operations on an object.

The overall terminology of OSI network management is relatively complicated, even though the end products are simple. In particular, it is very tedious to have to collect together terminology from different sources in a coherent fashion. For the benefit of the reader, in the next two subsections the author summarizes firstly, the development of the OSI standard and secondly, the basic structure of the application layer. Those who have a solid grounding in these areas may turn directly to Section 5.2.

5.1.1 Development of the OSI standard

From 1977, the *Open Systems Interconnection* (OSI) reference model of the *International Standardization Organization* (ISO) has been designated as the basis for the formation of standards for communication between communications media and applications. The objective of OSI is to facilitate

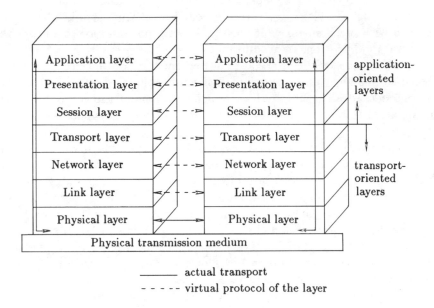

Figure 5.1 The ISO reference model.

communication in a heterogeneous environment based on application-supporting basic services. Over a decade later, standards have been released for wide areas of the architecture and are now being used very extensively in the message transport-oriented parts of communications systems (for example, wide area networks based on X.25 and local area networks based on ISO 8802). On the other hand, the breakthrough in the application-oriented layers is still only partial today.

The communication is implemented by a set of elements or entities, each with their own fixed place and task (Figure 5.1). In the framework of standardization of communication systems, the following must be defined:

- The division of the architecture into layers.
- The division of the layers into entities.
- The cooperation of the entities within a layer.
- The cooperation of the entities in adjacent layers.

The interface between two layers, seen from the top down, is a client/server interface. An entity in a layer provides a certain service. For this, it may use the assistance available locally or that provided (again in the form of a service) by an entity of the layer below. Lower-lying layers and higher layers cannot be used.

In addition to this interface, the observance of a control mechanism relating peer entities at different physical points in the same layer is also important. Such a control mechanism is called a protocol.

The communications architecture is defined to have seven layers. These layers each form a framework for standards, but are not actual communications standards themselves.

The lowest structural layer is the physical layer. This provides the communications-engineering assistance to transmission.

The link layer, which is already an abstraction from the physical connections, combines sequences of binary information into data packets and decomposes larger units arriving from higher layers into smaller packets, where this seems advisable. This layer incorporates elementary error detection and recovery mechanisms. The layer considers mainly two-point connections.

This is not the case in the network layer, the main task of which is routing (the determination of an optimal path through a possibly branched network). The optimal route depends not only on the number of intermediate nodes, but also on the load and the susceptibility of the individual stations and connections to noise.

The protocols of the next layer, the transport layer, have end-to-end characteristics because they relate directly to logical information sources and sinks. With the functions of this layer, the primary transmission-oriented part is complete.

Thus, the next layer, the session layer, is provided with a universal transport service. A session of the session layer denotes a logical connection between two intercommunicating entities of the highest layer. The main task of this layer is to provide assistance to the synchronization of the processes involved in the communication.

The presentation layer lies between layer 5 and the application layer. Its special services provide for a transformation of the data to an agreed standard format and for a uniform interpretation.

The last layer is the application layer which provides the distributed applications with logical communications support, in the form of certain services such as file transfer or remote job entry.

The system management is distributed vertically over the layers, since it requires information from each layer and should be able to access each layer.

Examples of stable application-layer standards include X.400 for message handling and FTAM for file transfer. Areas in which much is still open include transaction processing, data protection and network management.

It will be several more years before stable standards are reflected by the availability of reasonably-priced product lines.

5.1.2 Application layer: structure and elements (ISO 8649/8650)

The lower layers mainly move data. On the other hand, the application-layer standards are concerned with exchanging information whilst safeguarding its semantics (meaning) (see Figure 5.2).

For example, a large database might be distributed across a number of internetworked computers. A distributed application process might now be responsible for keeping the database up-to-date and maintaining its consistency.

In this connection, the application process may use services of layer 7 (for example, to request data from or to delete data on a server or to task another process with these jobs).

In the ISO terminology, an application process is an element of a real open system which is involved in the execution of or one more distributed information-processing tasks. This may be a program or a person (for example, someone who has to decide whether or not to reply to a letter).

The application process is a component of the local working environment. Its interface to an *Application Entity* (AE) is formed by a *User Element* (UE). The AE uses the protocols of the six underlying layers.

For application processes to cooperate they must have the common use of sufficient information for interworking. The set of such shared information is called the *Information Base* (IB). Of course, the processes must also develop a common understanding of the meaning of the information in the IB.

The application-layer standards provide schemes for the successful communication of processes. Such schemes define the rules for controlling the data exchange, the associated semantics together with the abstract syntax and the encoding rules for the data transfer.

In summary, layer 7 provides services which permit the negotiation of the semantics for the information exchange (for example, whether a file transfer should run with or without error control). Layer 6, with its services, supports the negotiation of a presentation (coding) of the information to be exchanged, agreed by all communication partners. Layer 5 enables the application processes to insert unambiguous, clearly distinguishable signals in the data stream (the application processes need these signals for synchronization and resynchronization) and to negotiate and manage the dialogue control which is used to support the information flow.

An application process is represented in the OSI model by one or more AEs. This means that every AE incorporates a different aspect of the communications behaviour of the application process.

In every AE, the application process must select an *Application Service Element* to execute its tasks. A service element is a primitive which is defined in the interface between two adjacent layers. An ASE is a set of functions to support a typical application. It represents various types of

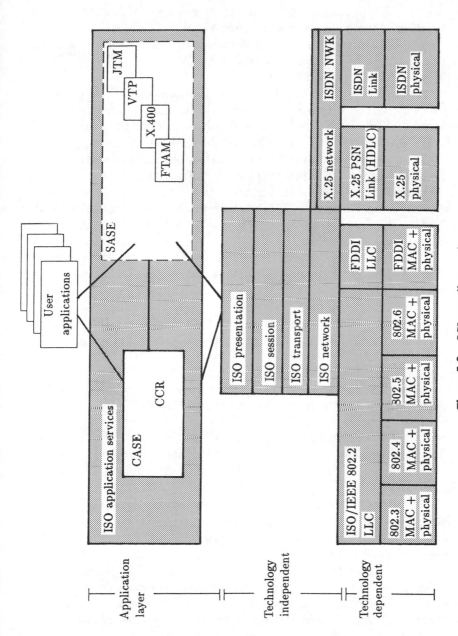

Figure 5.2 OSI overall scenario.

163

tasks which the user may wish to have executed, (for example, file transfer, mail service or transaction processing), together with the aids which will be required to carry out these tasks.

An AE contains a UE and one or more ASEs. The specific combination of these elements determines the type of the AE.

The UE represents the application process and acts on its behalf. It enables the ASEs to communicate with other ASEs. Thus, it is the source and sink of the information exchange.

An ASE is a coherent set of integrated functions which permit the interworking of AEs within a particular task. In the context of information processing, ASEs may be used independently of one another or jointly. The ASEs are already defined for FTAM and the X.400 mail system.

The *Association Control Service Element* (ACSE) is another type of ASE which facilitates the interworking of ASEs. ACSE correlates ASEs. For example, there is an ASE for restarting after errors (*Commitment, Concurrency and Recovery* (CCR)), which we discuss in more detail later. A FTAM ASE may operate on its own or with CCR. ACSE establishes and deletes the appropriate relation.

ASE is a portmanteau term for the frequently used *Common Application Service Element* (CASE) and *Specific Application Service Element*) (SASE) concepts. CASE denotes the common elements which are used by two or more computers within an application communication. SASE may be used to refer to elements in the individual areas (FTAM, MHS, VTP). Although CASE and SASE often appear in the literature, there are no objective criteria for distinguishing between the two, so that in the future only ASE will be used.

In an OSI environment, the entities must be uniquely identifiable. An entity may support several relations between applications. Every entity is linked to a presentation address which points to one or more *Presentation Service Access Points* (PSAPs). An AE has at least one name (the application title) by which it can be identified. The application title is always tied to the presentation address associated with the PSAP assigned to the AE.

The standardization of certain specific applications, such as X.400 or FTAM, has led to the definition of modules (CASEs) which are common to all applications. These modules cooperate with SASEs to implement the service demanded by the application process.

That different working groups have patently considered these functions independently from one another and have each developed their own model (in continuation of a glorious tradition of standardization), is clearly shown, for CASEs in particular, in the variety and diffuseness of the terminology. The following are presently defined:

- RTS: Reliable Transfer Service.
- ROS: Remote Operation Service.

- CASE: Common Application Service Element.

Here, however, CASE defines a number of functions and not a subcategory of the ASEs. (Now at least the call should go out for a committee to coordinate the terminology-forming subcommittees of the telecommunications-related working groups of the national and international, manufacturer-linked and manufacturer-neutral, application-oriented and application-neutral, technical and non-technical subcommittees of the standardization authorities!)

Much more could be said about the structure and the basic elements of the application layer, but this would not lead us anywhere. Thus, we refer to the relevant literature.

5.2 The OSI management framework

The OSI management framework (ISO DIS 7498-4) is applicable in the OSI management environment, which is conceived as part of the overall OSI environment. The management environment comprises all tools and services which are used to control and manage connection activities and managed objects. We return to these managed objects shortly. The management environment enables managers to collect data, to exercise control and to verify the existence of managed objects and receive reports of their status.

The network management facilities of the OSI NM environment are described under five functional categories: configuration management; error management; performance management; security management and accounting management.

The portmanteau word for these five categories of functions is 'facility', although there is no precise definition of this.

We shall describe the *Specific Management Functional Areas* (SMFAs) in more detail later (see Figure 5.3).

Firstly a word on the term 'managed object'. An object is an abstract concept which describes something specific or abstract. According to the concept of the object, this description also includes the functions which may be executed on this object. A managed object is an object within the scope of the OSI NM environment. The five SMFAs monitor and control the following four aspects of a managed object:

- The existence of the object.
- The object attributes.
- The object states.
- The relationships between the object and other objects.

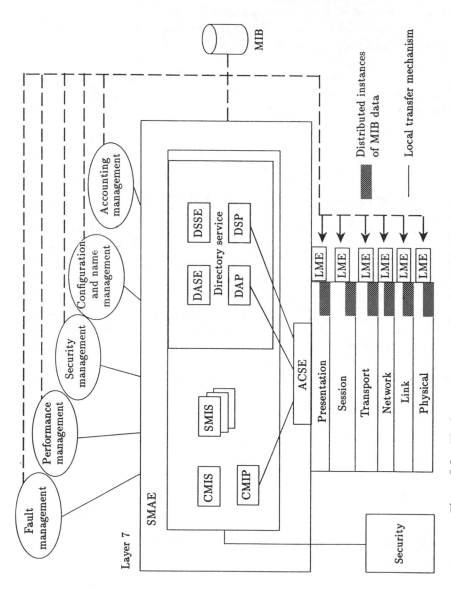

Figure 5.3 The layer management is supported by the layer management entities.

A managed object exists in the sense of the OSI NM if, and only if, it has an object identifier (name) and a corresponding set of management information which may be accessed by the OSI NM. Managed objects may be created and deleted. For creation, the user of the object must enter the name and the management information in the *Management Information Base* (MIB). Attributes describe the characteristics of the object, for example, the characteristic behaviour during the execution of an operation. An attribute has a name and a value. During the lifetime of an object only the attribute values may be changed; no attributes may be introduced or deleted. The status describes the instantaneous state of an object, in respect of availability and operability. Relationships with other objects define the connections between the object in question and other managed objects.

The framework defines the structure of the OSI network management in terms of three groups (Figure 5.4).

- The *system management* provides mechanisms for monitoring, controlling and coordinating all managed objects within an open system.
- The *layer management* provides mechanisms for monitoring, controlling and coordinating each of the seven layers of the OSI reference model.
- The *protocol management* provides mechanisms for monitoring, controlling and coordinating an individual communication transaction.

The framework incorporates the MIB concept. The MIB represents the information within the open system which is used, modified or transferred in the framework of the OSI management protocols. The MIB knows all managed objects and their attributes. Physically, it is not necessarily centralized, but may be spread across the system and the individual layers. Since the OSI model is not concerned with memory technologies the MIB is always viewed as being outside of the model (Figure 5.5)

5.3 OSI system management

The OSI system management provides mechanisms for monitoring, controlling and coordinating all managed objects within an open system. The OSI-system-management concept was considerably extended and reworked at the end of 1988. There are now two important conceptual groups: system management models and system management standards. In addition, minimal conformance requirements which a product must satisfy before it may be considered to be an OSI management product, were introduced for the first time.

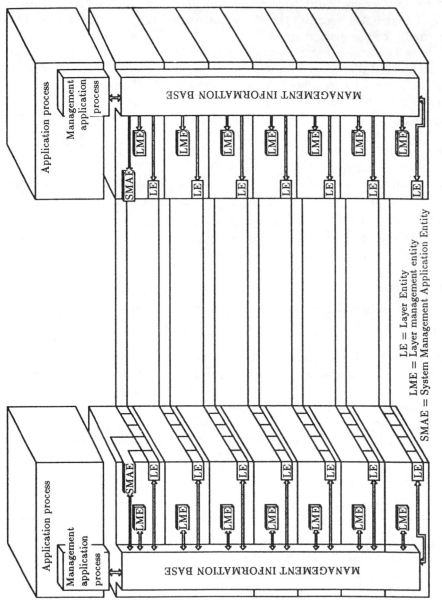

Figure 5.4 Model of the OSI management.

LE = Layer Entity
LME = Layer management entity
SMAE = System Management Application Entity

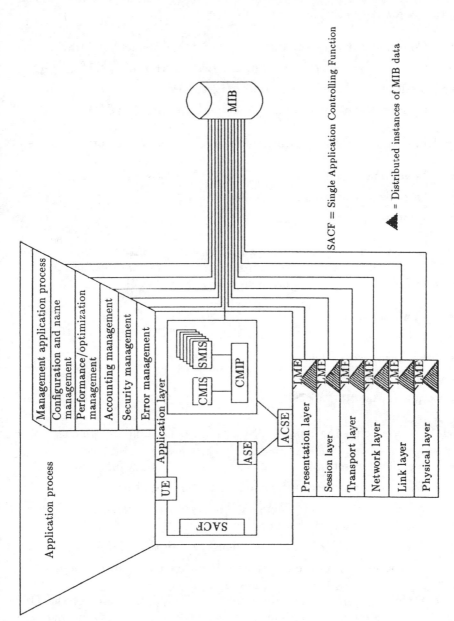

Figure 5.5 Embedding of the MIB in the communication system.

SACF = Single Application Controlling Function

◄ = Distributed instances of MIB data

169

5.3.1 System management models

OSI management models define various aspects of the system management. In addition, they specify supplementary conceptual and terminological conditions for the following areas:

- Common Management Information Service Element (CMISE).
- Specific Management Functional Areas (SMFAs).
- Structure of Management Information (SMI).
- Generic Definition of Management Information (GDMI).

The definition of system management comprises three conceptual models:

- Functional model.
- Organizational model.
- Information model.

The functional model introduces the concept of SMFAs, which, prior to 1988, were known as *Specific Management Information Services and Protocols* (SMIS/SMIP). ISO has defined five SMFAs:

- Configuration SMFA
- Error SMFA
- Performance SMFA
- Security SMFA
- Accounting SMFA

Each SMFA is defined in its own OSI management standard which:

- specifies the set of facilities to support the SMFA functions;
- describes procedures associated with these facilities;
- specifies the use of *Common Management Information Services* (CMIS) to support the functions;
- describes classes of managed objects within this SMFA; and
- uses subsets of all the functions to create conformance classes.

The organizational model describes the distributed character of the OSI management through the concepts of the managed open system, manager and agent processes and domains. This is important in that it relates OSI concepts to the real world, where management centres, systems and personnel are widely spread. It also describes the extent to which management tasks may be distributed across the various network carriers

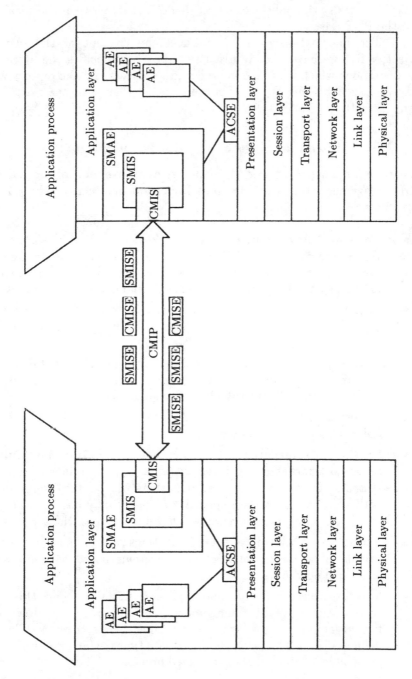

Figure 5.6 Communication between the System Management Application Entities (SMAEs).

such as PTTs. Even in Germany, with the opening up of Europe, the need to segment tasks is more likely to follow the American pattern, whereas today practically the only distinction made is that between the local area and the PTT area.

The information model introduces the concept of the managed object, which we have already discussed above. It specifies the attributes, the operations which may be executed on the objects and the reports which may be issued by this object. The objects together with their attributes form the MIB.

5.3.2 System management: standards, overview

The system-management working paper gives an overview of the following OSI management standards, the most important of which we shall discuss in detail below.

- *Common Management Information Services/Common Management Information Protocols* (CMIS/CMIP) are services and protocols for the dialogue between the points which initiate the management functions and the points which execute the management functions.

- Configuration SMFA is a set of functions to identify, monitor and control managed objects in support of the uninterrupted operation of connection services.

- Error SMFA is used to process error states. The original OSI proposal also included error recovery. However, this is now viewed as a configuration problem outside the scope of OSI.

- Performance SMFA is a set of functions to evaluate the behaviour of objects and the efficiency of the connection activities.

- Security SMFA facilitates the control and distribution of information so as to guarantee the integrity of information in various open systems. It informs managers, and others who wish to communicate with a system, that the required level of security has been attained and notes and reports events which are relevant to the security.

- Accounting SMFA is a set of functions which may be used to calculate the performance of open systems based on the costs of using managed objects.

- The *Structure of Management Information* (SMI) defines the logical structure of the OSI management information. It lays down rules for the naming of managed objects and their attributes. The SMI defines a set of subclasses and attribute types, which are in principle applicable to all classes of managed objects.

- A *Generic Definition of the Management Information* (GDMI) is currently being debated by the authorities. It would be a basic pattern or template for the interpretation of management information, from which every open system could deduce an incarnation. GDMI would be useful for everything that must in principle be present on all systems to enable them to participate in the OSI network. However, it remains far from clear today.

After this overview, we now discuss the individual elements, except GDMI, in more detail in the following paragraphs.

5.3.3 Common management services and protocols

CMIS and CMIP are the counterpart of the CASE functional elements for the management. They are the basis of all management functions and support the exchange of information and commands for network management purposes between two peer applications at the same level. In addition to CMIS and CMIP, the ACSE (ISO 8650) and ROSE (*Remote Operation Service Element*, ISO 9072) application-layer functional standards are used. ACSE and ROSE do not form part of the OSI NM specifications, but form the foundations for the basic functionality of the message exchange.

5.3.3.1 CMIS

CMIS is an ASE which may be used in the system-management context by an application process to exchange information and commands. A set of service primitives which form this ASE is defined. On top of that, appropriate parameters are specified. CMIS defines the information structure which appears necessary for a clean description of the environment.

Practically all OSI network management activities are based on the following ten CMIS service primitives.

Confirmed event report   Report of an event by a managed object to a peer application. An answer is expected.

Event report   As above, but without an answer.

Confirmed get   Request by the peer application for information from the MIB. An answer is expected.

Confirmed set   Request by the peer application to modify information in the MIB. An answer is expected.

Set   As above, but without an answer.

Confirmed action   Request by the peer application for execution of an action. An answer is expected.

Action   As above, but without an answer.

Linked reply   Request by the peer application for answers to multiple requests in correlated order.

Confirmed create   Request by the peer application to create a managed object. An answer is expected.

Confirmed delete   Request by the peer application to delete a managed object. An answer is expected.

The SMFAs use these CMIS service primitives. How they use them is explained below. Services are described in the CMIS-DIS in terms of service primitives plus appropriate parameters. When these facilities are considered more closely, both the variety of alternative uses and the high complexity of an OSI management solution become apparent (Figure 5.7). For further details, see the discussion in Section 6.6.

5.3.3.2 CMIP

CMIP is a request/response service between peer users in open systems. Furthermore, it permits the observation and recording of events. The standard defines an abstract syntax for CMIP protocol data units and procedures for transmitting management information between peer application entities. In addition, CMIP lays down procedures for the correct interpretation of protocol control information and basic conformance criteria which CMIP implementations must satisfy.

Basically, CMIP contains a prescribed procedure for every CMIS primitive. Together with the corresponding protocol data units, these procedures form sufficient information for implementation. Thus, in the literature, CMIP is often used as a basic term for CMIS/CMIP; however, this is incorrect.

All *Protocol Data Units* (PDUs) are formulated in ASN.1.

5.3.3.3 ACSE and ROSE

The OSI NM CMIP uses the ACSEs initialize, terminate and abort. The first primitive is used to construct an association (logical link) with a peer application. Without this connection, the ten CMIS primitives cannot be used. The two other primitives are used to clear this logical link either normally or abruptly.

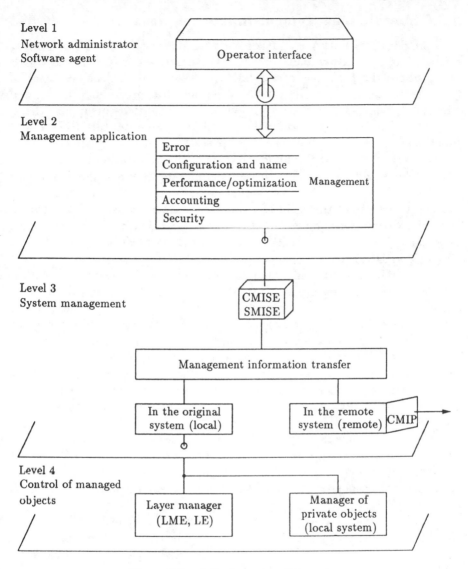

Figure 5.7 OSI management hierarchy.

ROSE makes the services Invoke, Result, Error and Reject available to the ten CMIS service primitives. These services in turn depend on other functions in the presentation layer. ROSE is generally used to establish a client/server relationship between two AEs and to erect interfaces. Invoke sets up the operation. Result is the answer to a successfully-executed operation, Error is the answer in the case of error and Reject is the reaction to the detection of a problem.

5.3.4 Specific management functional areas

ISO provides five SMFA standards for configuration, error, performance, security and accounting management. They describe how CMIS and CMIP are used for the functions of the SMFAs. Every SMFA specifies a set of facilities which support the SMFA functions, the procedures associated with these facilities and the way in which CMIS is used to support these, together with the classes of managed objects used in this SMFA and functional subsets for conformance purposes. Basically, the SMFAs are the counterparts of the SASE functional areas of the application layer.

The standards specify the appearance of the management tasks behind the objectives of each area. Thus, functional requirements are placed on the use of the facilities, which themselves consist of procedures and information. One important part of the provision of the management functionality is the exchange of *Management Application Protocol Data Units* (MAPDUs).

A MAPDU contains management commands, responses, notifications and other management information and is exchanged between a management process and an agent process. The management process resides, for example, in a console or OSI NM workstation, while the agent is specific, for example, to a certain application or a certain device. The MAPDU is the standard aid to message exchange between peer entities in the framework of the application-layer management protocols. Different functional areas use the same MAPDUs, if necessary. For example, both error and configuration management may wish to execute the same Set or Get primitives on error counters in the MIB.

In a management protocol, no distinctions are made between MAPDUs from different functional areas. However, the semantics of certain messages are in part fixed. Thus, for example, the error management may request that the degree of severity of the error should be reported in all error signals.

ISO intended that the SMFAs should be disjoint, and that they should in certain cases, use functions belonging to each other. Under the error management, on restart after error, services such as those provided by the configuration management may be required.

In practice, the requirements on and the capabilities of the network management are very different. Analogously to the known subdivision of the lower layers into classes, subareas are also defined for SMFAs which take account of the different requirements and capabilities.

5.3.4.1 Configuration management

Configuration management involves the monitoring and control of conventional normal operations in an open system or network. Thus, the OSI concept is in stark contrast to the configuration management in SNA-CNM, which also includes the design of extensions. The configuration management SMFA enables the network personnel to generate, observe and modify operational parameters and conditions which govern the mode of operation of connections in the open system. This includes, for example:

- The existence and names of network components.
- Relationships between network components.
- Addressing information.
- Operational characteristics such as the transmission speed of a line.
- Information about the usability of components.
- Conditions for back up operations.
- Routing control.

The configuration management involves the definition, collection, observation, control and use of configuration data. Configuration data includes the information about OSI resources which is required for the management of the system. Configuration data represents both static and dynamic conditions. System administrators may also use this configuration data for other purposes such as inventories, configuration planning, extension planning, network configuration, network design, system generation, operator support, etc.

The configuration management provides functions for other SMFAs and uses other areas if necessary. The configuration management monitors and controls a managed object, in terms of its existence, attributes, states and relationships to other objects. The configuration management classifies CMIS primitives into five categories (facilities):

- The object configuration facility is used to create, name and delete managed objects. The facility uses four CMIS services: Create, Delete, Get and Event report.
- The attribute management facility is used to inspect and set attributes and to report changes. The CMIS services Get, Set and Event report are used.
- The state management facility is used to observe the state of managed objects and to report changes. Here too, Get, Set and Event report are used.
- The relationship management facility is used to check and set relationships between managed objects and to report changes in such relationships. This requires the four CMIS services Create, Delete, Get and Event report.
- The software distribution facility (SDF) is a (not yet fully defined) facility to distribute software in the open system environment. It

is used to transfer a configuration to a peer user, to forward other software to peer users, to check software components at a remote peer point, for updating and maintenance and to execute remote loads and remote starts in the network. It requires both CMIS/CMIP and FTAM services.

The SDF is certainly in danger of falling partly or completely beyond the narrow scope of OSI NM. Programs and tools to execute functions, which at a higher level are known as supplementary configuration management functions (for example, inventory or extension planning), are completely beyond the scope of OSI NM.

5.3.4.2 Error management

The OSI error management has the task of detecting and identifying abnormal operations in the OSI environment. Errors may prevent an open system from carrying out its normal tasks. They may be permanent or temporary. Usually, they are noticeable via certain events. The error management facilities maintain the error log. They process error detection messages and act on them if necessary. Finally, they assist in the execution of diagnostic routines.

The error management defines a number of facilities, including procedures for error detection and diagnosis. Thus, the standard specifies the CMIS services which support these facilities and the classes of managed objects which are handled by the facilities. The standard also specifies a subset of the error detection and diagnosis facilities to form realistic conformance classes.

Network administrators, operators and repairmen may use the error management elements to detect abnormal system operations and to intervene in order to correct these. There are three main areas here: error detection, error diagnosis and error recovery.

Error detection follows three main routes. Firstly, conventional users may detect errors during the execution of normal operations, for example, from concurrent monitoring programs or from the generation of an error report. Secondly, errors may be detected when reliability tests are executed. Finally, errors may be detected when preset thresholds are exceeded.

Error diagnosis comprises the analysis of error and event reports on managed objects and the running of diagnostic programs which catch a managed object in a particular act.

Finally, the process of error correction involves a combination of measures extending as far as the replacement of hardware or software. In most cases, this process is supported by the configuration management.

The error management SMFA facilities include:

- The spontaneous error reporting facility which enables a user to send error reports to other users.

- The cumulative error gathering facility which enables a user to periodically call up information from the error counters of another user, using the CMIS Get service. Thus, it is possible to poll the error counters in other peer systems in order to detect error conditions.

- The error threshold alarm facility provides the user with various threshold functions. The user may set and monitor thresholds, send threshold reports and query the thresholds at a peer point. A threshold alarm is activated if a preset threshold is reached, exceeded or fallen below (according to the specification).

- The confidence and diagnostic checking facility enables the user to have tests executed on a managed object by a remote user, either in order to determine whether the latter is able to execute these functions reliably or as part of a diagnostic routine.

- The event tracing facility may be used to maintain a log of events.

- The management services control facility contains profiles for management services. It enables the user to activate, use and deactivate these profiles. There has been some consideration as to whether this general facility should or should not be incorporated in a different area.

5.3.4.3 Performance management

Performance management is used to evaluate the behaviour of managed objects and the efficiency of communications activities. In fact, its function is the medium- and long-term evaluation of OSI systems. This management area requires a regular provision of collected statistical data in order to analyze and, where appropriate, predict trends in the communication between open systems. Thus, it helps to guarantee the functionality in the medium-to-long term, by predicting and limiting bottle-necks and supports extension of the network with analytical assessment of scenarios.

OSI performance management contains the functions, parameters and message sets for monitoring performance data, collection and analysis of system statistics, tuning and control based on the statistical analysis and generation of network performance reports at different time periods and intervals. For efficient operation, it must determine performance data for special resources based on specific events and measurement results. This includes the possibility that the users may specify events, thresholds, observation intervals and observation periods. Procedures and resources must pre-process the data required by performance management before they forward it, so as not to overwhelm the performance management with useless data.

There are checkpoints so that if there is something wrong with the performance cut-off data of an open system, the users must be able to tune the system to improve the performance. For this, they must be able to alter resource allocations, resource parameters and resource-attribute values. However, such functions extend right into the configuration management and it is again questionable whether it is possible to maintain the strict division of the individual areas.

A network management system must be able to provide its users with reports on the efficiency of the system and its current and previous performance. These reports may refer to a single system in the network or to the whole OSI area, including the network or arbitrary subsets of it. For documentation of the overall operation, reports on a daily, weekly, monthly or annual basis are required.

We shall not discuss the facilities in any more detail here, since it will not lead us anywhere. They generally may be divided into functions to monitor certain events or resources and functions to evaluate the results of the monitoring functions. Furthermore, the standardization has not advanced far in this area.

In my opinion, it must be said quite clearly and emphatically, that the architects of the standard clearly know nothing at all about the methods and results of queueing theory, which are well-known from the operating systems area, or else they have not wanted to listen. It is well known that the tools of mathematical performance analysis may be used to predict performance patterns. Companies like IBM offer their clients software systems in which such tools may be used even without fundamental previous knowledge of mathematics. As long as the standard in this area is not made more specific, this situation will remain.

5.3.4.4 Security management

The term 'security' is often misunderstood. It concerns simple things such as the protection against random, unauthorized access by normal users, up to the securing of military or other highly-sensitive systems against highly-specialized attacks. There is no such thing as a system which is secure against all attacks.

For the purposes of delimitation and classification, there are published national and international criteria towards which evaluations may be oriented. These include the US government 'rainbow books' (Blue Book, Orange Book, Green Book, etc.) or the IT security criteria of the German ZSI (soon to be called BSI). These published criteria introduce security classes which describe the level of security of a system. Two such classes are generally described.

Firstly, the term security for these classes applies primarily to military systems and to 'stored' secrets (data). This leads to a relatively static perspective since dynamic changes and the handling of data outside its position in memory (functional integrity) are extensively disregarded.

Secondly, outside the military area there are other requirements which concern the security in the broadest sense and which are associated with the reliability of systems and their failsafe properties.

The insecurity which already exists for isolated systems increases exponentially in the network area. There are a large number of 'unknowns' here. The theme of security is certainly worth a book on its own. However, we have room for only two comments here. Firstly, we would refer to the relevant literature, (Ruland, 1988) and the excellent conference proceedings (Spies, 1985), which cover all the basics. Secondly, for those interested, we would at this point like to introduce the basic essentials of the security of objects in open systems, although initially this has nothing to do with the OSI standardization.

ISO currently has several working groups which are concerned with security (in the context of NM and that of security frameworks). To an observer their work appears uncoordinated, as indeed it is. A later section entitled 'OSI security management', summarizes the most important considerations in the OSI network management area.

Protection of objects in open systems   Here we consider another important aspect. The components of a computer system carry information which is stored in the computer system and processed. This information generally has a value which may be qualified and quantified in various ways. This value must be protected. This comprises not only the protection of the data, but also the protection of the integrity of the execution of operations. The discussion in this section is oriented towards the important works (Spies, 1985) and (Spies, 1986).

The above accounts for relationships between the objects which exist within a system and the subjects (users) outside a system which use these objects. These relationships may be formulated using access rights.

A system (also an open system or a distributed system consisting of computers and a computer network) may be described via its objects and the operations on these objects. The access rights are then defined as a family of relations between the subjects and the operations defined on the objects.

The requirement for object protection is determined by the fact that a subject should only execute the operations accorded to it by the relations. The requirement for the object performance of a system is determined by the fact that a subject should be able to exercise the rights assigned to it, in other words that a legal operation should also lead to the desired success.

The object performance is usually in the foreground. The requirement for object protection is a general formulation and a considerable strengthening of the terms 'data secrecy', 'data integrity' and 'data protection', which are usually used instead. It is easy to find examples. Certain information may have the property that it has a fixed value so long as it is known to only few subjects. Thus, only the latter may access (read) the protected object carrying this information. As soon as foreign subjects obtain the information, it becomes worthless to the original subjects. The

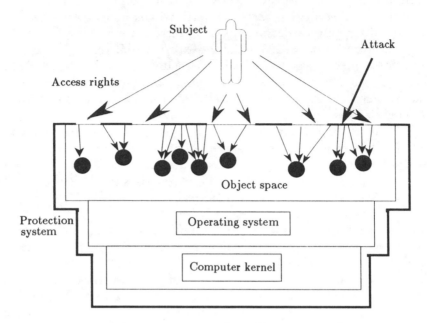

Figure 5.8 Protection of objects. Objects in closed systems.

implementation of object protection thus implies data protection for this information.

As the variety of the potentially valuable concepts and the components (objects) in a computer system increases, so too does the variety of possible attacks.

As far as information security is concerned, there are high requirements on the family of relations and on the data objects of the computer system. Initially, the family of relations must be coherently defined. However, this is not so simple, since in general additional time-related factors will also intervene. In many cases, access rights are only valid for a fixed period.

The operations on the data objects must be defined in such a way that information flows between the system objects on the one hand and between the system and its surrounding area on the other hand, and can be controlled by controlling the execution of operations.

Finally, the operations must be defined in such a way that the possibilities for deducing information by controlling the execution of operations, can be controlled. The information security requirement is met when conflicts, arising from the requirements for information protection

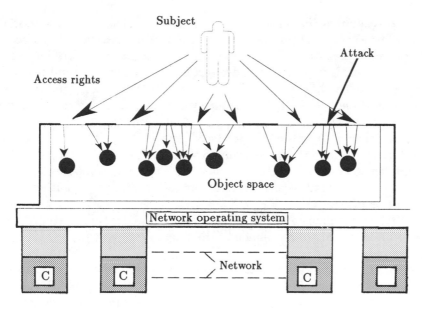

Figure 5.9   Protection of objects. Possible target: single system image.

and the requirements for information performance (which correspond to the above concepts of object protection and object performance applied to the information content of the objects), are resolved by rules and these rules may be implemented.

The rules defined by the family of relations assume that the subjects can be identified in the computer system environment and that the subjects and objects can be identified in the computer system. They also assume that the system objects possess definite known properties. These are absolute prerequisites for a secure, and thus usable, computer system.

Every observation of and action on the computer system is an access. Access may be authorized (by the family of relations, which specifies the rights) or unauthorized. Security means that every access is authorized. An unauthorized access is called an attack. For internal measures against attacks, it is important to detect the attacks as such. Measures to detect attacks include verification of the authenticity of subjects and objects together with measures to verify authorization. Attacks are particularly hard to detect if they are passive (for example, eavesdropping). Closed computer systems may be characterized as follows:

- All accesses to the system are executions of tasks, where a task is, for example, a program involving the system objects.

- All task executions begin with the verification of the authenticity of the client.

A closed system is immune to passive attacks. There are appropriate security measures, such as capabilities granted to the client by a secure and trusted administrator after verification of authenticity, without which access to objects is impossible. Under certain supplementary conditions, the client can transfer these capabilities further, with restrictions. However, the capabilities do not leave the computer system and their internal structure is hidden to the client.

Another approach is the security kernel. Here, it is assumed that some, but not all, objects are relevant to security. The security requirements are implemented by a small number of system components; these components execute all security-related operations from their authorization to their execution.

These mechanisms for the security of closed systems are of much general interest and we recommend (Denning, 1982) and (Spies, 1985) for further study.

Next, we consider attacks on open systems and their suppression. Firstly, we introduce certain concepts (following (Spies, 1986)) then we illustrate attacks on networks and discuss possible solutions, together with the general procedure for data security by encryption.

A distributed computer system consists of a set of points and a message network. The points should be systems with the properties of a protected closed system. Unfortunately, the message network has the following properties, which we describe in more detail later:

- Passive and active attacks cannot be prevented.
- All active attacks are executions of operations on system objects.

To be more precise, we assume that in our system there exist two processes, (subjects) p and q with a client/server relationship, where p is the client and q is the server. For the communications scheme between p and q, we choose the rendezvous (Figure 5.10).

The server q defines an operation, which it makes available externally. We suppose that the calling specification of the operation is as below, where the types 'in' and 'out' are assumed to be defined:

service op (X: in; Y: out);

The client p knows q and the operations provided by q, including the parameter types. p has a qualified access object q_ref as component, which authorizes p to call 'op' on q. p contains a call

$q\_ref.op(a,b)$;

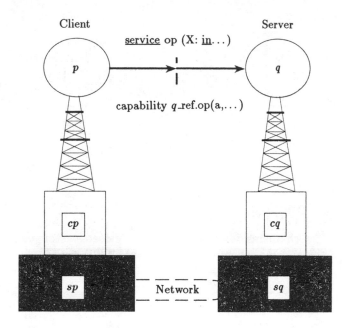

Figure 5.10 Objects in open systems. Cooperation of objects.

Thus, the interworking of p and q under the rendezvous scheme is clear: p calls the operation and waits, q executes it at a given time and returns the result to p, p then proceeds.

If p and q are now implemented at different points of the computer system, a message transfer system between these two points must be used. Let sp and sq denote these two points and cp and cq denote the objects which implement the communication between p and q. Then the following security requirements must be placed on this implementation (Figure 5.11):

- cp and cq are authentic.
- cp and cq operate for p and q only.
- The interworking between p and cp, q and cq is secure.
- cp and cq are functionally correct.
- The message exchange between cp and cq is secure.

All the requirements, except the last one, may be implemented locally using the same measures as in closed systems.

The message exchange between cp and cq may be subject to a variety of attacks with a variety of motives.

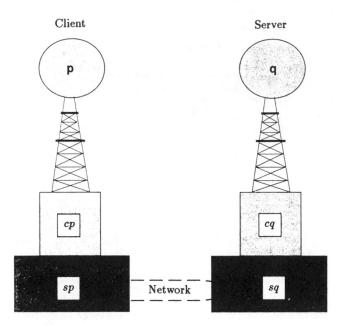

- *cp* and *cq* are authentic
- *cp* and *cq* operate for *p* and *q* only
- The interworking between *p* and *cp*, *q* and *cq* is secure
- *cp* and *cq* are functionally correct
- The message exchange between *cp* and *cq* is secure

Figure 5.11 Objects in open systems. Cooperation of objects.

Firstly, we assume that no other objects use the message network and that none wish to attack it from the outside. The correct functionality of the message network may be, to a large extent, secured using the various measures discussed in the previous chapters (including error control, restart after error, proof of correctness of protocol implementations, error detection and error correction codes at the line-level).

In practice, the assumption that there are only two subscribers in the network is wrong. Information which is to be exchanged between *cp* and *cq* must be protected using appropriate measures, such as cryptographic procedures, if is not to be read or falsified by other subscribers. Even the use of these procedures does not help against all attacks on a message network, above all against attacks from inside.

The object model has a facility to specify who may do what in the system, using which utilities. This specification is called a security policy.

Table 5.1   Security in ISO/OSI.

Security services	1	2	3	4	5	6	7
Authentication of the communication partner entity	N	N	Y	Y	N	N	Y
Access control	N	N	Y	Y	N	N	Y
Confidentiality of the connection	Y	Y	Y	Y	N	N	Y
Confidentiality without the connection	N	Y	Y	Y	N	N	Y
Confidentiality/fields	N	N	N	N	N	N	Y
Preventative flow analysis	Y	N	Y	N	N	N	Y
Data integrity of a connection	N	N	Y	Y	N	N	Y
...with recovery	N	N	N	N	N	N	Y
...without recovery	N	N	Y	Y	N	N	Y
Authentication of the sender	N	N	Y	Y	N	N	Y
Proof of transmission	N	N	N	N	N	N	Y
Proof of receipt	N	N	N	N	N	N	Y

If there is no such specification, it is a hopeless case, since the system must be told what to protect against whom or what.

Aids to the implementation of this security policy are of various types. PC LAN software packages contain at least the facility to allocate resources to users and to formulate usage rights.

Authenticity is often a problem, since passwords which provide access to the user environments created by the system may be falsified or listened in to on the line.

OSI security management   An OSI system is normally just a component of a company-wide, information-processing facility. A security strategy is advisable for the whole information-processing facility. The security strategy is subdivided into security policies for the individual areas.

Thus, there is a security policy for the OSI system. This security policy is described by the OSI security framework. The OSI security management supports the functions of the framework, in particular through the implementation of security aspects in the individual layers, interfaces, protocols and services (Table 5.1).

The implementation of these security aspects is again subject to the aspects of the security framework and often lies within the scope of the individual layers. Thus, for the security management SMFA, it only remains to implement the utilities and interfaces which permit and coordinate the use of the security functions of the individual layers. The standardization structure is currently quite shaky in this area.

The security policy of an open system may be empty in OSI, or it may be a powerful set of rules which specify the supplementary conditions for the communication. In addition, one should of course not forget that the open systems in different organizations have very different security policies and security strategies.

Core elements of the OSI security management include the security policy and security objects, such as, for example, qualified access objects. They are described by OSI security management services and mechanisms. There are three areas:

- Security-related object management uses the same facilities as the configuration management SMFA. Thus, it manages its own security-related objects, attributes, states and relationships.

- Security-related event and audit trail management works with facilities which correspond to those of the error management. It permits the generation, maintenance and forwarding of audit trails.

- Security management is a placeholder for everything that remains undefined.

Overall the author feels that this SMFA provides a sad, immature picture and will surely have to undergo a number of modifications.

5.3.4.5 Accounting management

The accounting management includes mechanisms to monitor and control information and resources which concern individual users of the OSI environment. This enables users and administrators to identify the use of resources (and, if necessary, restrictions on their use) and where resources incur costs to calculate these and allocate them appropriately. Of course, like the other functional areas, this only concerns items within the OSI environment and not those outside its scope.

There are two basic aspects: costs for a communications medium and transmission system and costs for resources in the end systems. Here, the end systems and the communications system may belong to different accounting domains. Every domain may have its own specification of costs and their handling. Thus, there is a requirement to exchange cost information between the domains.

Above all, in the application and network layers there are a number of accounting procedures which are service or network specific and allow users to activate accounting, collect accounting information, list and evaluate accounting information and process accounts. The accounting SMFA covers those management activities within an open system which actually concern the exchange of accounting information.

The standard specifies how CMIS and CMIP may be used for accounting management and thus defines a set of facilities and associated procedures to support the accounting management. It also specifies how CMIS services are used, the relevant classes of managed objects and subsets for conformance purposes.

If the accounting management is distributed across various systems, all systems may be required to control their own area themselves. Furthermore, a system may request information from other systems in order to square its accounts. The SMFA places practically no restrictions on this.

A system which generates data for accounting purposes is called an accounting management agent. Accounting managers are systems which interrogate accounting management data or obtain it in other ways. A system may play both roles.

Although the accounting management, unlike for example, the security management, is a very well-founded facility, this standard is not yet very well-developed. This is because accounting management started off later than the other areas. Before 1988, there are practically no references to the possibility that performance in an open system might incur costs.

5.3.4.6 Structure of the management information (SMI)

The SMI standard derives its importance from the fact that it defines OSI elements which may be used in all other areas of the OSI management. It is relatively abstract.

SMI defines the logical structure of the OSI management information, including in principle, all information which forms part of the communication between the OSI management entities. This structure is determined by managed objects, their attributes, the operations on these objects and the reports which may emanate from objects. SMI specifies the rules for naming objects and attributes.

SMI defines further object subtypes and attribute types which are basically applicable to all classes of managed objects. These definitions include the common semantics of the object/attribute types, the operations and the reports.

5.4 OSI layer management

The layer management may concern various entities associated with communication links. It comprises all the activities which are needed to monitor all OSI resources belonging to a particular protocol layer (for example, routing in layer 3).

The tasks of the layer management include:

- The collection of statistics and journaling.
- Recording and signalling of errors which cannot be immediately eliminated.
- Registration, deletion, allocation and release of communications resources on behalf of the system management.
- Reconfiguration under abnormal conditions.

The layer management is supported by the *Layer Management Entities* (LMEs). The LMEs, together, control the *Layer Entities* (LEs) together. There is one LME per protocol layer, which has a view of this layer. The LME permits the observation of layer-specific information such as state variables, protocol operations, events (errors, thresholds, changes of state) and parameters for performance analysis. The LME provides a facility for loading protocol parameters and activating and controlling resources. An LME supports the layer-specific decision taking which may be based on the observation either of local components and parameters, or of foreign LMEs belonging to other incarnations of this layer.

As conceived by the working group, the communication between LMEs in a specific layer should be executed using system management protocols of layer 7, which use all underlying layers. However, where not all seven layers are implemented a layer-specific management protocol may also be installed.

One major problem of this construction is that it relies on the existence of operational connections in the network. Of course, the LMEs could still operate autonomously for a time if a connection broke down. However, it is difficult, if after correction of an error, one wishes to bring all LMEs back to the same level. Special protocols are required for this. On the other hand, there are facilities and mechanisms for error recovery in the lower layers and some of these will certainly be used. This is also the reason why the protocols no longer belong to the management framework, but so-to-speak carry their own management with them and must be considered separately.

5.5 OSI protocol management

The protocol management consists of those protocol-internal mechanisms within one of the seven layers which are used to monitor a specific instance of a communications link. One example of this is flow control in various layers. The protocol management is specified and described in the standard for the protocol and services of each layer.

Thus, it is not a component of the management standard. Protocol management actions for layers 1–6 are described elsewhere in the literature. We do not wish to go into that further here. Instead, we concern ourselves with names in the OSI area.

5.6 Identification of OSI resources

Registration of names enables us to generate unique individual names to identify OSI resources. The name management identifies OSI resources by the allocation of OSI names such as protocol-layer identifiers. The address and route management ensure that an application name, which is appropriate for a process in an end system, is first attached to a Network Service Address Point (NSAP), then to a physical address and finally to a route.

This translation must also function reliably in an internetworking environment, with gateway systems and internetwork protocol converters.

Here, the name-management application process must integrate and control functional elements both of the directory services and of layer 3.

Directory services permit the dynamic binding of names in the application layer to various name attributes (for example, the point at which the name is implemented) and to other names or groups of names. At present, consideration is being given as to how far relational associations of attributes or logical data structures could sensibly extend this scheme.

ISO is developing a general model in which the name mappings are not necessarily restricted to layer 7. For example, directory services are also used to support the interprocess communication mechanisms of layer 5 and the mapping of NSAPs onto physical addresses and routes in layer 3.

Directory services might also be developed in such a way that they support system management functions, such as an integrated database including the most important data of the individual layers. Such a service would facilitate queries of the distributed data relating to various aspects such as addresses and file names.

There is an operational protocol between a *Client Service Agent* (CSA) and a *Directory System Agent* (DSA). A given DSA has an overview of only a part of the whole global data, but, may access other DSAs in remote parts of the network by corresponding requests from CSAs . Thus, another protocol, based on the CMIS protocols, is required for the cooperation between DSAs. The complete set of DSAs forms the directory system. The protocol between the DSAs must provide facilities such as the data chaining and file shadowing in order to achieve a certain transparency (Figure 5.12).

To round off, we now mention X.500 (ISO 9594), since most directory protocols will initially be based on this.

In an organizationally-large environment, it will always be necessary

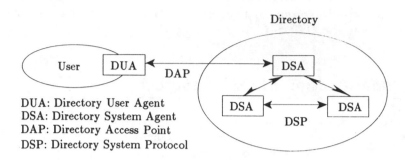

Figure 5.12 Directory model.

names and other characteristics of all persons involved in the communication, and all objects which are reachable via applications, may be quickly found. This information system goes beyond locally-available information and has a distributed implementation. The CCITT X.500 series recommendations are concerned exclusively with such information systems.

In X.500, a directory is a database from the user's point of view, the *Directory Information Base*. Every object known to the directory is represented by an entry in the directory information base. This entry contains all information relevant to the user. The entry is subdivided according to attributes.

The problem of naming surfaces again and again for distributed systems. In digital information-processing systems, it is senseless to permit ambiguous names. Thus, an object name in X.500 must be unique and valid worldwide and must remain stable for a long period. From the point of view of data protection, it is also important that not everyone knows where an object is physically located (this helps to prevent attacks over illegal routes). Thus, the naming should be independent of the physical position of the object incarnation and also of the network topology, or the distribution of the database. So as not to restrict the parallelism unnecessarily, it should be possible for naming to be carried out by several independent entities with precisely-defined areas of responsibility.

X.500 is such that every entity can store a tree for its area, representing the interdependencies of objects, as is also customary for file systems in some operating systems. The tree only contains relative names, the full names are obtained by concatenation with the root. This tree structure is particularly suited to mapping organizational entities. An object may have several names (alias names).

A construction known from other application-supporting services is used to support the distribution of the database. Every system contains an application process, the DSA, which executes the accesses to the part of the directory information base which it manages. If an inquiry comes from outside, the DSA may respond to it immediately if it relates to an object stored locally, otherwise the DSA may obtain the required information from a colleague. This variant hides the position of the information as far as the user is concerned. Another variant would be for the local agent simply to inform the inquiring application process which other agent is responsible. As in X.400, a user is always represented by an application process, the so-called *Directory User Agent*, (DUA).

In the simplest cases, the system management is just a user since, initially, no other assumptions are made about the users.

5.7 Summary

The OSI network management presents the interested observer with a very conflicting picture. Firstly, the logic underlying the proposals and the course of action is largely welcome. However, at certain places the OSI network management framework has some problematic loopholes, which we have described in this chapter. On the other hand, in the medium term, it is the only chance of a manufacturer-neutral integrated management solution.

Today the OSI network management has undergone its third complete conceptual permutation. One cannot be certain that this really is the last.

Certainly CMIS/CMIP is a stable basis for further progress. However, CMIS/CMIP must be weighed against SNMP, the *de facto* standard for the management of heterogeneous environments.

In the past, we have often had to acknowledge that the OSI euphoria was not altogether justified. In particular, OSI solutions are basically complicated solutions which require large amounts of computer time and memory space.

The first operational OSI management systems will surely require a workstation of the Sun 3 class or a UNIX computer.

For the user, the pure theory of the OSI management is less relevant than what the manufacturers wish to make of it. The reader will find this out in Chapter 7.

Chapter 6

Management in TCP/IP environments: SNMP

- The TCP/IP environment

- Introduction to SNMP

- The structure of SNMP

- SNMP products

- Limitations and problems of SNMP

- SNMP versus CMIP

- The future of SNMP

- Summary

In recent years, the US Department of Defense's protocol suite TCP/IP has been specially implemented for linkage of heterogeneous systems. It consists of a number of protocols for layers 3–7 and was originally developed by the US DoD to unify computer communication in the ARPANET framework.

The *Simple Network Management Protocol* (SNMP) is intended to provide network managers with a central point for observation, control and management of their installations. As such, it is fully independent of manufacturer-linked concepts.

Products based on SNMP facilitate the upkeep of complex internetworks and the reconfiguration of a broad spectrum of devices in the network from routers to workstations, depending on actual requirements. These products, which have been announced and in some cases delivered by a large number of manufacturers, are based on powerful workstations with a graphical user interface. Thus, the network manager may journey in comfort through the network and inspect weak points, ideally before errors occur. It is also important that the manager only needs to use a single central workstation and not devices distributed everywhere.

Although SNMP was originally conceived for TCP/IP environments, it has also been extended with control facilities for non-TCP/IP devices such as IEEE 802.1 bridges.

The first SNMP products were produced in 1988 by Cisco Systems, Advanced Computer Communications and Proteon. In the meantime, about forty suppliers now support SNMP.

The SNMP protocol itself is only one aspect of the overall management structure, the other parts of which form the *Management Information Base* (MIB) and the *Structure of Management Information* (SMI) specifications. The MIB is a collection of objects, which abstractly represent the devices in the network and their internal components. SMI is a set of rules to define the characteristics of network objects and how management protocols obtain information about these objects. The *Network Management Station* (NMS) is a central component, usually a workstation, which provides the administrator with an overview of the state of the network and with facilities for intervention. The individual network devices contain *agents*, small programs which execute the most important network management functions, such as the recording of state values on the spot.

SNMP stemmed from the TCP/IP protocol suite. It was originally conceived as a simple and fast facility for performance and error monitoring for Internet. However, in the first half of 1990, it received a considerable boost from commitments by large manufacturers such as IBM, DEC and Sun and from practical window-oriented network management products.

This chapter introduces the concept of SNMP, its structure and functions and points out the limitations of the concept. Finally, we consider SNMP products and their status in the market. A comparison with OSI CMIP completes the discussion of SNMP.

As in all chapters, we begin with a brief overview of the general area of SNMP. This general area is today determined largely by the TCP/IP protocol suite.

6.1 The TCP/IP environment

The TCP/IP protocol suite was not designed for a particular message transport system such as a LAN, but may be used on various transmission media, systems and networks and on various computers. This means that it is naturally suited for a doubly-heterogeneous internetworking environment, where the whole network consists of different parts linked by gateways, over which various computers from different manufacturers intercommunicate. The most important encouragement for the DoD protocol suite was its integration into the UNIX family. From Berkeley UNIX 4.2, the DoD protocol suite has been available to the user for problem-free communication of different UNIX systems. The portability of the operating system has also led to the portability of the communications software. This is a decisive step towards the simplification and unification of communication. Today, the DoD protocol suite realizes the target objectives of the ISO/OSI model; however, it does not correspond to the international standard. Instead, the individual protocols stand out by their relative simplicity. They are thus cost-effective to implement in a PC environment.

Corresponding implementations exist for almost all systems which

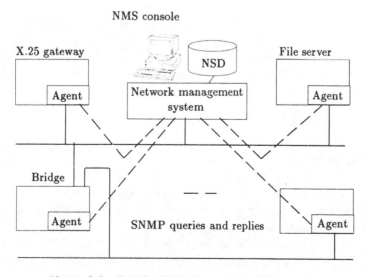

Figure 6.1   SNMP. The central management model.

ISO/OSI   DoD protocol suite

7	Telnet	FTP	SMTP	NSP
6	interactive	File transfer	Simple mail	Name server
5	terminal traffic	protocol	transfer protocol	protocol
4	TCP Transmission control protocol		UDP User datagram protocol	
3	IP Internet protocol			
2	Network as data transport resource, for example, X.25 WAN,			
1	IEEE 802 LAN, Other LANs, PBX, private data network			

Figure 6.2   DoD protocol suite.

use UNIX, in one of its many different variants (including SINIX and AIX operating systems) and for DEC VMS systems, MS-DOS, OS/2 and OS/2 EE, CP/M and IBM-VM and IBM-MVS. Thus, file transfer, electronic mail and line-oriented dialogue may be executed from a terminal under the various systems. One of the most common applications is the integration of (IBM-)PCs, DEC systems and IBM systems using Ethernet as a communications medium.

The DoD protocol suite has elements in layers 3–7 (Figure 6.2).

The *Transmission Control Protocol* (TCP) is used as a secure host-to-host protocol in packet-oriented, computer-communication networks and in local area networks. TCP is a connection-oriented, end-to-end protocol of layer 4 of the ISO/OSI seven layer model.

TCP is a reliable protocol for interprocess communication between host computers attached to different networks. It uses a simple, reliable datagram service provided by the layer below (IP). In principle, TCP supports many different communication systems and has been implemented on a wide spectrum of networks (dedicated lines, packet- or circuit-switched networks, LANs).

TCP expects an *Internet Protocol* (IP) in the layer below it, which provides facilities for receiving variable-length information segments enclosed in Internet datagram envelopes.

Internet datagrams may be used to address TCPs in different networks. IP is responsible for the fragmentation and regeneration of TCP segments which may be necessary when transporting the data through several networks and their gateways.

TCP is normally a module in the local system. The users access TCP like any other subsystem. If required, TCP can call operating system functions. TCP does not call the network device drivers directly, but delivers its data to the Internet protocol.

Typical application programs which use TCP (so-called 'clients') include the *Telnet* dialogue protocol, the *File Transfer Protocol* (FTP) and the *Simple Mail Transfer Protocol* (SMTP); these are all standardized.

Thus, TCP/IP provides a secure, process-to-process communication service for layers 3 and 4 in a multinetwork environment. It is a host-to-host transport protocol which runs over several networks.

One of the strengths of TCP/IP, its excellent security mechanisms, and the lavish routing mechanism affect each other simultaneously and unfavourably.

The *User Datagram Protocol* (UDP) enables application processes to exchange datagrams without establishing a virtual connection. TCP and UDP sit above IP.

The Darpa *Internet Protocol* (IP) permits the exchange of data across several networks. IP guarantees neither the delivery of the datagram to the destination nor the preservation of the original datagram sequence. Since IP must also support a transmission path over various networks, it is able to carry out appropriate fragmentation in the case of different permissible message lengths on different networks. The individual packets created in this way are transported independently and are given a special identification so that they may ultimately be pieced together again.

Telnet, SMTP and FTP are applications using both TCP and IP which may be accessed directly by the user.

Telnet   Telnet permits a bidirectional byte-oriented communication in the dialogue with other systems. The following connections are conceivable:

- between a terminal on host A and an application on host B;
- between a terminal on host A and a terminal on host B;
- interprocess communication between applications on hosts A and B.

FTP   FTP may be used to share files, to copy data and programs between different systems and for indirect access to resources on other computers. Telnet is used to establish the connection and to execute commands.

SMTP   SMTP is used to transmit mail to hosts which are attached to the same LAN (network) or which are reachable via a gateway, if the sender and recipient are not in the same network.

The main advantage of the DoD standard is that the standardization is not restricted to the lower layers, but that standards and applications (which in the meantime have been implemented on almost all DP systems) are also defined for the higher layers 5–7.

6.2 Introduction to SNMP

SNMP is based on the TCP/IP suite (Glaser, Hein and Vogl, 1990) and was designed for use in the framework of distributed data processing with PCs, workstations, minis and mainframes in the commercial office environment and in administration. In the US it is widely implemented in place of manufacturer-dependent programs to manage LANs, bridges, routers or servers.

SNMP is swimming on the TCP/IP wave. The relationship between SNMP and CMIP (the ISO/OSI information protocol, see Chapter 5) is coarsely analogous to the relationship between TCP/IP and ISO/OSI themselves. Ideally, one would like to base communication between heterogeneous installations on the OSI standard. However, TCP/IP is installed because it is more compact, simpler, cheaper and more available and may be implemented without grossly affecting the most immediately important performance characteristics.

The relationship between SNMP and NetView may be viewed in the same way. NetView is a tool for network management in closed SNA environments. SNMP controls open TCP/IP Internets. There are clearly points of contact between SNMP and NetView domains. It is important that the two management systems should obtain information from one another, since this would bridge the isolation at the most effective point. IBM is prepared to do exactly this in the framework of the increased TCP/IP activities.

The so-called *Internet Activities Board* (IAB) is responsible for the TCP/IP standardization. Internet is the US-wide network of the US government, which connects government, research and teaching establishments. The SNMP concept was not developed by a major manufacturer but was conceived in April 1987 by four people: Jeffery Case of the University of Tennessee, James Davin of the Massachusetts Institute of Technology, and Mark Fedor and Martin Schoffstall both of Performance Systems International.

6.3 The structure of SNMP

6.3.1 SNMP functions

In the narrow sense, SNMP is the protocol for interworking between the agents and the NMS. All SNMP systems use both the connectionless UDP and the connection-oriented TCP to exchange messages. The management software in the NMS monitors and controls devices by querying values which the agents assemble. The most important task of an agent program is to provide information about objects which correspond to the critical parts and actions of the device for which the agent is responsible (for example, the state of a Token Ring card or the number of collisions on the Ethernet over a given time span). The agents store this information and deliver it to a management program on request. Unrequested signals (alarms) are only issued by agents in critical circumstances such as unusual errors or breakdowns in the power supply.

An SNMP system supports three important types of command: GET, SET and EVENT. For example, GET REQUEST enables an NMS to query one or more objects or variables in an agent MIB required in the management context. GET NEXT enables NMS to query agent MIB tables and lists. GET RESPONSE is used for information retrieval in the MIB. SET REQUEST enables an NMS to modify a value of an MIB object or variable and may be used to boot or reboot devices. EVENT makes it possible for an agent to send its NMS an unrequested alarm in situations where an alarm is set off.

SNMP also functions as a proxy agent, thus permitting a management station to monitor and control network elements which do not implement the SNMP specifications. The proxy is able to convert protocols and provides the NMS with a uniform picture.

6.3.2 The SMI specifications

The SMI specifications are rules governing how network variables or objects should be defined for use via the network management protocol, how the protocol accesses the objects and how objects in the MIB are implemented.

The OSI description language, ASN.1, is used to describe the data formats for objects corresponding to an object information model (Gora and Speyerer, 1987). ASN.1 permits the system-independent definition of objects. In ASN.1 the SMI objects are given numbers called object identifiers. The philosophy behind SMI is for modularity and extensibility within the protocol. Unlike CMIP, SNMP only handles simple data types, for example, simple entries in a table. OSI NM implementations remain responsible for the creation, processing and maintenance of complicated composite data types.

The reason for this, in addition to the bounding of the complexity, is, above all, the fear that data types created by manufacturers might not be available on machines from other manufacturers. If the basic structure is kept simple, there are less restrictions on extensions. Thus, in the end, more applications can use SNMP.

It is easy to see how important ease of extensibility is. If a router is installed today, it will remain in place for some time. During its lifetime, other routers will be installed which correspond to other versions and may support other MIB objects. In order to permit future extensions in addition to existing objects and functions, SMI contains four classes of objects: directory objects, management objects, experimental objects and private objects.

The class of directory objects will only be used later. Management objects are those which are mandatory in every SNMP implementation. Experimental objects are used in internetworking experiments as candidates for future extensions. Private objects are unilaterally defined, for example, by manufacturers for their particular devices. Using these object classes, SNMP can be gradually extended in a sensible way; extensions may be essentially tested before they are entered into the above object classes.

6.3.3 The SNMP MIB

The SNMP MIB is a database-like collection of objects in the agents which may be observed and controlled from the management workstation. Thus, the MIB is distributed. These objects are mostly of a statistical nature; they include counters of packets sent, connections used and connection establishment attempts, together with the numbers of faulty packets and collisions in a LAN segment.

In addition to the MIB, there is also the *Network Statistics Database* (NSD) which is central to the management workstation.

The aim of the MIB is to create a unified, protocol-independent data space. Every device in the scope of SNMP is called a 'managed node' and has three software components (Figure 6.3): transmission protocols such as TCP/IP or UDP which carry out the actual work; a management protocol (SNMP) which permits the remote monitoring and control of the various transmission protocols and management tools which act in combination with the transmission protocols to implement monitoring and control. In the SNMP terminology, the transmission protocols are ironically called 'useful protocols' and contain objects which must be managed (for example, routing tables, information about physical interfaces, counters and parameters). These objects are defined independently of the SNMP management protocol. Thus, it is possible to modify the management protocol without having to modify the 'useful protocols' or the software for the management tools.

The MIB defines 126 groups of objects, some of which are permanently or temporarily obligatory. The objects themselves are hierarchically arranged; naturally, the same numerical identification cannot be allocated to several objects. The individual objects themselves form the lowest level of the hierarchy. At the highest level are tables composed of

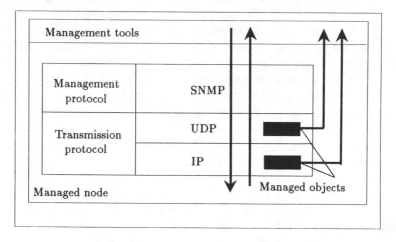

Figure 6.3   SNMP. Managed node.

entries. There are five types of tables; the IF Table describes the status of the interfaces to the agent; the AT Table contains values for address transformations; the IP Address Table contains the IP addresses of all the agent's interfaces; the IP Routing Table contains IP destination addresses, addresses of the next hop, the number of hops, etc; and the TCP CON Table contains the state of the TCP connections.

The two most important operations executed by the management software on the MIB are SET and GET functions. For example, a manager might be interested in the address of the next hop or in the total number of hops in an IP Routing Table. He can obtain this information using GET. Of course GET is seldom executed explicitly; instead, the software for the network management administrator interface of the NMS workstation uses this function.

6.3.4 The control functions

In an SNMP implementation, the NMS manager code runs on a management console (for example, a Sun SPARC workstation, which turns out to be the device most used for this purpose). The administrators and network managers perform their observation, monitoring, control and installation functions from the central point of the workstation.

In SNMP, observation of the network involves the polling of the devices, where information is continuously fetched from the agents and collected in the NSD for the purposes of correlation and planning. The network administrator may determine the polling rate. The agents reply to the polling queries, thereby using up all the data they have collected; whence, the storage space allocated to them remains small.

If a devices ceases to function and thus is no longer reachable, an alarm condition or a 'trap' is tripped. There are five important events which lead to a trap: the going down of a connection; the restart of a connection; the initialization of an agent; the restart of an agent; and authentication error when an unauthorized user attempts to gain access to an agent. SNMP allows the manufacturers to define other trap conditions. These might be events connected with the use of X.25, DECnet or 802.1 protocols.

Polling with traps is the SNMP method of isolating sources of error. The method is very effective and fast.

The data collected by polling or the reaction to certain events may stimulate network managers to modify certain network parameters. Parameters are essentially modified using the SET command, which, analogously to the GET command, may be used to set variables in the tables. For example, if a duplicated address is identified as the source of error in routing, this source of error may be eliminated by entering one or more new addresses.

The collected data may also be used to support long-term planning tasks. Here, the manufacturers may naturally provide their clients with extensive first hand planning assistance using this data. Finally, *Artificial Intelligence* (AI) programs are also conceivable, which would use the NSD data (amounting to previous experiences and rules) to generate proposals to the network manager for his further work. This will be of particular interest for large networks.

6.4 SNMP products

SNMP is simply the biggest surprise on the network-management market. Scarcely any well-known manufacturer has gone over completely to this protocol. At this point, we can only discuss the most important trends.

Typically, a supplier first develops SNMP-agent software for his products, leaving the NMS product until later. Many manufacturers have opted for the first operational agent-software codes from MIT, Carnegie Mellon or NetLabs as a basis. Some OEM products are made for special environments, such as, for example, UNIX. Others, such as SNMP Rel.2 from Epilogue or XNetmon from SNMP Research, are ported and may run in various environments such as Sun OS, DEC VAX VMS, IBM AIX, DOS or XENIX. They are mostly written in C. These products are often supplemented by a range of utilities, such as, for example, an MIB compiler which generates SNMP MIB data from manufacturer-specific data. This may avoid time-consuming, error-prone, manual conversions.

The basic functions of SNMP may be refined for the user in a variety of different ways. Simple systems provide only the network observation and the error isolation. More complicated implementations also permit performance and configuration management. The same is true for the user surfaces: simple surfaces may be character-based for the tough guys below the network manager. User-friendly surfaces use window techniques and coloured representations of the network, which may be zoomed into step-by-step. Alarms and problem points are emphasized in colour.

Distinction must be made between products for internetworking environments, products and plans for interfaces to other management systems, the role of the LAN manufacturers and the position of the software houses.

6.4.1 SNMP, large manufacturers and other management systems

What is the position of large DP manufacturers who, in many cases, have a network management concept for their own relatively homogeneous world which is different to SNMP? The answer to this question is surely the decisive key to the success or failure of this group of protocols.

IBM, DEC, HP and Sun have announced support both for SNMP and for OSI CMIP in their network management systems. All four have their own network management systems with capabilities considerably more powerful than those of SNMP. However, each manufacturer sees the need to support standards which permit clients to use and control a wide range of devices from various manufacturers. We shall come to these concepts in the next chapter.

For OS/2 EE 1.2, IBM has announced TCP/IP complete with an SNMP agent. This implementation allows OS/2 EE servers to communicate with an SNMP NMS. The network manager receives information such as error statistics or packet counters from the agent MIB. In the near future, IBM is to extend the host-based NetView management system with the facility to control TCP/IP SNMP and OSI CMIP nodes. This should also be seen as a reaction to the lukewarm acceptance of NetView/PC. The agent software contains no IBM-specific MIB extensions. It supports the SNMP GET function, which allows an OS/2 client to ask other SNMP agents for their MIB data. However, IBM does not support the SET function and thus elegantly avoids the security obstacles.

Hewlett-Packard supports SNMP and 'CMIP over TCP/IP' (also called CMOT), a hybrid which uses TCP/IP as a transport system for CMIP, in the Open View Network Management Server which was announced in Spring 1990. HP implements a communications infrastructure application programmer interface in the server, which allows various protocol stacks to be used independently of the highest layer of the Open View Management applications. The SNMP NMS software in Open View only runs in the HP-UX environment. HP plans to provide agent software for UNIX workstations, servers and gateways. The SNMP NMS module in Open View can use TCP/IP and OSI transport protocols on LANs or X.25 routes. HP supports the GET and SET commands in full. The Open View management server provides presentation and search services which poll the network and find all TCP/IP and SNMP nodes. The server then generates a map of the network and indicates the node status. The graphical user interface contains dialogue boxes and pull-down menus. The management server also carries out data and event management. The system journals the status of all nodes and records all important events. This information may be stored in a standard SQL database. Simple editorial aids enable the users to write applications which access the SQL database and generate reports about the performance of the network. The Open View SNMP implementation contains various MIB extensions, including the HP Metadata compiler which provides users with a simple means of introducing MIB objects and definitions in order to customize their management system.

Within the *Enterprise Management Architecture* (EMA), DEC had only planned to support its own existing network-management mechanisms and OSI CMIP; but, the explosive spread of SNMP has forced DEC to include SNMP in EMA for its TCP/IP client-base. DEC provides SNMP and CMIP support in the DECmcc management station (a collection of DECnet management products) and is also to incorporate SNMP in the DECmcc director which will represent DEC's EMA system. We discuss EMA and the role of the director in Chapter 7. As far as access modules are concerned, both SNMP and CMIP facilities are provided. The SNMP access module runs on the DECmcc director control console and enables the network administrator to monitor SNMP agents and to receive alarms. DEC supports both GET and SET, but has generated its own security restrictions, which, for example, do not permit everyone to reboot a node. In due course, DEC will also provide SNMP agent software to support bridges, routers, gateways and terminal servers. With DEC it is not possible to create a proxy agent to convert information from non-SNMP nodes. DEC provides an intermediate language to convert from SNMP MIB attributes into more natural language elements. With DEC, the functional modules reside above the access modules and control the construction of network domains, the construction of the network topology, the generation of alarms together with performance and error analysis. The user interface is formed using corresponding presentation modules.

Sun Microsystems' SunNet Manager, which was announced in 1989, is a protocol-independent management station which can use SNMP for communication with SNMP agents, but is not restricted to this. Sun uses its own network management and sees the SNMP NMS module as a proxy. This proxy property allows the network manager to integrate various SNMP MIBs and extensions in one database. With Sun, the communication with the database is executed on the basis of a remote procedure call. This also permits fast and efficient access by application programs on other stations. The SNMP implementation of the SunNet Manager supports GET and SET functions, error detection, network-performance monitoring and configuration management. More than twenty manufacturers, including Cisco, Netlabs, Synoptics and Wellfleet have announced that in the future they will use the SunNet Manager for their SNMP software.

6.4.2 SNMP in LANs

The further a network management system extends, the more useful it is. Thus, integration is of primary importance. SNMP was designed as an internetwork management system. Nowadays, an end point in an internetwork is seldom an individual station, but is more likely to be a LAN. What, then, is the position of the major manufacturers of LAN software on SNMP, when they have their own architectures and utilities for LAN management?

3Com and Novell have both announced that they are to provide their servers and internetworking units (gateways, bridges) with SNMP agent capabilities. Banyan is still undecided. The role of IBM has already been discussed.

3Com and Novell, however, do not want to bring the SNMP capability to the workstations.

3Com is afraid that a complete TCP/IP stack with SNMP in the workstation could take up too much memory space. However, this argument does not hold water, since firstly, the memory space restriction applies only to old DOS workstations and secondly, there are already efficient DOS implementations of agents which only take up around 25 35 kbytes. There should be no problems under OS/2 and the LAN Manager. 3Com supports SNMP agent software in the Netbuilder/2000 brouter, but has not announced an NMS. An NMS could only operate in conjunction with 3Com's own *Open Management Architecture* (OMA). According to 3Com, OMA will in the future manage client-server LANs and company-wide networks including hosts, bridges, routers, workstations, servers and other odds and ends. It should interwork with DEC's EMA, IBM's NetView and AT&T's UNMA.

Novell has recently introduced an SNMP monitor for remote Ethernet LANs. The LANtern is an OEM product which can be integrated into a network-management station from any manufacturer. It resides in a physical Ethernet segment, which enables it to observe the mode of operation of the physical and link layers in the Ethernet and to find the reasons for malfunctions such as permanent broadcasts, noisy transmissions, IP address duplication and routing problems. LANtern uses SNMP to communicate with a central network management station such as the SunNet Manager or ACS4800. Since LANtern is not defined in the standard MIB, all LANtern statistics belong to the extensions. It is possible to observe the number of packets, and the number of errors and collisions on the physical network segment and between two stations. The various protocols used can be determined and displayed. LANtern stores all network statistics in a database, where they may be called up by each SNMP management station in the network. It supports all standard SNMP commands including SET and GET and is able to generate traps and alarms based on predefinable events and signal them to the NMS.

Another important manufacturer is Synoptics, which is represented here by SEL. Synoptics has selected SNMP for its Lattisnet network-management station to execute the monitoring of the two lowest layers and the network planning and control. Synoptics has implemented SNMP agent software for the Lattisnet LAN concentrators which link the various physical media. Lattisnet supports Ethernet as a universal cabling system, Token Ring and FDDI. The Lattisnet network management station can poll concentrators and local Ethernet bridges, activate and deactivate ports using the SET command and display the number of extension cards in a concentrator.

Thus, it is clear how manufacturers of LAN hardware and software can support SNMP. Currently, Novell and 3Com have an absolutely overwhelming market share of the PC LAN software. If one includes IBM, then the companies which together represent about 85% of LAN software installations are uniform in their support for SNMP. This should answer the question as to the role of SNMP in LANs. One should not forget, however, that SNMP in the LAN can only be made responsible for the management of the resources of the lowest 2–4 layers. The application-oriented services and resources must still be controlled by individual management systems, the capabilities of which are oriented to the network software used and the servers. Thus, for example, the implementation of access protection for files on file servers or the implementation of alternate exclusion of two concurrent processes is never a task for SNMP.

6.4.3 SNMP products for internetwork environments

Internetwork environments consist primarily of bridges and routers. Suppliers supporting SNMP in this sector include Proteon, Cisco, Hughes, Wellfleet and ACC.

Proteon was one of the first suppliers to support SNMP, partly because one of the first SNMP developers previously worked for Proteon. In addition to SNMP the *Simple Gateway Monitoring Protocol* (SGMP) is also supported in the routers. However, SGMP was discarded in 1990. In addition to the agents, Proteon provides the Overview network management system based on an 80286 PC. The Overview surface is fully graphically-oriented. The network manager can define an internetwork topology hierarchically. The fault manager detects faults and helps to remove them. The availability of network resources is displayed. Proteon has implemented the standard MIB extended by a 'Private Enterprise Tree'. Proteon has published the main specifications in order that other manufacturers can support Overview. In addition to X.25 Token Ring and Ethernet connections, the Proteon solution also supports FDDI.

Cisco Systems has also introduced SNMP NMS software based on a Sun 3, which is also intended for use on DECstations and other UNIX workstations. Cisco supports SNMP agents on all multiprotocol routers, bridges, terminal servers and protocol converters. The fully graphical NMS software is called NetCentral and provides a dynamic real-time area map of each node and each connection. The Sybase SQL database is used as the NSD database. Thus, it is possible to write widely portable network management programs.

Both Proteon and Cisco limit the variety of parameters available in the SET command, so that a network administrator cannot delete resources accidentally.

Today, security remains a weak point of SNMP. We shall look at this again shortly. The manufacturers are attempting to improve this with additional measures, particularly in relation to the protection of the NMS workstation.

Hughes LAN Systems, which is both an internetwork and a LAN supplier has introduced the 9100 Network Management Center on a Sun 3, with which it hopes to control up to 18 000 devices. Hughes has agent software for its bridges, terminal servers and LAN servers. The 9100 has a character-based interface, optional windows and pop-up menus. It is also characterized by the Unify relational database and the Unify 4GL ACCEL. ACCEL may be used to construct complicated monitoring and reaction programs. Hughes has also provided for stronger security controls.

Wellfleet markets multiprotocol routers and bridges with SNMP agents and SNMP NMS software which runs on a Sun 3 workstation or on a Sun SPARCstation server. Wellfleet has extended the MIB so that, in addition to TCP/IP, DECnet, XNS, Novell's IPX and MAC level bridging are also supported. However, these extensions are restricted to Wellfleet devices. In addition to the usual networks, Token Ring- and Ethernet-to-FDDI bridges are also supported.

Advance Computer Communications (ACC) offers the SNMP agents in the IP routers and the ACS 4800 NMS system, which also runs on well-known Sun devices and has capabilities similar to those of the other products.

6.4.4 The position of the software manufacturers

Finally, it is interesting to see what the software houses, who specialize in OEM products in the TCP/IP area, are doing about SNMP.

Spider systems markets its TCP/IP stack complete with an SNMP agent. In mid-1990, Spider began to market licences for a Central Management Station Software package, which runs on the Spider Monitor

220 and collects, stores and analyzes network performance data. The SNMP product runs with Berkeley Sockets and can interwork with any relational SQL database. It supports various window interfaces such as X-Windows and OSF Motif. It can run under DOS, OS/2 and UNIX. The Spider Ethernet Analyser can decode and analyze SNMP packets running over Ethernet. In the future it will also support Token Ring and FDDI. Spider implements all current SNMP specifications and provides MIB extensions (such as a support for X.25, in which remote TCP/IP segments may be observed via the NMS Monitor) and utilities to set up one's own MIB extensions.

Finally, Wollongong markets the WIN/MGT software, complete with SNMP agents and NMS capabilities. This software is equally accessible to OEMs and end users. The WIN/MGT NMS software runs on a Sun 3 with Openlook, on a DECstation with Ultrix and DECwindows and on PS/2 systems with SCO-UNIX and Open Desktop. Agents may operate under VAX VMS, DOS, Macintosh and 386 Unix. The SNMP agent software comes with MAC Pathway Access 1.2, TCP/IP 386 Streams 4.1, WIN/Route 2.1 and WIN/TCP/IP for DOS 4.1 (it is clearly not too large in this case!).

6.5 Limitations and problems of SNMP

Even though SNMP was very recently equipped with many different extensions, it cannot disown its origin, the TCP/IP networking environment. It was not designed, for example, to implement configuration management at a high level, and its capabilities are restricted to the monitoring of networks and the isolation of errors.

Thus, it does not represent an overall network management strategy in the sense of DEC's EMA or IBM's NMA, but rather an urgently-needed aid to the integration of various subnetworks and the devices linking them (bridges, routers).

Like all TCP/IP elements, SNMP was constructed with a view to functionality and with less attention paid to security. This mainly concerns the possible misuse of the SET function. The manufacturers of SNMP products have already taken this into account so that, either the SET function cannot be used at all, or it can only be used with an encrypted authorization control. Since this control is specific to the NMS, this does nothing for the openness of the concept if it is implementation dependent. However, even this does not protect against the copying and installation of a complete NMS.

One of the main properties of SNMP is the simple polling process between NMS and agents. This process runs over UDP, which means that there are no sessions between the communication partners, the establishment, execution and release of which could be protected. The polling rate may be set by the administrator so as to obtain a best possible balance between control intervals and use of the transmission bandwidth.

On the other hand, the data in the agent MIBs is seldom classified as security-related, since it is structural data of an internetwork environment, which from experience with X.25 networks, is usually left 'lying around'. Total control here is certainly uncalled for and not economically viable.

As always in the network, the protection of data and applications must always be implemented from 'on high' or from outside, in other words, within the applications themselves and within the framework of basic application-oriented services (such as FTAM or FT) which support them, since in most cases in a distributed environment, the paths which applications will use to intercommunicate are unknown.

6.6 SNMP versus CMIP

CMIP is the basic protocol for message exchange between management facilities in the ISO/OSI network management. It is clear that, currently, many more products support SNMP than support CMIP. Thus, there is now no question of replacement, but only of the medium-term development. CMIP is increasingly an element of the international standardization and in the course of time it will draw implementations after it.

It is anticipated that in the coming years there will be a coexistence of NetView, SNMP and CMIP, which will be just as stable as the coexistence of SNA, TCP/IP and OSI protocols. For control of a domain in a network, one will choose the most useful protocol. Here, from a structural view, CMIP will be viewed as the last integration stage.

SNMP is a tactical solution for the network manager's current problems. It has been optimized with respect to simplicity. The main functions are contained in the agents and in programs outside SNMP which edit the data of the NMS database. SNMP only has a modest object structure and lacks complicated composite objects. There is no standard way of introducing new devices; the manufacturers must provide for this themselves in corresponding agent programs and MIB extensions. It is relatively difficult for users to place a device under the control of SNMP if there is no manufacturer-produced agent for this device.

However, the main difference is that SNMP is a centrally-oriented management solution, while CMIP represents a scheme for decentralized network management. The SNMP management has a star-shaped structure with the NMS station in the middle. Thus, the boundaries of the area of influence of SNMP are fixed from the outset. The area of influence of CMIP is given by a hierarchically-oriented, tree-like management structure. For networks over a certain size and complexity, such a solution is preferable on both ideological and practical grounds.

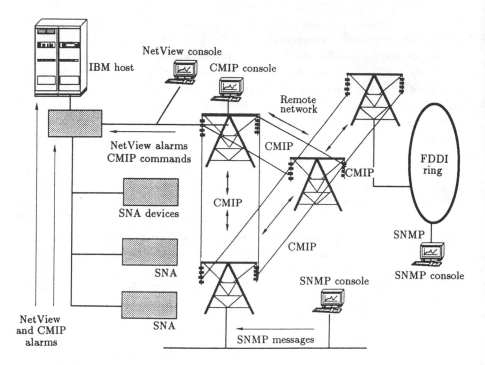

Figure 6.4   SNMP, CMIP and NetView: friendly coexistence.

Even manufacturers of PC LANs have seen this. Thus, for example, the latest version of NetWare allows one to define group administrators, who stand below the main supervisor but control the resources of the group.

For the future, one must think one step further. A company-wide network consists of various subnetworks, including, for example, terminal networks controlled by SNA and NetView. There are Token Ring networks which replace the terminal subsystems and have certain additional server-oriented functions. Up to now these are controlled internally by the IBM Token Ring LAN manager. There are Ethernets with TCP/IP and SNMP management. Now a server in the Token Ring sends its host NetView messages and a gateway to the Ethernet in the Token Ring generates SNMP messages for the NMS. The NetView and the SNMP control areas must be integrated where necessary. CMIP is well-suited for the exchange of messages between the areas.

Both SNMP and CMIP are defined in ASN.1. As far as the formation of composite types is concerned, SNMP imposes a number of restrictions on the designer. This is not a purely theoretical difference. Once definitions and attributes are set, SNMP does not permit them to be applied to further generic applications. When one defines a bridge in SNMP, the definition is fixed and should not be modified. If one wishes to define a self-learning bridge, this must be done from scratch, since the other object definition cannot be referenced in a different context. Under CMIP, for the definition of the self-learning bridge, one could simply take the definition of the unintelligent bridge and extend it by specifications to describe self-learning characteristics. Through its generic characteristics, CMIP also supports dynamic objects, while SNMP is very limited in this area. Virtual connections changing during the day in a remote network are an example of dynamic objects.

However, CMIP and SNMP do have a number of things in common. Firstly, both are tools for the communication between resource-specific agents and the logical management facilities. Both support the commands GET, SET and EVENT with largely equivalent functionality. In CMIP, however, these commands have considerably more extensive object fields (parameters). In addition, CMIP also has the commands CREATE, DELETE and ACTION. CREATE and DELETE are the outward signs of the fundamental difference from SNMP. A manager may use the CREATE command to permit a CMIP agent to create an object. The object is the management's view of a resource. Whether CREATE actually constructs the object, or only incarnates it from a template stored in some database, is irrelevant. The manager will, for example, use CREATE to activate an application program or a protocol stack. The function of DELETE is clear. The manager uses ACTION to have an object execute certain operations, for example, a test. CMIP automatically generates a new object as soon as a new resource enters the network.

Where SNMP has SMI, CMIP has DMI *Definition of Management Information*. DMI has a practically inexhaustible area of influence. Furthermore, CMIP has considerably more facilities to filter information and to single out subareas. However, we shall not discuss that further here.

It should be clear that CMIP can do far more than SNMP; thus, it also has correspondingly greater implementation costs. How do they compare in practice?

In daily operation, SNMP and CMIP have a basically comparable performance, which depends largely on how skilfully the ASN.1 specifications are converted. SNMP and CMP are certainly both as reliable as the quality of their implementation and of the protocol stack permit. Both are basically dependent on the underlying transport protocols; in the case of SNMP this is TCP/IP and the LLC connections, while CMIP is available with OSI stacks and also with TCP/IP (CMOT). As far as extensibility is concerned, SNMP is extremely manufacturer-dependent, while CMIP depends on the willingness of its users to learn.

6.7 The future of SNMP

The future of SNMP appears very rosy, since most of the major computer manufacturers (IBM, DEC, HP, Sun), the major manufacturers of LAN software (Novell, 3Com, IBM), the major manufacturers of internetwork environments (Cisco, Hughes, Proteon, Wellfleet) and the major manufacturers of TCP/IP software (Spider, Wollongong), together with some manufacturers of LAN hardware (SEL, Synoptics), strongly support SNMP.

It is clear to me that this support is the result of the groove in which the frightfully sluggish standardization of OSI (CMIP) is stuck and of the ever increasing internetworking of users who cannot or will not wait any longer.

SNMP will survive and continue to be developed strongly as long as the TCP/IP protocol suite exists.

The further developments coming from the *Internet Engineering Taskforce* (IETF), (a group within the IAB which is responsible for the SNMP standardization), mainly concern SNMP MIBs for Token Ring and DECnet Phase IV devices.

Gary Krall, marketing director of ACC and member of the IETF puts it like this: 'With the support of key manufacturers like DEC and IBM, SNMP will continue to snowball'.

In fact, in mid 1990, a new stable version of the MIB, MIB II was introduced, where the main extensions relate to private objects.

There are now no restraints on the use of these extensions. Over 200 manufacturers have already applied for and received private extensions. All have committed themselves to publishing the private extensions, but scarcely any are doing so. This leads to the paradoxical situation whereby, there is a common network-management industry standard but it will in many cases be impossible to control heterogeneous environments without further ado, since the manufacturer's private objects will not be understood by central management stations of other manufacturers.

6.8 Summary

We have seen that there is broad support for SNMP amongst a wide range of manufacturers. We have also learnt the limitations of SNMP and seen that there is another concept which in all probability is heading towards us, namely CMIP. What should today's network manager do about tomorrow?

Of course, one could fall into a fruitless ideological discussion. In practice, SNMP will often be installed where it is useful and where other products are lacking.

A correct long-term decision can only be based on a carefully-generated, user-specific overall object model. It is only possible to evaluate whether or not the structure of SNMP will also fulfil future needs within the framework of such a model.

However, it is pragmatic simply to install SNMP and to wait until such clear limitations appear in the day-to-day use that it makes economic sense to think about what one should use next.

We are well acquainted with this procedure, which in the past has not led to the worst solutions.

The future role of SNMP will largely be determined by how the open integrated management platforms of manufacturers such as DEC, HP or Sun use these products. More details of these platforms are given in Chapter 7.

Chapter 7

Manufacturers' OSI-oriented schemes for integrated network management

- The structure of integrated multivendor network architectures

- AT&T: Unified Network Management Architecture

- DEC: Enterprise Management Architecture

- Hewlett-Packard: Open View

- Siemens: development of TRANSDATA management

- Other management schemes of other companies

- Decisive medium-term developments

In Chapters 3 and 4, we described classical network management in IBM, DEC and Siemens, together with IBM's view of the future. Each of these structural approaches is based on a proprietary network-architecture strategy. The management of open systems in a heterogeneous environment, as described in Chapter 5, thus has at best a secondary role.

Currently, all manufacturers offer their clients the perspective of OSI communication. Here, the reality is very different for each manufacturer. When one speaks today of open communications, one should not neglect the TCP/IP suite which, despite conceptual deficiencies, in many cases now leads to satisfactory communications solutions in heterogeneous environments, where other approaches have scarcely made an impression.

In this chapter, we shall describe the schemes of AT&T, DEC, HP and Siemens as examples of the most important approaches to integrated management. Because of the introductory nature of this book, it is not our intention in this chapter to provide a full list of existing products for these strategies or to compare these products. Instead, we wish to provide the reader with an impression of the conceptual range of these products even for his environment. Thus, the discussions of the individual strategies are preceded by a brief introduction, which shows how one may go about constructing an integrated network management system.

At the end of the chapter there is a short overview of the management 'standards' of other companies.

From past experience, it should be clear that, if possible, we should not again make the mistake of choosing manufacturer-linked proprietary management architectures, as was done initially in the case of communications architectures; instead, comprehensive concepts should be developed. The current choice of alternatives is not very wide and is restricted to the really large manufacturers. However, the author is firmly convinced that amongst the few alternatives there will still be a market shake-out when we move from strategies to the product arena.

AT&T is attempting to build a network management based on the guidelines of the ISO/OSI reference model. On the other hand, AT&T knows that large SNA networks will also exist for a long time. Thus, AT&T intends to interlink SNA network management and OSI network management.

In Chapter 4, we briefly discussed network management in existing DECnet Phase III and Phase IV systems. DECnet is currently being extensively converted to an architecture and protocols following the guidelines of the ISO reference model and international standards; however, considerable attention is also being paid to the TCP/IP suite. Consequently, here too there is also a new strategy for the network management. Section 7.3 describes this strategy, EMA. EMA is decentralized. This contradicts the strong hierarchical view of other management strategies such as NetView.

HP's Open View is the approach which takes greatest account of the findings of modern software development of complicated systems. Its graduated model provides a conceptual basis for the creation of integrated and flexible network management.

In Germany, for Siemens (now SNI), as for IBM, the main problem is the installed base. A network management strategy must take account of these existing environments. On the other hand, the clients (who are mainly in the public sector) are demanding access to international standards for which Siemens strove very early on. A two-track procedure has been adopted for network management in imitation of the procedure whereby one constructs a protocol stack in accordance with international standards, in addition to the in-house stack for communications protocols, and then gradually removes the in-house protocols when possible. This procedure also provides for integration in the UNIX-based management workstation.

No importance should be attached to the order in which we discuss the concepts: it is purely alphabetical. For the benefit of the reader, all the concepts are, as far as possible, introduced against a uniform plan.

7.1 The structure of integrated multivendor network architectures

It is useful to prefix the discussion of the strategies of the various manufacturers with a consideration of the facilities which are generally provided. This section is based on the description in (Herman, 1990) which is particularly appropriate.

Most networks in companies and organizations today consist of a relatively heterogeneous collection of components from various manufacturers, where every manufacturer would like to feel that his own network management system is used and preferred. This tendency towards heterogeneity is considerably more widespread in the USA than in Germany, but with the spread of LANs we shall soon reach a similar position.

The interface between a device or software in the network and the management system is often called the manager–agent interface; this is because for each device or software suite involved there is an agent that collects information for the management and executes management commands (we have already seen this for SNMP). Management information flows in both directions across this interface. For a manager to work with an agent both must implement the same management information protocol and agree on a particular presentation of the management information to be carried under this protocol in the form of data. This agreement over syntax (the protocol) and semantics (the data definitions) must be adhered to before a management system can work with a particular device.

In the case of SNMP, SNMP is the protocol and the structure of the data is specified by the SMI specifications. In OSI, CMIS and CMIP are the protocols and the structure of the data is taken from the OSI SMI for the managed objects.

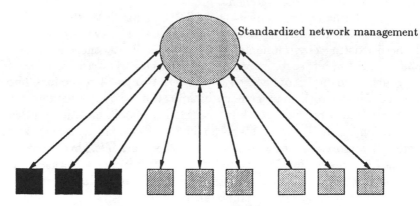

Devices and services from various manufacturers

Figure 7.1   Multivendor management.

Today, however, manufacturer-specific management systems must usually be used since there is no widespread industry standard for management protocols and the data presentation. Thus, all manufacturers have developed their own management systems which are quite often device or subnetwork specific. Here, one thinks, for example, of IBM where there are managers for SNA connections, for local area networks and for ESCON connections and these managers are not integrated in any way whatsoever.

There are four basic approaches to integrated management:

- A universal interface to a standardized manager directly from all devices or subnetworks (Figure 7.1).

- An integrated manager (general manager) with a uniform interface to element managers, which themselves possess standardized or specific interfaces to the network elements (Figure 7.2).

- A management network in which the element managers are linked amongst themselves and not to one but to several integrated managers (Figure 7.3).

- The platform approach, in which the network elements use various protocols to access a multivendor network-manager platform, which itself provides a universal *Application Program Interface* (API), on which standardized and manufacturer-specific network-management applications can run (possibly from different manufacturers who have nothing to do with the network elements) (Figure 7.4).

The first alternative with the universal interface requires a truly-uniform network-management standard. If every system in the network

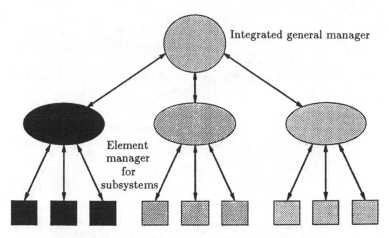

Devices and services from various manufacturers

Figure 7.2   Multivendor management (general manager).

supported protocols and data structures based on this standard, a uniform general manager could be used. But, currently, because of the powerful installed base, this approach is unrealistic. It would take decades to replace all devices to the extent that they could conform to a new uniform standard, even if one started now.

This will scarcely happen since manufacturers such as IBM appear to have decided to continue to use their own existing management interfaces for monitoring and controlling their own products. In the meantime, however, there are a number of standards for IEEE LANs, TCP/IP internetworks, OSI networks and UNIX systems but only in a few subareas. For example there is a common standard for TCP/IP, namely SNMP (see Chapter 6), which is generally accepted and which permits the implementation of powerful manufacturer-independent network managers, even for the broad area of bridges, routers and gateways. Questions arise as to whether the current SNMP euphoria will be stable in the long-term and whether the goal of including extended environments such as Token Ring networks will be reached.

In the short term, the general manager seems to be the faster way to success since this requires only relatively few standardized interfaces linking the element managers with the integrated general manager. Because of their modular software design, current element managers are easy to equip with such interfaces. Moreover, the element managers filter out important details for the general manager and carry out element-specific tasks on their own. In the previous scheme, the standardized manager suddenly had to take

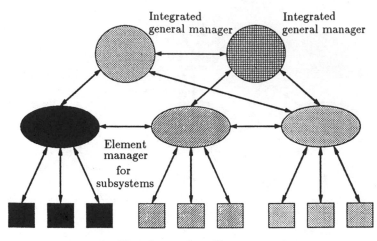

Figure 7.3   Multivendor management (network management).

on all the fine control tasks. The installed base of network elements may remain untouched. OSI CMIS/CMIP is a candidate interface.

The OSI network-management-framework approach goes a step further; it aims for a flexible management network. From the practical point of view, this is clearly the most robust approach, since breakdown of the standardized manager or the general manager could sooner or later have far-reaching consequences for the network. However, the breakdown of a component in the management network has less extensive consequences. A hierarchically organized management network of this type with no self-imposed restrictions could lead to unnecessary growth of the management installations, more expensive and more unnecessary redundancy than desired and even arguments over competence. It is likely that the management network will increase the number of network management installations rather than decrease it.

The platform approach offers a real possibility for reducing the number of management systems. A management platform forms a standardized environment for the implementation of network and system management applications. The management platform defines a set of open application program interfaces which will be published, thus allowing many suppliers, software developers and indeed companies and organizations to generate high-quality, modern management software without having to struggle with the details of management protocols, management data definitions or complicated peculiarities of the user interfaces. The platform supplier will (hopefully) implement a set of tools and services to take over

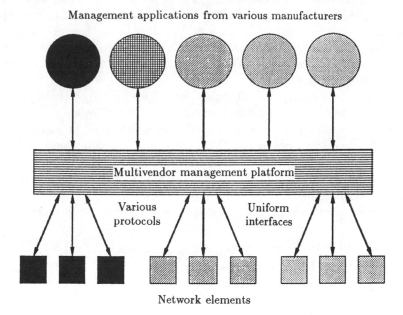

Figure 7.4   Multivendor management (platform strategy).

these functions. At the present time, the leading proposals for management platforms (such as DEC's EMΛ) want to implement different standardized and non-standardized management protocols to reduce the need to alter existing network elements.

7.2 AT&T: Unified Network Management Architecture

The *Unified Network Management Architecture* (UNMA) is AT&T's strategy for the integrated network management of voice and data networks in a heterogeneous environment. The objectives of UNMA go beyond those of NetView and also beyond those of ISO: basically, NetView wants a relatively-homogeneous data network and ISO a heterogeneous data network. AT&T on the other hand, is convinced that voice networks or better-integrated voice and data networks will contribute extensively to information processing.

UNMA is a three-tier architecture which follows the ISO management framework, insofar as this is defined and stable. The core component of UNMA, which was announced at the end of January 1990, is the ACCUMASTER Integrator. The Integrator should be assigned to the management of the physical network rather than to the management of the logical links. In its first implementation it uses terminal emulation to permit access (possibly for other products) to logical management components such as NetView or Net/Master.

For the future, AT&T also envisages a large base of SNA installations, but hopes that, for example, DEC and all other manufacturers will move in the direction of OSI. Furthermore, it cannot be ruled out that IBM will take other steps in the OSI direction and shape the management to be more compatible with the OSI framework.

Both NetView and UNMA allow the user to observe the physical and logical aspects of the network separately.

There are three basic structural areas for the network management:

- the end user area;
- the area of local data exchange;
- the remote-network area.

SNA and other management schemes usually stop shortly before the remote networks, the control of which they leave to higher-ranking logical components. On the other hand, according to US analysis, UNMA in its first form is straightaway a tool with which to control the remote network area. However, this is of secondary interest to the European market. In the US, AT&T is drawing on its own experiences as a provider of network services. However, these experiences are only very hypothetically transferable.

Before we go into the details, let us look first at the development of the strategy

7.2.1 The development of UNMA

Regardless of the academic consideration of the conceptual approach, the question is WHEN? UNMA depends on the progress of the international standardization. Five more years will pass before the network management, with all the trimmings such as data protection, is well-defined and stable, since, as we know from other standards, stability can only be attained after a product test phase. It will then be perhaps 2–5 years before the major manufacturers can provide corresponding implementations. The SNA users can scarcely wait so long and will install NetView or refinements of it in large numbers. Thus, the general importance of UNMA, despite all conceptual preferences, should not be overestimated.

For the US, the following assumption about the future is being made: the greatest pressure as far as OSI is concerned will come not from private companies but from the US government, via the GOSIP activities. For its part, GOSIP is independent of the ISO/OSI position. However, if this situation arises, it could well be that AT&T will have an appropriate offering to market, while, so far as is known, IBM is not preparing anything. But, even with IBM we can no longer be sure that there will be no major surprises *à la* AIX TCF, if only client pressure matters.

The development of UNMA since its announcement can be briefly summarized. The end phase of the preparatory work for UNMA can be dated back to 1987. At that time, AT&T already wanted to achieve a very strong OSI orientation. Unfortunately, most OSI management standards were still stuck in their infancy, as we saw in Chapter 5. In order to proceed with UNMA, AT&T then froze a certain subset of the existing standards which it called the *Network Management Protocol* (NMP).

In January 1989, the ACCUMASTER Integrator was announced. This was the first product to be based on achievement of the integration objectives of OSI. Based on AT&T's 3B system and using Sun workstations, it implemented a graphical surface, an integrated relational-database system and real-time connections into the AT&T network. The use of an expert system to correlate alarms was an interesting experiment. It is already clear that the Integrator is only of limited applicability as far as Germany is concerned since connections to the AT&T network are less widespread. One important aspect for AT&T was the strategic alliance with Cincom to create the connection to the SNA management. However, this connection is only really sensible if Net/Master is used in the host environment instead of NetView. Because of the general inertia of NetView it was easy for AT&T to insist on the implementation of a superset of the NetView functions.

In 1990, the Integrator base was supplemented by further NMP connections to important networks such as T1 networks or AT&T client networks. AT&T always places connection to its clients in the foreground. The network-management forum strengthened AT&T's position further. For example, UNISYS announced that it would not develop its own network management strategy but would adapt UNMA and the integrator. Over the next two years the NMP specifications will certainly be in line with the state of developments.

7.2.2 The structure of UNMA

UNMA has a three-tier structure (Figure 7.5). Tier 1 consists of the network elements, the customer premise equipment such as modems, multiplexers, LANs, hosts and PBXs or other networks in the local or remote area (Local Exchange Carrier (LEC) networks, interexchange services, PTT or international services). Here, one sees particularly clearly that UNMA has developed from the spectrum of AT&T's US network facilities. Scarcely anyone in Europe can imagine that there could be an extra LEC between LANs and public networks.

Tier 2 consists of the Element Management Systems (EMSs), which,

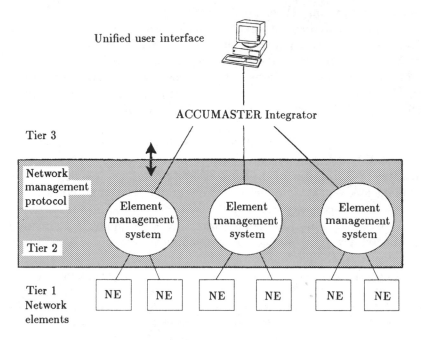

Figure 7.5 AT&T's UNMA: the three-tier architecture .

as their name suggests, manage network elements. An EMS implements local network management capabilities, in particular for operations, management and maintenance and provides functions to be used from tier 3. Today, the existing networks contain a number of EMSs which are a result of the various manufacturer-linked network architectures. In a large user network one may even find different components for controlling a group of systems such as LANs. Today, every EMS works away on its own. This prevents the administrator from obtaining a unified end-to-end-oriented perspective of the network.

Tier 3 is designed to provide the desired complete end-to-end perspective, by communication between the EMSs and the Integrator (the core of UNMA). The Integrator communicates with the EMSs via a common protocol stack. This stack, called NMP (*Network Management Protocol*), is AT&T's implementation of the 1988 OSI management specifications. Integrator systems themselves also communicate via this protocol stack. The communication between tier-3 and tier-2 elements is essentially carried out via NMP. Tier-2 elements may communicate with their subordinate tier-1 elements via their own local protocols, insofar as these are suitable. A standardized communication at this level is not currently provided for, but could be developed in the future.

The ACCUMASTER Integrator allows complete access to the EMSs. Thus, it may be placed below, for example, NetView. Another tier-3 element is the unified user interface which is intended to generate a logical overall picture of the network or the subnetwork. In the ACCUMASTER Integrator product, this is implemented by a Sun graphics workstation.

AT&T has published several documents on NMP, which should permit other manufacturers to extend their EMS products for linkage to the Integrator. It is presumed that the current NMP is the implementation which is heading towards the next OSI management standard.

NMP is based on the seven-layer OSI model and is implemented on layers 4–7. This makes NMP independent of changes in layers 1–3. NMP itself will probably have to be modified several times in due course, since it is based on proposals for standards that are not yet ready.

AT&T divides its application-layer services into two classes: transaction services and file transfer services. Simple transaction services are based on CMIS, ROSE and ACSE (see Chapter 5). Extended transaction services use additional synchronization mechanisms (two phase commit, chaining) from CCR. The file transfer services need ACSE and FTAM. These individual elements are described, for example, in (Beyschlag, 1988).

In addition to implementing NMP over layers 4–7, AT&T has published application message sets for configuration and error management, to which we shall return. These two functional areas are somewhat further advanced in the standardization than the others.

7.2.3 UNMA and the network management problem area

The main problem areas of network management have been described in all the previous chapters. UNMA defines nine functional areas which are correlated with the problem areas. The first five are also covered by the OSI proposals:

- Error management
- Configuration management
- Performance management
- Accounting management
- Security management
- Planning
- Operations support
- Programmability

- Integrated control

The last four areas clearly show that practice is being take into account here.

The eventual goal of error management is to guarantee a tolerable level of network availability. In particular, this includes fast error detection and problem delimiting. The ACCUMASTER correlates alarms from various systems in order to isolate the event which activated them. UNMA provides for the full recording of all events, alarms and reactions.

The configuration management is intended to help change the network configurations as a result of changed requirements or problem isolation. For this, the systems must collect information about the state of the network and indicate changes. The UNMA definition of this functional area has four aspects: network inventory management; change management; name management and current connections. Inventory management keeps a record of all devices, systems and services in the network. Change management records the removal of telephones, modems, terminals, circuits and other network components. Name management is the basis for the network directory and the current connections are relations between logical and physical components of the network.

The foremost task of performance management is to isolate problem areas before errors occur. For this, network-operation performance data must be continually obtained and suitably processed. The advantage of UNMA is that very different systems may be observed. Moreover, UNMA allows user-definable performance measures and thresholds. UNMA provides running performance data and also performance data from the recent past, which the user may use to analyze performance trends in the network.

Accounting management is intended to provide for the correct distribution of the costs to those responsible for them. In particular, UNMA allows the user to compare different bills from different network service providers with actual services.

Security management includes access control, authorization facilities, partitioning of the logical network, key management and encryption, together with security logging. UNMA records all logons and logon violations so as to prevent unauthorized access to the network. There are also different access levels. Network administrators may run the network centrally and also, following a partitioning, from various control centres.

Network planning is another very important area which is not covered by the OSI efforts; however, that is not tragic! The planning process includes first and foremost the construction of the model of the network and the analytical evaluation of the effects of possible changes. Results from performance management must also be brought into this. UNMA distinguishes between three areas: capacity planning, contingency planning and strategic planning.

As far as operations support for the network management centre is concerned, UNMA includes four areas:

- The creation of cycles in the network management centre (for example, recording of errors, specification of maintenance work, etc.).
- Analysis of the work of the centre and of the information flow within it.
- Analysis of the personnel situation in the centre.
- Preparation of the user-training and the development plans.

The programmability must be adaptable to the network management entities of the client installation since no two large installations are the same. UNMA provides parameterizable systems and services and other user-oriented options in many areas. UNMA supports C.

The objective of integrated control is to form a single virtual network from the many individual components and the various subnetworks, even though these subnetworks may now have different management systems. The Integrator is the UNMA tool for this.

The nine functional areas outlined form a good benchmark for the evaluation of network management schemes and systems. Here, UNMA goes far beyond ISO/OSI and IBM's CNM. If it succeeds in attracting a sufficient number of other manufacturers to this scheme in good time, and if at the same time the objectives are met with products, then UNMA is certainly an important scheme.

7.2.4 UNMA products and services

UNMA is an overall strategy and involves products for network end clients, for network management on the client side and for the network service providers.

The ACCUMASTER Integrator is a product for the client area. It is a UNIX system and runs on an AT&T 3B2/600. Implementations for other machines are planned. It also includes a Sun workstation for coloured representations of the network. There are two basic functional areas: alarm integration and correlation, and configuration management. The alarm correlation compares alarms received by the Integrator, determines the most likely causes of the alarms and suppresses secondary alarms. The Integrator uses device profiles (stored in an Informix database,) together with its own correlation logic. Operators may also help to isolate problems more rapidly. On the other hand, this feature is not infallible, since there is a small probability that the actual problem point may be ignored (Figure 7.6).

The Integrator extracts logical network information, for example, from the UNMA application and combines it with physical network data which it obtains via NMP interfaces.

The UNMA software application developed by Cincom resides in the

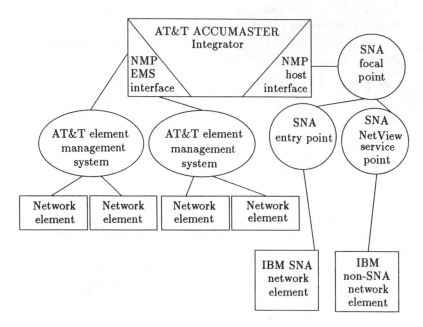

Figure 7.6 Integrator: relationships between UNMA and SNA.

IBM host and enables the ACCUMASTER Integrator to interwork with either NetView or Net/Master. The application supports the extraction of logical information from the IBM system by SNA clients and its delivery to the SNA management application in the ACCUMASTER Integrator. Of course, the same also holds for other logically-based management systems. Net/Master Advanced Network is a prerequisite for the use of the UNMA application. The two together are prerequisites for the use of the Integrator and cost over £33 000. A typical Integrator configuration for the management of various systems costs well over £170 000.

NetPartner NMS is a product for the carriers of LEC networks. It was mainly designed for Centrex clients; thus, we shall not discuss it further here.

Other products are targeted towards the establishment of network management centres, whose services may be rented.

7.2.5 Market perspectives for UNMA

AT&T has published details of UNMA and NMP in various documents. Without going into these proposals and implementations in more detail, we note that, from experience, the OSI communication standards leave much scope for interpretation. This means that, for example, AT&T's implementation and other implementations of the same elements (for example, by DEC within EMA) will not necessarily interwork immediately, without problems.

Thus, AT&T must campaign for interworking. For, in the future, other OSI-based approaches will also play a considerable role. At the moment, things look bleak for the general support of the NMP, since many of the software houses concerned, and other manufacturers, lack the capacity to follow different approaches.

AT&T is therefore at pains to take on as active a role as possible in relevant forums and meetings. The OSI/Network Management Forum was founded in 1988 by AT&T, HP, Unisys, Amdahl, British Telecom, Northern Telecom, Telecom Canada and STC PLC; it now has over sixty members, although in May 1989, these did not include IBM and DEC. The main aims of the forum are to drive forward the standardization process and to ensure the interoperability of products. For the next step, object definitions are planned. AT&T will, if necessary, modify NMP according to the views of the forum.

In the meantime, DEC is continuing to work on EMA, and is trying to find as many supporters for its architecture as possible. EMA uses a flexible directory-entity approach, which supports several directors (DEC's network management systems) to manage entities in network domains. Here, EMA specifies an OSI-based standard format for the data exchange between directors. At present, DEC does not foresee any interworking between the directors and the Integrator.

The forum, as one might have expected, has been criticized by various parties and the whole theatre is highly reminiscent of the various groupings at the time of UNIX standardization.

It is also presumed that IBM will not support AT&T directly.

7.2.6 Criticisms of UNMA

Here we give a brief summary of the main criticisms of UNMA.

Firstly, we must see UNMA's importance to the European market in relative terms. AT&T developed UNMA not least in order to provide clients with ready-made tools which would enable them to improve cooperation with third-party and public AT&T networks and to provide better services themselves. Thus, the first wave of network products is strongly oriented towards such networks and scarcely applicable to local conditions. To say that the monopolist Telecom might one day provide something to improve the clients' management facilities would be pure speculation. Should this occur (against all expectations) it will tend less towards UNMA. AT&T's distribution is small and value-added networks, such as MEGANET, are also specific to certain user groups or scarcely represented.

Currently, UNMA is the strategy which is truest to OSI. This may have a positive effect in the future, but may go wrong in the medium term if, for example, users choose SNMP management even as an interim solution. At the moment, the OSI orientation limits the number of element managers implemented, but this may change suddenly.

The main conceptual limitation is the purely-centralized approach. For example, the current implementation does not allow any additional (for example, regional) Integrators which could be used for local backup proposes. NetView has had this facility for a long time. While the software is modular it does not use any distributed operating system formulations such as remote procedure call or the like, which play a central role with HP, DEC and Sun. That is also why the purely-central approach cannot be overcome so quickly.

Installed on a 3B the Integrator can only be used economically for large networks. A version which only runs on Suns has been announced but not yet seen. The Integrator is provided with its full functionality by AT&T and there are no facilities for third-party software houses to introduce management-function modules in the highest tier. AT&T does not intend to provide open APIs. One exception is the access to the database system.

With the restriction to OSI, the specification of the construction of a general manager, as shown in Figure 7.2, the rejection of the platform approach and the link with Cincom, AT&T is imposing limitations on the scope of its strategy. These may lead to acceptance problems.

Next we come to EMA, the new strategy of Digital Equipment.

7.3 DEC: Enterprise Management Architecture

The *Enterprise Management Architecture* (EMA) is DEC's strategic plan for integrated network, system and application management. Even in DECnet Phase IV, the terms system, network and application were more tightly interwoven than, for example, with IBM. This is largely because DECnet was primarily designed for the cooperation between DEC computers, whilst the control of units was only a secondary aim. Thus, the development of EMA is very different to that of SNA. It is also understandable that DECnet and the *Digital Network Architecture* (DNA) are better suited to OSI, since here too the communication between (heterogeneous) systems based on application-oriented basic services come to the fore.

EMA may be used to control networks with a hierarchical or a horizontal organization. In practice, a mixture will often occur.

EMA contains an implementation of the OSI management standard protocol, CMIP, for information exchange between network management entities, which facilitates the communication between EMA components and foreign components.

Thus, EMA has a better OSI linkage than NetView and is more flexible than AT&T's UNMA.

7.3.1 The development of EMA

EMA was introduced at the end of 1988 and was DEC's first step towards the integration of many existing network management products. Thus, DEC was the last main applicant to introduce a network management architecture. The reason for this was that a plan to convert the installed networked base (approximately 200 000 computers) from DECnet to OSI was proposed at the same time.

DEC is the first firm to describe a distributed architecture for network and system management. EMA uses advanced architectural models for name service, distributed identification assignment, distributed timing service and remote procedure calls. It is also, functionally and structurally, strongly related to HP's Open View.

The first EMA product, DECmcc was introduced in mid-1990, its version 1.1 was announced for the first half of 1991. The acceptance of EMA, for example, by small network-equipment suppliers and public suppliers in the US, can be termed to be good. DEC is working for linkage with SNA in cooperation with the new 'owner' of the Net/Master product, Systems Center. Although Systems Center will certainly make considerable extensions to the Net/Master platform, as in the case of AT&T's UNMA, here too we note a limitation in the SNA area.

7.3.2 The structure of EMA

EMA has a decentralized organization (Figure 7.7). The basic elements may be implemented on various computers and in many cases the implementation of a single basic element may be distributed across several systems. This flexibility mainly takes account of the fact that companies and organizations are increasingly installing computers with very different classes of performance, from PCs to hosts. EMA is based on a model with entities which are managed and directors which manage. The set of directors has a role comparatively similar to that in NetView, although it is implemented in a totally different way.

An entity consists of two parts: the managed object (for example, a modem, a communication path, etc.) and its agent, the management software for the object to be managed. The agent may have a certain level of local management capability. Primarily, however, it is an executive organ for management operations. The management operations are divided into events and directives. According to the EMA guidelines, agents and target objects need not be implemented in the same system. Thus, the agent may communicate with its target object over an almost arbitrary communication path, using an appropriate protocol. The only important thing is that

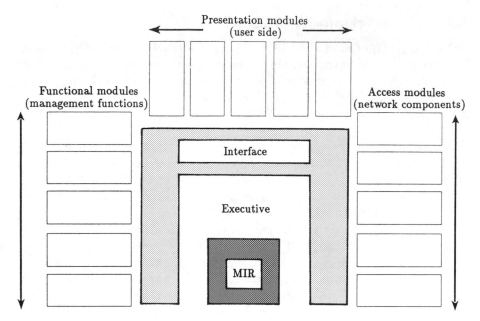

Figure 7.7   DEC: basic structure of EMA.

the director to which the agent is subordinate also receives the corresponding information.

The director is a software system which functions as an interface between users and the managed entities and systems. The director consists of five components:

- the Executive;
- the Management Information Repository (MIR);
- and three types of management modules:
    - presentation modules,
    - functional modules, and
    - access modules.

While an entity refers more to a specific resource (from the modem to the DECnet node), a director is more a logical concept based on a set of software components which may be (but need not be) implemented in a physical node.

7.3.2.1 The executive

The executive, the core of EMA, is a major DEC control program with various routines supporting standard interfaces which coordinate the work of the management module. These supporting routines are implemented by a remote procedure call. This is basically a critical feature, since EMA permits peer-to-peer communication between many distributed directors. A director may retrieve information from another director's access module or use functions of another director's functional module. Thus, a director may use objects which are implemented at remote points. The executive's communications support for intermodule communication is a tool which is often used to implement the desired flexibility of the EMA design. The executive uses a distribution mechanism to support the intermodule communication. It determines the target procedure, passes control to the target procedure and returns the response to the source procedure.

The executive generates and maintains information in the MIR.

7.3.2.2 Management modules

Management modules are the extension entities of a directory. These entities should be able to interwork without specific, pre-defined knowledge of one another. The executive controls the intermodule communication as described above.

Presentation modules   Presentation modules are the user interface for EMA directors. A presentation module may be written so that it supports a certain console type, a certain application or even communication with non-EMA components. A director may have several presentation modules. The advantage of this construction lies mainly in the fact that the support for external units and objects is independent of the entities which are managed. This also makes (for example) the ability to adapt to the user or the further processing of management information (possibly with the assistance of AI) dynamic.

DEC is to define a basic set of presentation modules. The publication of the interfaces and the definitions is awaited, since this will enable the creation of other corresponding modules.

Functional modules   The functional modules cover the five functional areas prescribed by the OSI management standard: configuration, error, performance, accounting and security management. However, EMA allows a module to execute more than one function. Strictly speaking, this is not provided for in the OSI management standard. On the other hand, this is understandable, since in the past the OSI bodies have been deeply engaged in drawing up clear lines of separation between the functional areas. This flexibility also prepares EMA for the future. To wit, it is not impossible to design a functional model which uses an expert system to correlate information from several OSI functional areas. Functional models may be written by DEC, by users or by third parties.

Access modules   Access modules communicate directly with typical communications components such as PBXs, multiplexers, modems, LAN bridges and logical components in the network, such as systems and applications. They use specific protocols for this and at the same time permit the director to remain protocol independent. Access modules are functionally comparable with the programs which third parties must write in order to be able to communicate with NetView/PC. However, there are some fundamental positive differences. Access models convert device- and system-specific information into a data format which can be interpreted both by directors and by other management modules. They thus permit the bidirectional interchange of information between devices and directors. The reverse flow was first promised for NetView/PC Rel. 2.

When an access module is attached to an EMA director, it must be registered. During the registration process, the access module must tell the director what it wishes to manage and how. It notifies the director of the object classes which it wishes to manage and the management operations which will be supported for these objects. In addition, the access module must supply the MIR with data for use by the other modules.

Access modules may be designed both by DEC and by third parties. DEC recommends the use of CMIP for the communication with the director, but this is not mandatory. Access modules are EMA's tool for controlling heterogeneous multivendor networks. The use of CMIP will help to attain this goal. With the first release, DEC itself will probably provide products to manage DEC devices based on access modules (Figure 7.8).

7.3.2.3 Management Information Repository

The *Management Information Repository* (MIR) is an object-oriented configuration database for information about network entities and management activities. According to DEC, it is independent of any specific implementation and any specific DBMS. This is very different from NetView for which VSAM is a prerequisite and from ACCUMASTER Integrator, which uses an Informix database.

The above mechanism (described for access modules) for registration with the director also applies to the other classes of modules and is mainly used to fill up the MIR. Modules may access the MIR using the executive's distribution mechanism. Four types of data are stored in the MIR, where the first three types correspond to groups of data in the OSI MIB and the fourth is local to individual management modules.

Class data assigns network installations and devices which are to be managed to coherent classes. Examples of such classes include bridges,

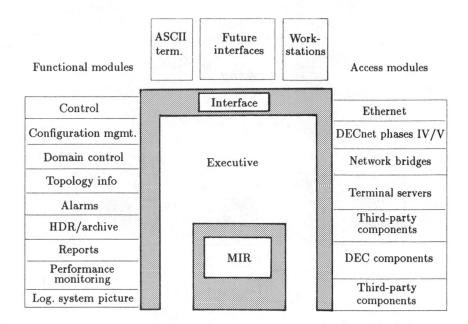

Figure 7.8   Overview of DEC EMA.

terminal services, T1 processors, DBMSs, etc. The database's relational structure naturally also permits searches for objects using criteria such as the executable management operations.

Instance data is configuration data, such as network addresses, node names, disk controllers etc., which lies in the area controlled by a director.

Attribute data is the management information relating to entities to be managed, which is received and stored over the course of time. It is usually made available by the access modules which obtain the information either by polling or from event signals (for example, in case of error).

Private data includes all particular information belonging to a certain management module. There are no special structural recommendations for this.

7.3.3 Problem areas and management domains

In EMA, DEC has taken a view of domains which is somewhat different from the usual concept. In EMA, a management domain is a 'user-specified sphere of interest in network management and control'. This sphere of interest includes at least a director, network components and entities which serve a

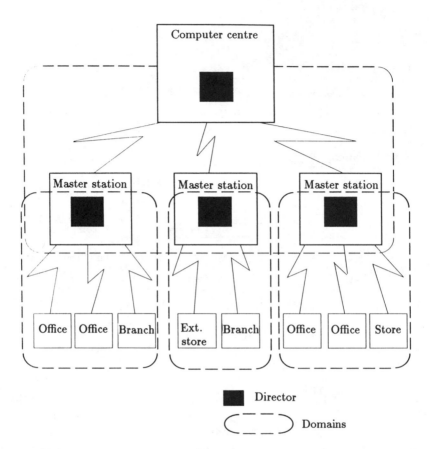

Figure 7.9 EMA domains.

common purpose (Figure 7.9). This purpose is completely arbitrary and is only specified by the user. At this point, the reader will have in mind the IBM concept of a domain, where the purpose of the domain is determined solely by IBM. Moreover, the IBM SNA domain refers strictly to an SSCP which must be fully implemented in a single host. The director on the other hand may be spread across several machines.

The definition of EMA domains is based on global entities. A global entity is any component of the network which has a unique name or a unique address. There is no class above these global entities, which represent the highest level of addressable units in EMA. However, domains may themselves be graduated, so that global entities of a subordinate domain may form a relative subclass.

Domains may be selected in accordance with the following criteria:

- *Functions* Grouping of network and management components according to their functions, for example, performance, error, configuration, security or accounting management.

- *Organizational structure* Grouping of network components according to the organizational units which they use, for example, computer centre, master station, branches.

- *Technology* Grouping of components according to technological criteria.

- *Geography* Grouping of components according to geographical criteria.

A domain may contain other domains, refer to other domains, overlap other domains and share data with other domains (for security reasons, this last possibility is in practice often very limited). EMA does not provide rules for forming domains. In fact, there are a number of practical restrictions on the size of a domain, the volume of network-management traffic which it may handle and the size of the MIR used by the domain.

7.3.4 Products and services: from DECnet to EMA

In Chapter 4, we summarized the features and facilities of DECnet Phases III and IV, together with the most important network-management aspects. For almost a decade, since the beginning of DECnet Phase III, DEC has also developed wide-ranging products for network management, for example, products for the VMS operating system which provide for trouble-free use of X.25 connections. The software produced for DECnet always resides in individual nodes, even if it can be used by other nodes.

DEC has announced that it is to use existing products as a basis for a migration path between Phase IV and EMA. DECnet already has a layer model which looks similar to the OSI management framework. In layer 7, DEC defines a network-management sublayer which uses the NICE protocol for tests, downline loading and upline dumping. Most of the management functions executed by DECnet nodes are concentrated in the network-management sublayer, only a few remain in other layers, for example, the Digital Data Communications Message Protocol (DDCMP).

NICE is published and does much the same as OSI's CMIP. DEC will presumably replace NICE by CMIP in DECnet/OSI Phase V.

In addition to the integrated network management components, DEC also has a number of 'free items' such as the remote bridge management software, Ethernim, terminal-server managers, remote-system managers, LAN traffic monitors and the network management control centre/DECnet monitor.

Nevertheless, two important elements were missing before EMA: DEC itself provided no assistance to the control of non-DEC components (in the sense of event messages, observations, etc.) and no other important manager supported DEC's NICE protocol.

EMA incorporates DEC's strategy for an integrated network management and a bridge to other manufacturers. EMA is an ambitious plan.

7.3.5 EMA: market perspectives

EMA incorporates three design objectives:

- Distributed processing, including for network management.
- Open interfaces, by publication.
- Support for third-party control software.

Thus, EMA follows a completely different path to the IBM strategy and is also more open than AT&T's scheme. The consistent use of the platform approach offers the best prospects for the future. There are strategic alliances, mostly with PBX manufacturers (Siemens, Telecom Services Bureau Int.) or suppliers of public carriers (DCA/Cohesive, Stratacom, Timeplex).

We shall have to wait for the first products to see how far these objectives are implemented in practice. In any case, there will be considerable discussion outside of the IBM community as to which management concept (EMA, UNMA or Open View) should now be followed.

The many existing contented DECnet users form a stable client base and at the same time guarantee the completion of Phase V/EMA.

In the opinion of many experts, DEC currently has the most advanced and most carefully-developed approach to integrated network management. This has taken longer than with other manufacturers, thus there are also fewer compromises. DEC has basically created a network management 'operating system', which can be supplemented with network management application modules, network management user interfaces and practically any interfaces to controlled units, subnetworks or software. In addition to the OSI protocols, the TCP/IP suite is also supported with an SNMP connection module.

7.3.6 Criticisms of EMA

These may be briefly summarized. In order to achieve a high degree of functionality and scaleability, DEC has dug deeply into its own product range. The DEC EMA director currently only runs with the VMS operating system on corresponding computers. IBM largely uses its own technology but before the announcement of System View did not want to sell this openly. Thus, DEC must try to free itself from the proprietary stigma. The director is next to be implemented to run with ULTRIX, DEC's own version of UNIX. DEC may appeal to the fact that there are currently no standardized application-program interfaces for many functions which EMA needs or provides.

7.4 Hewlett-Packard: Open View

The manufacturers of information-processing equipment believe it is important to provide their clients with a strategic broad outline of future developments. In addition to IBM, Siemens, and DEC, HP is also a manufacturer whose client base expects such a broad outline. For the future, HP also sensibly sees a coexistence of existing *de facto* standards for network management, with management facilities based on the guidelines of the OSI management framework.

HP's network-management architecture is called Open View. HP has developed two interesting models as part of its Open View concept, namely the organizational model and the operational model. These models represent an abstract view of management at a high level and may be viewed as a broad outline of the development of network management products. The first Open View products were very well received by the experts.

The organizational model is intended to help the designers to identify management functions and their interrelationships. On the other hand, the operational model provides ample details to support data-flow and coexistence analysis. Both models support graded degrees of integration of various systems within a common network-management architecture.

Like EMA, and unlike NetView and SNMP, Open View has a decentralized organization. Like EMA, it incorporates a large number of different functional utilities and management tools, including various user interfaces. Open View is oriented towards international and industry standards and is flexible in its physical implementation.

7.4.1 The development of Open View

With its announcement of Open View in 1988, HP breathed new life into the scene and came straight into conflict with IBM (then still NMA) and AT&T as to which strategy was best. HP was the first company to introduce a platform approach, believing that clients now use different protocol stacks and will also want these in the future. Moreover, HP also criticized the fact that management standards such as OSI had until then been concerned with the exchange of information between management facilities and scarcely considered the function of these facilities.

In order to be able to show something, a DOS-based service called

Open View Windows for a graphical user interface was introduced, which could be linked with other applications using a published application-program interface. The main aim of the Open View strategy is that third-party manufacturers should be able to write network management modules for the Open View environment and incorporate them in that environment.

The success of the DOS version was limited, disregarding the fact that all other manufacturers felt obliged not to come up with major new ideas for the user interface. In 1990, a substantially-extended and more powerful version based on the UNIX operating system was introduced which found the necessary acceptance (see Figure 7.10).

At the end of 1990 came the first real proof that Open View is indeed an open concept in every sense, namely its porting to a Sun workstation and the announcement that Open View would be made available for other systems if the market required it. If one thinks of a system /6000, this could be unpleasant for IBM, for then Open View would be, so-to-speak, a movable platform which could also be used in non-host-oriented environments.

HP is not committing itself to any specific protocol stacks: it is already delivering solutions for TCP/IP with the Open View platform and has announced OSI for when the standards are stable.

7.4.2 The structure of Open View

As previously mentioned, Open View is a strategic platform approach. The UNIX version has the following four main components:

- Presentation services
- Database management
- Distributed communications infrastructure
- Communications protocols

The presentation services contain the Open View windows applications and the OSF/Motif window user interface for other management applications. The database management includes database- and result-management services. OSI and TCP/IP are preferred as communications protocols. There are no constructive reasons for ruling out other protocols.

The *Distributed Communications Infrastructure* (DCI) now provides application program interfaces (APIs), via which network management application programs may use the other three components. As the name suggests, it is also possible to use networks without having to provide the management applications with knowledge about these networks. Interworking of different management applications, independently of their locations, is also possible using the DCI. Thus, management functions may be flexibly distributed to management servers.

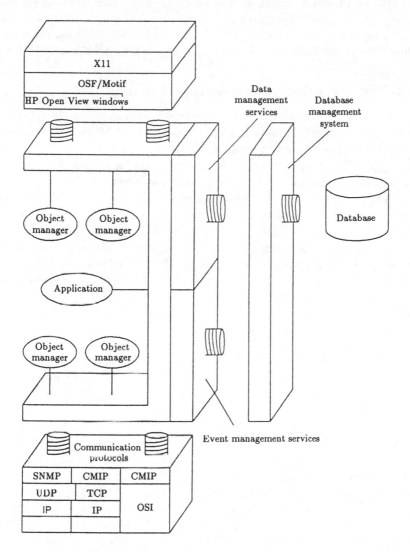

Figure 7.10   HP Open View network management server.

Another important feature of the Open View architecture is the use of object-oriented programming techniques. As proposed by OSI, network elements are described as objects even when they are not managed by OSI protocols. In order to send and receive management data, modules termed object managers transport the objects between the object-oriented procedures, regardless of the physical path actually used by the network element described by an object.

To describe the possible advantages of such an object-oriented approach in practice, we shall consider the two most interesting basic models, the Open View organizational model and the Open View operational model and we shall use a small example to discuss the various perspectives of network management relating to a device.

7.4.3 The Open View organizational model

The organizational model has three main components: user interfaces, management applications and management services. Management services are usually provided by two groups of components: objects and data stores. The organizational model uses these components to model the functional and relational composition of a network-management solution.

These components are of a high logical level and in this model do not describe a design or implementation scheme. Here, HP is following a generally-recognized technique of computer science used in the design of high-grade software, known as 'stepwise refinement'. At the beginning of a complicated design task all the details are ignored (in this case: communication protocols, communication profiles, communication resources) and an initial logical superstructure is designed. Later, the design is refined in steps until all the details are included. This is what happens in the Open View operational model. This method also permits the integration of various other advanced design techniques.

In particular, the object-oriented formulation is also used to design and link together management services so as to create new management services. This goes far beyond the 'managed objects' approach followed in the OSI NM model.

The main components are shown in Figure 7.11. A user interface represents the technology which links the users with the management facilities. Here, the questions at the design stage relate mainly to the nature and training, organization and knowledge of the users. In the earlier chapters we saw that it is sensible to distribute the organization of larger networks and to delegate tasks. At the lower levels of the hierarchy, management users (or administrators) may simply be normal users with some additional knowledge. Thus, they require totally different tools to a fully-professional supervisor and in particular should only have management capabilities which are restricted to their direct environment. In the framework of the model, management activities are essentially conducted by the users, via a corresponding interface. Sometimes the user interface to the management is the same as that used to access the user's conventional applications (for example, a windows surface on a workstation). In such a case, this surface is also included in the organizational model.

A management application represents that part of a network-management solution which supports a specific network activity within a certain user interface. A management application accepts inputs from the user and prepares output information. For this, it uses the facilities provided

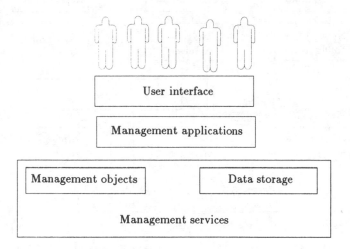

Figure 7.11   HP Open View: organizational model.

for it by the management services, the user interfaces and the basic resources of its environment (for example, the operating system).

Management applications are controlled, initiated and terminated directly by the user. Moreover, a management application may support several user interfaces. In principle, a management application may use all management services and in this respect is only restricted in the framework of a security policy.

The management services represent network-management support facilities which are implemented using objects and data stores. They are basically the most important components of the architecture. In addition to management applications, a management service may also support other management services. The distinction between applications and services, which is not as clear-cut in other manufacturers' models, provides for high modularity and flexibility in the shaping of the management environment.

Objects represent elements in the network which behave according to a fixed specification. Everything which can be monitored and/or manipulated by control algorithms is considered to be an object. This includes attributes, actions and events which are described in an object-oriented specification. Such specifications are stored, for example, in an MIB. Objects may describe specific elements (modems, computers, lines) or composite subclasses (LAN managers, subnetwork managers, etc.).

Finally, data stores represent storage and retrieval facilities within the network management framework.

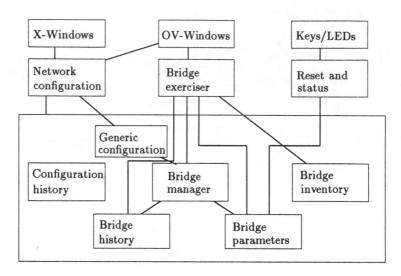

Figure 7.12 HP Open View: example of the organizational model.

Figure 7.12 shows an example of an application of the organizational model, namely the management of a LAN bridge where three different management applications use a management-services infrastructure.

The user accesses a configuration application via the X-Windows interface. This application itself uses the services of a generic configuration object and a store which provides information about the history of this configuration. The Open View windows interface provides its users with access to the configuration service and to a bridge control service. The control service uses the bridge manager and an object which holds the bridge parameters. Furthermore, the stores may be used for the bridge history and for an inventory of the bridge. A fully-local interface consists of an LED status display and a reset key, which use a corresponding application that itself accesses the parameters.

7.4.4 The Open View operational model

The operational model shows how the components of the organizational model are developed and implemented and how different network management solutions are able to coexist with one another. In addition, there are aids for data-flow and decision-flow analysis.

The permanently-changing, dynamic management environment requires a high degree of flexibility in the operational model. The operational model consists of the components shown in Figure 7.13. The outer box represents a physical system. The part of the network management

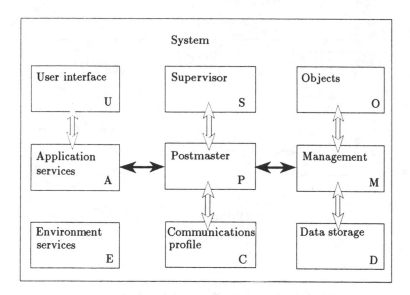

Figure 7.13   HP Open View: the operational model.

which this physical system contributes to the whole is divided into nine components within this system. The bold arrows represent standardized interfaces within the architecture. The other arrows represent system- or implementation-specific interfaces. The user interface, (U), represents the man-machine-interface. The management application, A, represents that part of a solution which supports a specific management activity via a particular user interface.

The environment services, E, represent general facilities within a system environment which may be used directly by one of the other components, for example, sort programs, terminal emulation or file transfer. The supervisor, S, is the monitoring part of a system which is responsible for the maintenance and upkeep of the system components. It is also responsible for the upkeep of the management software services within the system infrastructure.

The postmaster, P, is a basic object-oriented, message-forwarding facility. It operates like a message-driven switch and obtains its routing information from an object-controlled routing table. This table belongs to the supervisor. This does not imply changes to the existing communication protocol. The communication profile, C, includes a set of communication services which support the transaction-based routes of the postmaster. Every C is a complete profile for exchanging network management

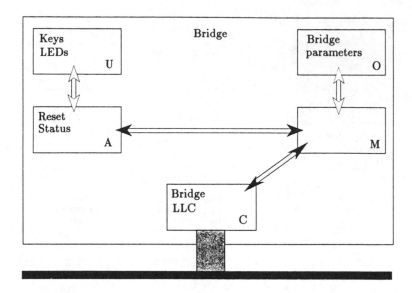

Figure 7.14 HP Open View: the operational model.

information with other systems. The profiles may be chosen explicitly or implicitly when the message reaches P. The routing table may be manipulated under the control of S so as to restrict the choice of profiles. Every system itself chooses which profiles it wishes to support and how (dynamically, statically, individually, simultaneously).

The objects, O, are the objects of the organizational model. The set of management services, M, contains all the services which are available in this system, and the data store, D, contains the stores available to the management.

Figure 7.14 shows the application of the operational model to the organizational model of the LAN bridge management discussed above. It is actually very simple.

The bridge itself is a possible system. It has a reset key and an LED status display which form a simple user interface. The software or logic of the board which controls the LED and reacts to the reset key is modelled as management application A. The bridge can accept control messages from the LAN. For this, it uses the communication protocols which are described as communication profile C. The specific bridge parameters which may be queried or set, appear as bridge parameter objects. The components P, S, D, and E are not present in the bridge.

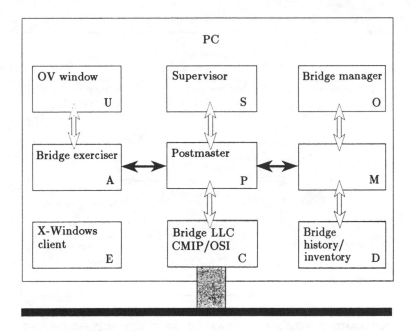

Figure 7.15 HP Open View. The operational model (Example).

Another possible system is a PC-based management station in the LAN which is able to control the bridge using control messages (Figure 7.15). Open View windows is the user interface U. To support this functionality, a bridge-manager object is incarnated on the PC together with a characteristic set of operations or services (M), such as 'SET PARAMETER' or 'SET CONFIG DAT'. Then, a management application A is generated, which enables the user to execute the functions and to observe the results of their execution. For the communication between the bridge-manager object and the bridge-parameter object, the PC must provide a common communication profile, C, between itself and the bridge. The PC also contains a postmaster, P, for object-oriented message handling. Data stores, D, for the bridge history and the configuration lie on the PC hard disk. The services of these stores are denoted by M. A supervisor, S, is used to query and control the postmaster's routing tables. Additionally, there is one more X-Windows client, which is the only environment service in the PC.

Finally, the last system is a workstation with an X-Windows user interface (Figure 7.16). A general configuration object, O, helps to identify the specific bridge-parameter object. One of the two workstation management applications, A, allows the user to execute the functions of the

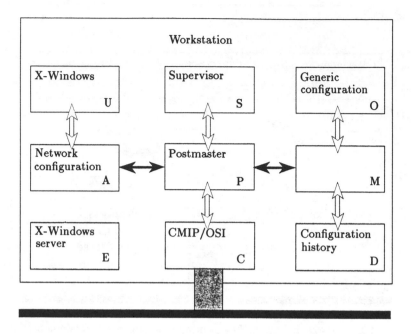

Figure 7.16   HP Open View. The operational model.

general configuration object. The other permits the execution of the bridge-manager object functions. Like the PC, the workstation also contains a postmaster and perhaps a number of components M, S, C and D which we shall not discuss further here. The management services, M, which are implemented on the PC management platform, are also available on the workstation. Here OSI CMIP is used as the communication profile.

This all shows the flexibility of the scheme. It is never necessary to modify whole environments, only individual objects and relations. An embedding, for example of SNMP, is no problem, neither is the later change to CMIP.

7.4.5 Open View products and services

Only a brief summary is given here. Open View Windows/DOS is a development environment for element-management solutions. The approach involves menu-based commands, dialogue boxes and consistent symbols. Development guidelines and support are provided. The only prerequisite is a PC-AT or a PS/2 with Windows 3. In the medium term, this product will be replaced by the extended UNIX version, which is a step with a low threshold. SNMP functionality is also available.

The big brother, so-to-speak, is the HP Open View network-management server, which runs on HP 9000 computers with HP X terminals under HP-UX. This is an extensive development environment for integrated management applications and element-management solutions. Software developers can use it to integrate isolated element-management solutions, develop specific applications or to provide direct management of certain network devices. In addition to the documented API interface, the so-called 'Application Design and Consulting Services' are intended to support application development. The strong object-orientation allows programmers to concentrate on the important things. Once implemented, details of object presentations can be used over and again. The event management service module collects events and forwards them to the network-management applications. The data management services support the Internet SNMP MIB, but permit other extensions. The server supports both SNMP and CMOT (CMIP over TCP/IP) access. HP plans to implement the OSI network-management-forum CMIP protocols when the software standard is stable. The whole software costs around £15 000, even if you don't have a UNIX computer and have to buy one, this is a very competitive price. The system is hardware independent.

The HP Network Node Manager (NNM) is an example of an element-management system. It also runs on UNIX computers, for example the HP 300, 400, 600 and 800 lines with HP-UX 7.0, or higher, using HP Open View Windows based on OSF/Motif. It is a system for monitoring TCP/IP internetworks, LANs and HP 9000 systems. On being switched on, it finds the local TCP/IP nodes and gateways and marks them out. This process may be applied to other LANs within one's own region or to LANs which can only be reached via a WAN. Moreover, NNM also provides for remote control of HP 9000 systems using the remote system administration capability.

The NNM is only one offering from a broad spectrum of Open View network-management products, test and measurement facilities and support services for multivendor LAN and WAN environments.

7.4.6 Open View: market perspectives

The unique construction of Open View, based on the DCI distributed system environment, enables clients to begin with a very small, partial network-management solution which may then be allowed to grow slowly. In practice, very different machines may be used ranging from a small PC-based UNIX system upwards. The true distributedness provides a wonderful facility for neutralizing the security problems of system-management centres. IBM SAA and SystemView Centres are currently exposed to great danger and must be very carefully screened against attacks from outside. An Open View environment with 20 or 30 management servers can scarcely be put out of action, particularly since, because of the distributed-system environment, network-management systems may undertake the tasks of machines which are out of use or broken-down.

Until now, HP has concentrated on providing a multivendor platform for OSI- and TCP/IP-based internetwork environments. This is, above all, supported by the fact that for practically a decade, HP has been a market leader for LAN analyzers and TCP/IP-based solutions. Naturally, Open View is well placed to build on and extend these positions. The choice of UNIX systems is the best possible choice, since this operating system will become the standard of the next ten years from PCs to hosts, as it already is in certain subareas. The independence from the hardware is a major advantage over DEC's EMA and an even greater advantage over the IBM solutions. It appears that HP would willingly leave the management of SNA environments to IBM, and that of open networks to AT&T, so as to dominate HP's primary market segments, since nowhere is SNA connection mentioned. If the pricing policy remains, those interested have reason to be happy.

In summary, Open View provides a powerful and flexible basis for the implementation of later management products.

7.4.7 Criticisms of Open View

There are not many criticisms. Open View is, first of all, a strategy and the products are primarily development environments. Naturally, HP will still have to invest a good deal before functioning applications for problem, change and configuration management can be made available. The platform itself still lacks some parts, such as a database management system and a distributed directory system. However, the author is convinced that HP can close the loopholes quickly should the current, very rickety standardization in these areas come to manageable results. The HP scheme is somewhat ahead of its time. This is paid for by the fact the companies such as IBM, DEC and AT&T have shown no inclination to take up the model. On the other hand, HP has only a comparatively small market penetration. It would be a shame were the brilliant Open View concept to founder in the market.

7.5 Siemens: development of TRANSDATA management

TRANSDATA networks are classically tree-structured systems and possess classical management facilities to guarantee and optimize the operation of the network.

However, the times of homogeneity are also over in the TRANSDATA world. SINIX systems locally networked with IBM compatible PCs, ISDN

PBXs and SINEC communication systems for industrial manufacturing, communicate with TRANSDATA networks and systems.

Consistently, from early on, in addition to the manufacturer-specific protocols of the NEA group in BS 2000, Siemens has also implemented open protocols for other systems according to the specifications of the OSI reference model. These have long been available for use for communication between Siemens systems and above all for interworking with other systems. The protocol stack has been consistently developed upwards in accordance with the current status of standardization. The most recent announcements include file transfer, according to OSI FTAM, as a further development of the Siemens FT product line, electronic mail according to X.400 MAILIX for SINIX and MAIL-2000 network management according to OSI.

7.5.1 The development of TRANSDATA management

In Germany, Siemens is one of the most important DP manufacturers, as its installation base shows. Like other manufacturers, Siemens also supports an in-house network system architecture for computer communications (TRANSDATA), to secure its own investments, manufacturer-neutral standards according to the OSI reference model as guidelines for existing and future products, together with product lines in the industrial-communications and ISDN-technology areas (also based on standards). Accordingly, it is crucial that the network management should be adapted to the latest requirements.

To support the management of heterogeneous environments and the integration of optimized management tools for use in particular subnetworks within such heterogeneous environments, the ISO management standards and interfaces within the OSI management framework are an almost mandatory choice.

In Chapter 4, we introduced the management in classical Siemens TRANSDATA networks. We now extend that introduction with a description of the latest developments as far as the implementation of standards for the higher OSI layers is concerned, for computers with the BS 2000 and SINIX operating systems. We then describe the latest developments in the TRANSDATA network management: TRANSDATA CNM.

7.5.2 New communications products

Siemens was an early supporter of international communications standards, and for the BS 2000 and SINIX operating systems has long offered communications products for the lower layers based on such standards, in addition to products based on its own in-house NEA communication protocols. Neither has linkage with the IBM world been forgotten.

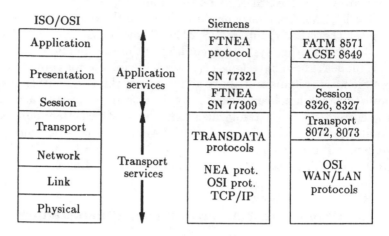

Figure 7.17   Siemens file transfer.

For the lower protocol layers, Siemens currently provides the following transport facilities:

- ISO transport systems in LANs or WANs.
- NEA transport systems for WANs.
- TCP/IP transport systems for LANs.
- SNA transport systems for WANs.

The latest extensions mainly concern the implementation of standards for electronic mail and file transfer.

Two file transfer protocols are available in the higher protocol layers:

- FTNEA protocols, based on Siemens standards for layers 5–7.
- FTAM protocols, based on ISO/OSI for layer 7 for use with corresponding products for layers 5 and 6.

The FTNEA protocols run on all the given transport subsystems while FTAM requires ongoing support of the OSI protocol stack.

To secure investments and to facilitate their use, FTNEA and FTAM have a common user surface, in other words, there is basically only one form of file transfer which operates with the different protocols. The FTNEA protocols are implemented by the FT BS 2000 and FT SINIX products. The FTAM protocol is implemented using the FTOS BS 2000 and FTOS SINIX (file transfer, OSI support) add-ons, with a partially-different functionality

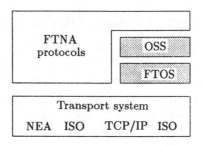

Figure 7.18   Siemens file transfer (user interface).

in each case. The FTAM implementations are supplemented by the protocol-independent functions (for example, job management, simultaneous file transfer, information about running actions) already available for FTNEA.
Siemens aims towards the following conceptual objectives:

- Implementation of an open system and creation of a common FT product basis. Here, in addition to the existing facilities for connection with third-party systems (for example, DEC and Nixdorf systems and PCs), general openness to all systems which support the OSI standards is intended.

- Unified functionality, together with uniform user interfaces, within homogeneous and heterogeneous connection scenarios.

- High availability, including according recovery after errors.

- Virtualization of the objects to be transmitted using the ISO/OSI virtual file principle, including for conventional FT systems.

- Integration of the existing FT worlds (FT BS 2000, FT SINIX, SNFT, FT PCD, FT DKS, SINEC FTS, FT MSP, FTSIE, TCom FT) into the future FTAM world.

- Provision of proven FT auxiliary functions including for FTAM communication: symmetry (anyone can initiate file transfer), request storage (with facilities for sorting and prioritization), automatic restart and check points, data transmission with follow-up processing, data compression, communication of results, defined interruption of file-transfer requests, various interfaces for issuing requests, file transfer over LANs, access protection, management functions and information services.

The extensions for electronic mail and document exchange are also based on international standards: X.400, X.500 and EDIFACT for the most important operating systems, BS 2000 and SINIX. For further information about these extensions and about file transfer, see the bibliography.

7.5.3 The structure of Siemens TRANSDATA CNM

TRANSDATA Computer Network Management (CNM) is based on the ISO/OSI recommendations. The implementation of network management standards that have already been released, and those that are still subjects of the standardization process, provides a stable platform for future developments. Most important for the TRANSDATA user is the knowledge that the new products will interwork with the classical management products in the TRANSDATA framework.

Siemens plans to provide CNM products graded according to their use, where the core will always be in a SINIX system. OSF/Motif with colour graphics and windows technology will be used as the user surface. NM agents execute tasks locally.

The most important features of the new concept include:

- Network management according to ISO/OSI standards.
- Interworking with previous components.
- NM centres and NM agents.
- Agents for both OSI and NEA protocols under BS 2000, PDN and SINIX for LAN and WAN configurations.
- NM centres based on SINIX/X-Windows/Motif with:
- NM information base (repository) for a global view of all static and dynamic objects, attributes, relationships and rules.
- NMA applications configuration management, performance management, security management, status monitor, session monitor and bridge monitor.
- Uniform open interfaces for specific management applications.

In principle, the SINIX system management can be reached using the standard UNIX rlogin mechanism, including from other SINIX stations. Clearly this is subject to very strong security restrictions.

The uniform open interfaces include CMIP for communication with ISO-conforming agents and units together with the NM Communication Protocol (NMCP) for communication with TRANSDATA agents.

In addition to the particular incarnations of the MIB in the individual layers, there is an Informix database for management information.

To complete the trio, (as for all other manufacturers), in addition to a manufacturer-specific protocol stack (NEA protocols in the case of Siemens) and OSI protocols, communication links via TCP/IP are used and supported.

7.5.4 TRANSDATA CNM and the network management problem area

TRANSDATA CNM implements the functions needed to control and manage a TRANSDATA network with BS 2000, PDN and SINIX, together with OSI-conforming components from other manufacturers. The functions correspond to the functions of the OSI network-management framework (as previously described) and extensions based on the user interfaces which these functions make accessible to an administrator.

The status monitor monitors the network and its components. The network-management information base (MIB) provides the status monitor with information about objects and the relationships between these objects. The status monitor generates a section across the network for screen display at the user interface. It obtains state information from the agents in the individual nodes. The nodes, states and changes are presented in a coloured, self-explanatory way. Particularly critical changes to the states are displayed in a special window of the monitoring console even when these changes take place outside the section currently being displayed.

The configuration management is used to acquire, modify and delete data about the network objects, attributes, parameters and relationships. The user interface provides ready-made formulas for describing objects and a special object description language. The specification of such data is, in principle, relatively expensive but fundamental for the OSI network management. Support by appropriate utilities would be welcome at this point, since this would remove the user's fear of generating the specific object world and would thus increase acceptance. The data generated is stored in the NMIB.

The performance management covers performance data such as overloading, the crossing of thresholds and response times. This data is also displayed on a screen. The data may be stored for later evaluation.

The security management relates primarily to TRANSDATA CNM itself, since other functional areas such as FT or FTOS have well-developed security measures. Rights and passwords may be recorded and managed. When an NM service is accessed, the service checks the authorization itself; access to agents is also checked at this stage. This double checking is mainly needed to make it difficult for an attacker located between NM service stations and agents to make the agents work for him without the knowledge and authorization of the central station.

The session monitor journals the applications which have registered with the transport system, the connections for these applications and the associated parameters.

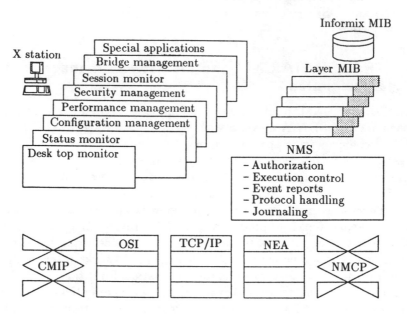

Figure 7.19 Siemens TRANSDATA CNM (overview).

The bridge management displays the data of special devices and layers (for example, the LLC).

7.5.5 TRANSDATA CNM: products and services

The central building block of TRANSDATA CNM is the Network Management Service (NMS). This may be accessed via the INMS programmer interface by all applications, and provides services such as authorization, execution controls, event reporting, protocol handling, logging, object-oriented access and access to the transport access system for CMX with the OSI, NEA and TCP/IP protocol stacks.

TRANSDATA CNM is available in three product groups:

- CNM B is the basic agent which must be present in every network component. It provides for basic services such as communication with the remote network management centre (NMC), execution of a set of basic commands (activation, deactivation, loading, dumping) and simple auxiliary functions. There are various forms of CNM B for different environments.

- CNM E is the extended agent. It must be installed in systems for which auxiliary functions (for example, preparation of data for the performance monitor or the extension interface) are required. There are also several versions of this.

- Finally, CNM NMC is the network management centre.

These conceptual extensions take adequate account of the structural change in TRANSDATA systems and provide a basis for integrated network management.

7.5.6 Market perspectives, criticisms

At present, SNI does not intend to provide a platform for multivendor management which would be accepted by other manufacturers in the sense that they could hang products, extensions or interfaces on to it.

On the other hand, CNM is heavily based on standards and also includes TCP/IP, so that transitions are possible at any time.

Siemens' clients form a sufficient basis for the economic success of the concept. Unfortunately as of now (the end of 1991) there are no deliverable components so that the quality of the implementation remains to be seen.

One might criticize the central approach and the lack of platform APIs, together with the lack of a gateway to SNA. However, since, as a strategy, TRANSDATA CNM is far removed from products, one or other of these things may change.

7.6 Other management schemes of other companies

In addition to the proposals of AT&T, DEC, HP, IBM and SNI (Siemens), many other manufacturers also have integrated network management models, for this is a topic where nobody wishes to be left behind, at least as far as words are concerned.

These schemes range from the subnanometric region to really interesting ideas and it is, with few exceptions, clear (see also NetView) that it is not the quality of an idea but the number of suppliers on the market which counts. For, such schemes are mainly concerned with the control of existing networks and systems and the previous distribution of market segments is a decisive factor.

Sun's products are always particularly innovative and worthy of attention. As we have already seen in this chapter, most network-management applications run on Sun workstations. Sun does not intend to produce a complete philosophy for integrated management from scratch. In October 1989, the SunNet manager was introduced as a platform for the construction of element management systems, particularly for LAN and workgroup systems. Like the DEC and HP strategies, the SunNet manager is based on a distributed architecture which uses Sun's remote procedure calls and is part of the Open Network Computing Package for logical connection of networked computers. Unlike as in the case of HP, the RPC concept is used less to interlink distributed managers (there may be some) than to generate connections between managers and distributed agents. This allows the management software to call procedures over the network without knowledge of the underlying communications hardware and software. As one might expect, the SunNet manager also runs on a Sun workstation with the SunOS distributed operating system. Open Look is available as a user surface and SNMP is the primary management exchange protocol, although DECnet should also be supported. There are strategic alliances with Synoptics, FiberComm and Concord, all progressive LAN manufacturers. The SunNet manager is mainly of interest to small, independent LAN suppliers, who are looking for a management platform to sell with their system without having to cover expensive development costs themselves. Because of Sun's reputation, it will also set yardsticks in other areas. One major advantage of the SunNet manager is the present specification of SMNP.

Sun Microsystems is the last manufacturer in this chapter to have brought out a product.

In 1990, the tiny company 3Com introduced its *Open Management Architecture* (OMA) and expressed its wish to build the first OS/2 management platform. In addition, 3Com has, together with IBM, developed quite unique specifications for LAN management, the basic tenor of which maps the CMIP protocol onto the logical link control (since there is no full OSI stack in LANs) and restricts the domain concept (for no understandable reason). Thus, CMIP is shrunken onto SNMP and an 'implementation of the international standard' is produced. It is to be feared that the LAN Station Manager and the LAN Network Manager announced by IBM for 1991 will be based on these specifications; there is scarcely any other way of explaining the smallness of the Station Manager. This is a blow in the face of the standardization bodies and clients will, in my opinion, simply lap it up, since very few clients take the trouble to read these specifications and work out the differences from OSI CMIP.

7.7 Decisive medium-term developments

It is important for those interested in network management platforms to be able to assess which of the available alternatives is in their best current and future interests.

For many, the problem of choice will not have such a high profile, since they are already clients of one company or another. In Germany, the manufacturers listed cover practically everything. It is not possible to give general guidelines here.

General trends include the development of OSI, the development of SNMP and the development of Distributed Management Environments (DMEs).

OSI and its associated management models must first be used in practice and prove themselves on a wide front from there before they can be generally accepted. For most customers, OSI today is still only a promise which the manufacturers are bandying about more or less earnestly.

In many cases, manufacturers and users now refer to the DoD protocol suite when it comes to the question of heterogeneous networking. Amongst the users, a regular TCP/IP community has grown up which defends its protocols loudly against criticisms of conceptual weaknesses. SNMP is the natural product for this community. It is to be feared that SNMP will not be limited to this community, but will spread relatively rapidly via LAN management, even to areas where it is unwanted. The SNMP culture is basically controlled by industry and four individual gurus and thus is faster to react than the slow process of international standardization. As an absolutely catastrophic scenario, the author envisages such a rapid spread of SNMP that, in the long term, the international standards cannot be implemented. Then, after several years, people will notice that SNMP has clear limitations, is no longer up-to-date and must be revised.

One final important development, neglected by practically everyone, is the further development of distributed operating techniques for a *Distributed Management Environment* (DME), in which the managers and agents are independent of each other and can intercommunicate. DMEs are the anchor for all management application processes and the key to their power and flexibility. A common remote procedure call concept in the framework of a standardized operating system (such as UNIX) would make it possible to run management application modules on different management platforms; this would in many cases be optimal. In 1990, the OSF attempted to take a first step towards the specification of such an environment. Surprisingly, the authorities did not specify tried-and-tested RPCs of Sun Microsystems but preferred other concepts. It is hard to say how this process will end. A DME would then be mandatory for all OSF operating systems (including IBM) and would form a (practically new) platform for management applications.

In summary, it may be said that of the alternatives for the construction of multivendor management systems described in the introduction to this chapter, the platform approach will win the day as a result of its higher flexibility. One exception to this, as always, is IBM.

Abbreviations

ACF/VTAM	Advanced Communication Facility/Virtual Telecommunication Access Method
ACSE	Association Control Service Element
AE	Application Entity
AIX	Advanced Interactive Executive
APPC	Advanced Program to Program Communication
ASE	Application Service Element
ASN.1	Abstract Syntax Notation One
CASE	Common Application Service Element
CCR	Commitment, Concurrency and Recovery
CMIP	Common Management Information Protocol
CMIS	Common Management Information Services
CMISE	Common Management Information Service Element
CMOT	CMIP over TCP/IP
CMS	IBM operating system
CNM	Computer Network Management
CP/M	PC operating system for 8-bit processors
CPMS	Control Point Management Services
CSA	Client Service Agent
DCA	Document Contents Architecture
DDM	Distributed Data Manager
DIA	Document Interchange Architecture
DNA	Digital Network Architecture
DoD	Department of Defense (USA)
DQDB	Distributed Queue Double Bus
DSA	Directory System Agent
EMA	Enterprise Management Architecture
EMS	Element Management System
ES	Extended Services
FDDI	Fibre Distributed Data Interface
FTAM	File Transfer Access and Management
FTP	File Transfer Program
GDMI	Generic Definition of Management Information
GOSIP	Government Open Systems Information Profile
IEEE	Institute of Electrical and Electronic Engineers
IP	Internet Protocol
ISDN	Integrated Services Digital Network

263

ISO	International Standardization Organization
LAN	Local Area Network
LDM	Network Logical Data Monitor
LE	Layer Entity
LEC	Local Exchange Carrier
LME	Layer Management Entity
LMS	Local Management Services
LPDA	Link Problem Determination Aid
LU	Logical Unit
MAPDU	Management Application Protocol Data Unit
MHS	Message Handling System
MIB	Management Information Base
MIR	Management Information Repository
MSA	Management Services Architecture
MVS	Multiple Virtual Storage
NCCF	Network Communications Control Facility
NCP	Network Control Program
NFS	Network File System
NICE	Network Information and Control Protocol
NMA	Network Management Architecture
NMP	Network Management Protocol
NMS	Network Management Station
NPDA	Network Problem Determination Application
NSAP	Network Service Address Point
NSD	Network Statistics Database
ODA/ODIF	Office Automation Architecture/Office Document Interchange Format
OMA	Open Management Architecture
OS/MVS	IBM operating system
OS/2 EE	OS2 Extended Edition
OSF	Open Systems Foundation
OSF Motif	UNIX surface of the OSF
OSI	Open Systems Interconnection
OSI/CS	OSI Communications Subsystem
PU	Physical Unit
PUMS	Physical Unit Management Services
RIPL	Remote Initial Program Loaded
RJE	Remote Job Entry
ROS	Remote Operation Service
ROSE	Remote Operation Service Element
RTS	Reliable Transfer Service
SAA	System Applications Architecture
SAP	Service Address Point
SASE	Specific Application Service Element
SFT	System Fault Tolerant
SMFA	Specific Management Functional Area

SMI	Structure of Management Information
SMTP	Simple Mail Transfer Protocol
SNA	System Network Architecture
SNA CNM	SNA Computer Network Management
SNADS	SNA Distribution Services
SNI	System Network Interconnection
SNMP	Simple Network Management Protocol
SSCP	System Services Control Point
TCF	Transparent Computing Facility
TCP	Transport Control Protocol
UDP	User Datagram Protocol
UE	User Element
UNMA	Unified Network Management Architecture
VM	IBM operating system
VMS	DEC operating system
VNCA	VTAM Node Control Application
VSE	IBM operating system
VTAM	Virtual Telecommunication Access Method
VTP	Virtual Terminal Protocol

Bibliography

Almes *et al.* (1985). The EDEN System, a technical review. *IEEE Trans. Software Engineering*, 11(1)

Baumgarten U. (1990). Die Entwicklung von UNIX im Umfeld von IBM und Token Ring. In *Proc. Token Ring Tage 90*, (Datacom)

Bennett (1990). SNMP. *Telecommunications*, (2)

Beyschlag U., ed. (1988). *OSI in der Anwendungsebene*, Datacom Verlag, Pulheim

Bitterwolf E. (1990). Netzwerk-Management in grossen, heterogenen Datennetzen. In *Proc. Netzwerk-Management Forum*, (ComConsult)

Borowka P. (1990). Ausfall- und Fehlersituationen in Netzwerken, Erfahrungen, Ursachen, Lösungsansätze für heterogene Netze. In *Proc. Netzwerk-Management Forum*, (ComConsult)

Büker N. (1990). Netzwerkmanagement in der Praxis. In *Proc. Netzwerk-Management Forum*, (ComConsult)

Cheriton (1984). The V kernel: a software base for distributed systems. *IEEE Software*, 1(2)

Danthine A., ed. (1987). A general management architecture for a backbone wideband network and its interconnected LANs. In *Proc. IFIP WG 6.4 Workshop on High-Speed Local Area Networks*, Aachen, 1987, North Holland

Datapro (1989). AT&T unified network management architecture (UNMA). In *Datapro Network Management*, McGraw-Hill, Maidenhead

DEC (1985). *DNA und DECnet Informationsschrift*

Deitel and Harvey M. (1984). *An Introduction to Operating Systems*. Addison-Wesley, Wokingham

Denning D. E. (1982). *Cryptography and Data Security*. Addison-Wesley, Wokingham

DIN (1982). *ISO 7498 Informationsverarbeitung – Kommunikation Offener Systeme, Basis Referenzmodell*. Beuth Verlag

Drols H. (1990). Einführung von LAN-Services und Benutzerakzeptanz. In *Proc. Token Ring Tage 90*, (Datacom)

Effelsberg W. and Fleischmann A. (1986). Das ISO Referenzmodell für Offene Systeme und seine sieben Schichten. *Informatik Spektrum*, 9, 280–299

Enslow P. H. (1978). What is a distributed data processing system? *IEEE Computer*, 11(1), 13–21

Erhard (1990). Netzwerk Philosophie, I: Offene Kommunikationswege als Infrastruktur der Firmenkultur. *Datacom*, (4)

Fitzgerald and Rashid (1985). The integration of virtual memory management and interprocess communication. In *Proc. 10th Int. Sym. Operating System*

Principles (ACM), New York

Glaser G., Hein M. and Vogl J. (1990). *TCP/IP. Protokolle, Projektplanung, Realisierung.* Datacom Verlag, Pulheim

Gora W. and Speyerer R. (1987). *Abstract Syntax Notation One.* Datacom Verlag, Pulheim

Häge H. (1990). Netzwerk-Management in der IBM Welt: Produkte, Tendenzen, Alternativen. In *Proc. Netzwerk-Management Forum*, (ComConsult)

Härtig H. and Kühnhauser W.E. (1986). *Distribution in the Birlix Operating System.* NTG Technical Report, Volume 92, VDE Verlag

Härtig H. *et al.* (1986). *Structure of the Birlix Operating System.* GMD Annual Report, 1985, Selbstverlag

Hegering H.-G. (1987). Benutzeridentifikation und Abrechnungsdienste in einer verteilten Systemumgebung. In *Proc. GI/NTG Tech. Conf. 'Kommunikation in Verteilten Systemen'*, Aachen, 1987. Springer

Heigert J. (1988). Directory und Netzwerk-Management. In (Beyschlag, 1988)

Herman J. (1990). Enterprise Management vendors shoot it out, *Data Communications* (11)

Hindin E.M. (1990). IBM brings mainframes in from the cold, *Data Communications* (11)

Huntington J.A. (1989). OSI-based net management. Is it too early, or too late? *Data Communications* (3)

IBM (a). *SNA format and protocol reference manual: management services* (SC30-3346-0)

IBM (b). *NetView general information and planning* (GC30-3463)

IBM (c). *NetView program products general information* (GC30-3350)

IBM (d). *NetView primer* (GC24-3047)

IBM (1990a). *IBM SAA: An introduction to SystemView* (GC23-0576)

IBM (1990b). *SystemView executive brochure* (G520-6775)

IBM (1990c). *IBM SAA: SystemView and the OS/2 environment* (G01F-0281)

IBM (1990d). *IBM SAA: SystemView and the Application System/400 system* (GA21-9607)

IBM (1991a). *IBM SAA: SystemView end-user dimension consistency guide* (SC33-6472)

IBM (1991b). *IBM SAA: SystemView concepts* (SC23-0578)

IBM (1991c). *IBM SAA: data model reference* (3091)

Jander M. (1990). IBM raises net management to a higher power, *Data Communications*, (11)

Kanyuh D. (1988). An integrated network management product. *IBM Systems Journal* 27(1)

Kauffels F.-J. (1985). Schwachstellen der Informationssicherheit in lokalen Netzen. In (Spies, 1985)

Kauffels F.J. (1989). *Einführung in die Datenkommunikation* 4th edn. Verlag K. Lipinski (Datacom)

Kauffels F.J. (1990). *Rechnernetzwerksystemarchitekturen und Datenkommunikation* 3rd edn. Mannheim: BI

Klemba K.S. (1989). Open View's architectural models. In *Proc. IFIP Sym.*

Integrated Network Management, Boston, 1989

Krall (1990). SNMP opens new lines of sight. *Data Communications Spec. LAN Strategies* (3)

Kröger R. (1984). *Konzepte für die Architektur von Rechensystemen unter besonderer Berücksichtigung von Züverlässigkeit und Verteiltheit.* Computer Science Report 39, Institüt für Informatik der Universität Bonn

Maekawa, Oldehoeft and Oldehoeft (1987). *Operating Systems, Advanced Concepts.* Benjamin/Cummings, Menlo Park

McCann (1989). OSI-based network management. In *Datapro Network Management*, McGraw-Hill, Maidenhead

Melchard W. (1990). Strategisches Netzwerkmanagement in SNA-Netzen, IV *Datacom* (4)

Mullender and Tanenbaum (1986). The design of a capability-based distributed operating system. *The Computer Journal* 29(4)

Needham and Herbert (1982). *The Cambridge Distributed Operating System.* Addison-Wesley, Wokingham

Nehmer J. (1985). *The Multicomputer Project INCAS Objectives and Basic Concepts.* SFB 124 Report 11/85

Peichert L. (1990). Integriertes Netzwerk-Management mit EMA, Lösungen von Digital Equipment. In *Proc. Netzwerk-Management Forum* (ComConsult)

Peschi R. and Danthine A. (1987). High-performance interface to the MAC of a wideband backbone network. In *Proc. IFIP WG 6.4 Workshop on High-Speed Local Area Networks*, Aachen, 1987, North Holland

Peterson and Silberschatz (1985). *Operating Systems* 2nd edn. Addison-Wesley, Wokingham

Popek G. and Walker (1985). *The LOCUS Distributed System Architecture*, MIT Press, Cambridge

Popek G. *et al.* (1983). The LOCUS distributed operating system. *ACM Operating System Review* 17(5)

Popescu-Zeletin, Le Lann and Kim, eds. (1987). *Proc. 7th Int. IEEE Conf. Distributed Computing Systems*, Berlin 1987. IEEE, Los Angeles

Preshun (1990). Considering CMIP. *Data Communications Spec. LAN Strategies* 3

Rao A.V. (1990). An introduction to expert systems in network management. In *Datapro Report on Network Management*, NM-20-200-301, McGraw-Hill, Maidenhead

Rashid and Robertson (1981). ACCENT: a communication-oriented network operating system kernel. In *Proc. 8th Int. Sym. Operating System Principles*, (ACM), New York

Rose and Fuss (1990). OSI Netzwerk-Management. *Datacom* (4)

Ross R.W.Jr. (1989). Integration of the physical layer into network management: AT&T's approach. In *Proc. Datacom Congress*, Cologne, 1989

Routt T.-J. (1988). SNA network management: what makes IBM's NetView tick? *Data Communications* (6)

Ruland Ch. (1988). *Datenschutz in Kommunikationssystemen.* Datacom Verlag, Pulheim

Ruland Ch. (1989). Datensicherheit in lokalen Netzen, Part 1 *Datacom* (12)

Ruland Ch. (1990). Datensicherheit in lokalen Netzen, Part 2 *Datacom* (1)

Scott (1990a). Taking care of business with SNMP *Data Communications Spec. LAN Strategies* (3)

Scott (1990b). SNMP brings order to chaos. *Data Communications Spec. LAN Strategies* (3)

Siemens (1989). *MAIL-X (SINIX) Version 1.0/1.1* (U2536-J-Z90-3)

Siemens (1990a). *TRANSDATA communication network management*

Siemens (1990b). *File Transfer – ein Thema für alle DV-Anwender* (U5776-J-Z12-1)

Siemens (1990c). *SINIX-Systeme – Kommunikation* (U3020-J-Z92-4)

Siemens (1990d). *SEDI (SINIX)* (U6166-J-Z90-1)

Siemens (1990e). *MAIL2000 (BS2000) Version 1.1* (U4369-J-Z50-2)

Sloman M., ed. (1984). *COST: Management of Local Area Networks*, Final Report of COST 11bis, LAN Group, Part II

Spies P.P. (1985). Datenschutz und Datensicherung im Wandel der Informationstechnologien. In *Proc. 1 GI Tech. Conf. 'Datenschutz und Datensicherung im Wandel der Informationstechnologien'*. Springer

Spies P.P. (1986). *Informationsverarbeitung in Verteilten Systemen*, Internal Report II/86/1, Bonn

Strauss P.R. (1989). NetView/PC: users are just saying 'no', *Data Communications* (1)

Suppan J. (1990). Wirtschaftlicher Netzwerk-Einsatz von der strategischen zur ökonomischen Kommunikationslösung. In *Proc. Netzwerk-Management Forum* (ComConsult)

Suppan-Borowka J. (1986). Netzwerkmanagement in MAP, *Data Communications* (3)

Tanenbaum and Renesse (1985). Distributed operating systems *Computing Surveys* 17(4)

Terplan K. (1987). *Communication Networks Management*. Prentice Hall

Terplan K. (1989). Allgemeine Konzepte des Netzwerkmanagements. In *Proc. Datacom Congress*, Cologne, 1989

Terplan K. and Huntington-Lee J. (1990). Can third parties change SNA management's stripes? *Data Communications International,* April 1990

Tripathi (1987). Distributed operating systems. In (Popescu-Zeletin, Le Lann and Kim, 1987)

VandenBerg Chr. (1990). MIB II extends SNMP interoperability, *Data Communications* (10)

Wakid, Brusil, La Barre (1987). Coming to OSI: network resource management and global reachability, *Data Communications* (12)

Weidenhammer D. (1990). Netzwerk-Management mit SNMP, die Lösung der nächsten Jahre. In *Proc. Netzwerk-Management Forum* (ComConsult)

Wolf K. (1990). Integration von BS2000, SINIX/UNIX und MS-DOS/OS/2-Systemen durch OSI-orientiertes Netzwerk-Management. In *Proc. Netzwerk-Management Forum* (ComConsult)

ZSI (1989). *IT-Sicherheitskriterien*, Bundesanzeiger Verlag

Index

access
  control   134, 228
  mechanism   42
  module   236
  rights   80
accounting   46, 104
  management   104, 188, 228
  SMFA   170
  utilities   37
ACCUMASTER Integrator   225, 229
ACF/VTAM   44
ACSE   164, 173, 174, 227
administration   45
administrator   35, 50
AE   162
agent   201, 204
AIX   27, 72, 114, 126, 198, 204
  PS/2   73
  TCF   72
  V.3   73
  /RT   73
  /370   73
analysis   45
API   220
APPC   27, 93
application layer   161, 162
application management   60
ARPANET   196
ASE   162, 164, 173
ASN.1   174, 201
AS/400   95, 127
AS/6000   74, 95, 96
autonomy, cooperative   40, 66

bottle-neck detection and avoidance   42
BS 2000   27

capability   184
capacity planning   45
CASE   164, 173
CCR   164, 227
change management   105

CLIST   112
closed system   184
cluster controller   91
CMIP   174, 196, 205, 211, 232, 236
CMIS   170, 173, 174, 178
CMISE   170
CMIS/CMIP   172
CMOT   205
CMS   73
CNM   90
command facility   110
communications controller   91
company standards   84
component
  configuration   77
  installation   77
  tests   86
configuration management   37, 105, 176, 227
configuration SMFA   172
control   44
control manager   44
conversation   93
CPMS   106
CP/M   198
CSA   191

data
  link layer   144
  processing, distributed   12
  protection   4, 161
  security   5
DATEL services   19
DCA   93
DCE   29
DCI   242
DDM   114
decentralization   5
DECnet   20, 107, 141, 204, 239
DIA   93
DIB   192
directory
  information base   192